SHARING RESIDENTIAL PROPERTY

AUSTRALIA
The Law Book Company Ltd.
Sydney : Melbourne : Brisbane : Perth

CANADA
The Carswell Company Ltd.
Toronto : Calgary : Vancouver : Ottawa

INDIA
N. M. Tripathi Private Ltd.
Bombay
and
Eastern Law House Private Ltd.
Calcutta

M.P.P. House
Bangalore

ISRAEL
Steimatzky's Agency Ltd.
Jerusalem : Tel Aviv : Haifa

PAKISTAN
Pakistan Law House
Karachi

SHARING RESIDENTIAL PROPERTY

JEAN WARBURTON, LL.B.,

Solicitor, Senior Lecturer in Law
University of Liverpool

with a foreword by
The Rt. Hon.
Sir Christopher Slade

LONDON   SWEET & MAXWELL   1990

Published in 1990 by
Sweet & Maxwell Limited
183 Marsh Wall, London, E14
Computerset by P.B. Computer Typesetting,
Pickering, N. Yorks.
Printed and bound in Great Britain by
Butler and Tanner Limited, Frome, Somerset

British Library Cataloguing in Publication Data
Warburton, Jean
    Sharing residential property.
    1. England. Real property. Coownership. Law
    I. Title
    344.206432

    ISBN 0–421–41020–5

PREFACE

Watching judges alter and strain old concepts and rules of law to join the latter half of the twentieth century is fascinating, no more so than in relation to interests in land where the law has developed over centuries. Listening to practitioners describe the difficulties and hardships suffered by their clients who have been sharing residential accommodation is more worrying.

This book is an attempt to state, analyse and apply the law relating to informal land arrangements and to suggest solutions to the more common problems raised by the sharing of accommodation. There are no neat legal answers but it is now possible to indicate which rights and remedies are likely to apply in which factual situations and to give some indication of the lines along which the law may develop.

In writing this book I have had considerable help from a number of sources, not least the local practitioners who took the time to discuss their cases with me. I am particularly indebted to Lord Justice Slade, not just for writing the foreword to this book, but for taking the time to read and comment on the manuscript in a way which clarified my thinking in several areas. My colleague Tim Evans read the chapter on proprietary estoppel and Tony Twemlow of Cuff Roberts North Kirk read the chapter on bankruptcy; both chapters benefit from their knowledge and expertise. His Honour Judge Michael O'Donoghue read the section on procedure and above all highlighted the perils and pitfalls which Chancery procedure can present to the uninitiated. Finally, my thanks are due to Kevin Grice for intelligent conversation throughout the writing of this book and for maintaining a sense of perspective.

Jean Warburton
Liverpool
June 1990

FOREWORD

"Behold how good and how pleasant it is for brethren to dwell together in unity:" (Psalm 133 v. 1).

The Psalmist forbore to comment how nasty and unpleasant can be the sequel if co-occupants of a dwellinghouse fall out with one another. In far too many cases that will be the first occasion on which advice is taken by any of them as to the legal consequences of their co-occupation. In far too many cases also this will be too late.

In writing this comprehensive study of the law relating to "Sharing Residential Property", Miss Warburton has undertaken a courageous task. Not only is she one of the pioneers in this particular field but, as she says in the introductory section, the relevant law is still in a stage of transition. Its basic structure emerged at a time when rights of ownership was ordinarily restricted to the *pater familias*. While that was so, our law could generally insist on the observance of strict formalities for the creation of interests in land; the advantages of certainty in this context were and are obvious. Since then, however, changing social conditions have necessitated an increasing degree of intervention by equity to prevent the ostensible owner from relying on his paper title against co-occupants in circumstances where such conduct would be dishonest or unconscionable. Such intervention has largely been by means of the developing concepts of constructive trust and proprietary estoppel. Present day social trends have brought about an acceleration of the process.

As I think this book well demonstrates, the present state of the relevant law is neither wholly clear nor wholly satisfactory. Perhaps the most striking illustration of the uneasy conflict between the competing demands of certainty and flexibility in this field is to be found in section 53 of the Law of Property Act 1925, of which subsection (2) exempted "the creation or operation of resulting, implied or constructive trusts" from the stringent requirements of a written instrument imposed by subsection (1). In particular, for all their advantages, the uncertain limits of the concepts of constructive trust and proprietary estoppel present difficult problems both for the courts and for practitioners asked to advise disappointed co-occupants.

Having regard to the elusive nature of her subject, it is inevitable that some of the propositions of law stated by the author may not meet with universal acceptance. All her readers, however, will appreciate the care, enterprise and erudition which she has devoted to a difficult project. For all its relative brevity, this work is a storehouse of learning and contains a valuable collation of references to relevant recent authorities, which is probably unique of its kind. It also offers some good practical advice. I have no doubt that it will be a useful vademecum for any practitioner concerned with this field of the law and would expect it to be of interest to others.

The Rt. Hon. Sir Christopher Slade
January 1990

CONTENTS

TABLE OF CASES

TABLE OF STATUTES

TABLE OF STATUTORY INSTRUMENTS

1 FACTS, LAW AND PROCEDURE

Introduction

The sharing of residential property can take many forms but, unless there has been careful planning, the result is very often serious disagreement between the parties. The lawyer normally becomes involved at the disagreement, rather than the planning stage, when one of the parties may be faced with losing his or her home. There is no one simple legal answer but a variety of possibilities, the relevance of which depends on the form of the parties' original arrangement. The potential legal rights and remedies are set out below, followed by a list of questions designed to elicit the type of information which will be required from the client. Once the probable form of the arrangement has been obtained, it should become clearer which of the potential rights and remedies are relevant. The details of those rights and remedies can then be found in the subsequent chapters. The procedural steps to be taken will depend upon whether the client is an owner seeking possession, or a non-owner seeking to remain in occupation. The rules are, therefore, examined from both points of view. Finally, various preventative measure, which can be taken before a sharing arrangement is entered into, are considered.

A.   The problem

People share residential accommodation for all sorts of reasons. Young people share flats and houses because they cannot afford to buy, or because they regard the relationship as merely a temporary one. Whilst the matrimonial home is now usually held in joint names, cohabitees often share property which is owned by only one of them. Families may feel obliged to share their property with a relative who would otherwise be homeless. A single householder may have a live-in housekeeper. The increasingly elderly population means that it is now far more common to find 'granny flats' or older people sharing their property with younger relatives or friends.[1] The terms

Informal arrangements

on which the property is shared are rarely thought through let alone discussed with a lawyer or put into writing. The informality is such that Croom-Johnson L.J. in *Rogers* v. *Eller*[2] coined the phrase "family non-arrangements." In some instances there may be no time to seek legal advice, for example, if a relative suddenly becomes ill, whilst in other

---

[1] For the problems inherent in elderly parents buying their council house with financial assistance from their children see L.S. Gaz. Nov. 9, 1988, p. 30.
[2] C.A., unreported, May 20, 1986.

cases the obtaining of advice may be seen as a cold and calculating step in an otherwise happy emotional relationship. The problem remains, however, that the nature of the law itself stops many people wanting to become involved with it.[3] The combination of living in close proximity and the lack of clear terms of agreement means that such sharing arrangements have a high degree of breakdown. This is shown by the fact that the most frequent reason for a household becoming homeless is that parents, relatives or friends are no longer able or willing to provide accommodation.[4]

The breakdown of such informal sharing arrangements has not always presented legal problems. Initially, the courts refused to recognise that a person had acquired any right in land unless the relevant formalities had been complied with. In more recent years, equity has recognised the informal creation of interests in land by means of resulting, implied and constructive trusts and proprietary estoppel. Until relatively **Legal involvement** recently, the courts have simply refused to become involved, either on the grounds that family arrangements were outside the realms of contract,[5] or on the grounds of public policy that the courts would not concern themselves with arrangements which encouraged immorality.[6] It is now clear that the courts will enforce arrangements between members of the same family[7] and give effect to their legitimate expectations.[8] The courts also apply and enforce the same legal principles, whether the parties are married or cohabiting.[9]

The major cause of the legal difficulties relating to the sharing of residential property is that the law is still in a stage of transition and has not yet fully come to terms with informal land arrangements. The main structure of property law was laid down when rights of ownership were restricted to the **Changing ideas of** *paterfamilias*.[10] Rights of ownership have now widened to the **property rights** extent that we have been described as living in "a real-property-mortgaged-to-a-building-society-owning democracy."[11] Ideas of what amount to property rights and who is entitled to legal protection to remain in peaceful occupation have also changed. This change in attitude is reflected in the legal status and protection afforded to a statutory tenant.[12] There has been no corresponding legislation to support the position of those sharing residential property without a tenancy and the extent of the courts' intervention has not been constant over the years.

As may be expected, the courts initially took a rigid approach to informal land arrangements and were only

---

[3] See *Gissing* v. *Gissing* [1971] A.C. 886, 896 *per* Lord Reid.
[4] Central Statistical Office, *Social Trends No. 19* (1989), p. 139.
[5] See *Balfour* v. *Balfour* [1919] 2 K.B. 571, 579 *per* Atkin L.J.
[6] See *Benyon* v. *Nettlefold* (1830) 3 Mac. & G. 94.
[7] See, for example, *Hardwick* v. *Johnson* [1978] 1 W.L.R. 683; Dwyer, "Immoral Contracts" (1977) 93 L.Q.R. 386.
[8] See, for example, *Griffiths* v. *Williams* (1978) 248 E.G. 947.
[9] *Bernard* v. *Joseph* [1982] Ch. 391, 402 *per* Griffiths L.J.
[10] *Williams & Glyn's Bank Ltd.* v. *Boland* [1981] A.C. 487, 508 *per* Lord Wilberforce.
[11] *Pettitt* v. *Pettitt* [1970] A.C. 777, 824 *per* Lord Diplock.
[12] See *Johnson* v. *Moreton* [1980] A.C. 37, 66–67 *per* Lord Simon of Glaisdale.

prepared to intervene in limited circumstances for limited purposes. For example, the remedy of proprietary estoppel was only available if the five probanda were proved,[13] and a licence would be enforced against the grantor but not against a third

Court intervention

party.[14] Attitudes changed slowly[15] until Lord Denning became Master of the Rolls when, suddenly, a very liberal attitude was taken to non-owners seeking to remain in occupation. Licences became binding on third parties[16] and jurisdiction was claimed to impose a trust whenever justice and good conscience required it.[17] Recent years have seen a rejection of a broad equitable jurisdiction in relation to informal land arrangements and the re-introduction of a more structured and rigid approach.[18] For example, detailed conditions for the acquisition of a beneficial interest under a trust for sale were set out by the Court of Appeal in *Grant* v. *Edwards*,[19] and in *Ashburn Anstalt* v. *Arnold*[20] they severely limited the circumstances in which a licence will bind a third party.

Realistic solutions

The courts are showing themselves increasingly more aware of the background against which their decisions have to operate[21] and the effect of those decisions on all the persons interested in that particular property, some of whom may not be a party to the action.[22] Thus it has been said that any solution which the court imposes must be realistic.[23] This realism is shown by the courts' refusal to grant a remedy which will force the parties to live together when relations have reached such a point that it would be totally impracticable.[24] It can also be seen in the recent House of Lords decision in *A. G. Securities* v. *Vaughan*,[25] which recognised that, in some instances, a licence accurately reflects the needs of those sharing accommodation. Whilst there has been a call recently for a generally more flexible attitude to cases involving the sharing of residential property,[26] the major trend appears to be to restrict the exercise of judicial discretion to proprietary estoppel but to widen the circumstances in which proprietary estoppel may provide a solution.[27]

---

[13] *Willmott* v. *Barber* (1880) 15 Ch. D. 96; see below Chap. 7, Part A1, p. 110.
[14] See below Chap. 2, Part B1, p. 24.
[15] For the history of the courts' changing attitude to claims to a beneficial interest in property used as a family asset, see *Pettitt* v. *Pettitt* [1970] A.C. 777, 819 *per* Lord Diplock.
[16] *Errington* v. *Errington and Woods* [1952] 1 K.B. 290.
[17] *Hussey* v. *Palmer* [1972] 1 W.L.R. 1286, 1290.
[18] *City of London Building Society* v. *Flegg* [1988] 1 A.C. 54.
[19] [1986] Ch. 638; see also *Burns* v. *Burns* [1984] Ch. 317; *Lloyds Bank plc* v. *Rosset* [1990] 1 All E.R. 1111.
[20] [1989] 1 Ch. 1.
[21] See *Williams & Glyn's Bank Ltd.* v. *Boland* [1981] A.C. 487, 510 *per* Lord Scarman.
[22] See, for example, *Re Sharpe (A Bankrupt)* [1980] 1 W.L.R. 219, 226 *per* Browne-Wilkinson J.
[23] *Rogers* v. *Eller* C.A., unreported, May 20, 1986 *per* Croom-Johnson L.J.
[24] See, for example, *Dodsworth* v. *Dodsworth* (1973) 228 E.G. 1115.
[25] [1988] 3 W.L.R. 1205; see below Chap. 3, Part G1(e), p. 50.
[26] *Lloyds Bank plc* v. *Rossett* [1989] 1 Ch. 350, 386 *per* Nicholls L.J.; see also Eekelaar, 'A Woman's Place—A Conflict Between Law and Social Value' [1987] Conv. 93, 99.
[27] *Grant* v. *Edwards* [1986] Ch. 638, 656 *per* Browne-Wilkinson V.C.

B.   The law

Potential legal remedies

The claimant will be seeking some right or interest in land. The potential legal rights available to a person sharing residential property range from nothing more than a bare licence at one end of the scale, to the fee simple arising under the doctrine of proprietary estoppel at the other. Once it has been established that a claimant has a right in the property, that right will need to be enforced, against the owner or a third party, by means of the usual remedies. Thus, for example, a contractual licence will be enforced by either an action for possession or an action for damages, depending upon whether the claimant has found alternative accommodation. A number of different legal concepts can be used to support or protect a person sharing residential accommodation and, in some instances, the concept which gives rise to the right in the land can also be said to be a remedy. Thus, for example, proprietary estoppel can be regarded as a remedy which grants a right to the claimant which itself may require to be enforced by further legal remedies. A constructive trust can also be regarded as an equitable remedy which gives rise to an interest in the property. The doctrine of part performance, by comparison, is an equitable remedy which enforces a pre-existing contract to transfer an estate. The rights and remedies which are potentially available to a claimant, together with their essential elements, are as follows:

(a)   Bare licence[28]—permission only;
(b)   Contractual licence[29]—a contract;
(c)   Equitable licence[30]—a form of proprietary estoppel;
(d)   Lease[31]—a contract and exclusive possession;
(e)   Part performance[32]—a contract;
(f)   Express trust[33]—clear declaration;
(g)   Constructive trust[34]—clear acceptance of the interest;
(h)   Resulting trust[35]—contribution to the purchase;
(i)   Implied trust[36]—common intention and detriment; and
(j)   Proprietary estoppel[37]—encouragement or acquiescence, reliance and detriment.

It is not usual to find any documents relating to the terms on which the parties are to share the accommodation but this lack of writing operates as a bar to only one of the potential legal solutions and then only in limited circumstances. A bare licence and a contractual licence do not need to be evidenced in

---

[28] See below Chap. 2, Part A, p. 20.
[29] See below Chap. 2, Part B, p. 24.
[30] See below Chap. 2, Part C, p. 35.
[31] See below Chap. 3.
[32] See below Chap. 4.
[33] See below Chap. 5, Part A, p. 71.
[34] See below Chap. 5, Part B, p. 74.
[35] See below Chap. 6, Part B, p. 83.
[36] See below Chap. 6, Part C, p. 89.
[37] See below Chap. 7.

writing because neither creates an interest in land.[38] Whilst a lease must normally be by deed, informal leases for less than three years are enforceable, even if oral.[39] An oral express trust and an oral contract for the transfer of land entered into before September 27, 1989[40] and supported by acts of part performance are both enforced, because equity will not allow a statute to be used as an instrument of fraud. The creation of resulting, implied and constructive trusts is specifically exempted from the requirement of writing by statute.[41] Finally, interests arising under the doctrine of proprietary estoppel do not require writing because the interest is actually granted by the court.[42]

Oral arrangements

A contract is an essential element for the creation of a contractual licence and a lease and for the doctrine of part performance. Thus, for a claimant to use any of those remedies, the parties must have had an intention to create legal relations. If the parties are members of the same family or cohabitees this is unlikely, although not impossible.[43] For example, in *Nunn* v. *Dalrymple*[44] the Court of Appeal held that an oral agreement between members of a family giving the claimants exclusive possession of a cottage in return for regular payments and renovation of the property, created a lease and not merely a bare licence. In the more usual case where the existence of a contract is very doubtful, proprietary estoppel should be considered. If the sharer has contributed in some way towards the purchase of the property, either financially or by carrying out substantial work on the premises, a beneficial interest under either a resulting[45] or an implied[46] trust may also be relevant.

Intention to create legal relations

The choice of legal right or remedy may, to a certain extent, be dictated by the practical remedy sought by the claimant who is sharing the property. If the claimant is seeking to remain in occupation against the original owner, it may be sufficient to establish the existence of a contractual licence.[47] That right will not be adequate, however, if the claimant is threatened with an action for possession by a third party.[48] In that situation, if there is no lease, proprietary estoppel[49] should be considered. Where a claimant has contributed a capital sum towards the purchase of the property but has now left the premises, the establishment of a beneficial interest under a resulting or an implied trust will ensure that he receives the return of his capital when the property is sold.[50] If the

Right or remedy required

---

[38] Law of Property (Miscellaneous Provisions) Act 1989, s.2(1)(6).
[39] *Ibid.*, s.2(5)(*a*); Law of Property Act 1925, s.54(2); see below Chap. 3, Part C, p. 42.
[40] *Ibid.*, s.5(3).
[41] *Ibid.*, s.2(5); Law of Property Act 1925, s.53(2).
[42] See below Chap. 7, Part C, p. 122.
[43] See below Chap. 2, Part B2, p. 26, Chap. 4, Part B, p. 65.
[44] (1989) 21 H.L.R. 569.
[45] See below Chap. 6, Part B, p. 83.
[46] See *Grant* v. *Edwards* [1986] Ch. 638; see below Chap. 6, Part C, p. 89.
[47] See below Chap. 2, Part B, p. 24.
[48] See below Chap. 8, Part F2(b), p. 146.
[49] See below Chap. 7.
[50] See below Chap. 6, Part D2, p. 105.

claimant is seeking to remain in the property, however, that equitable interest will not be fully effective because a beneficial interest under a trust for sale carries only limited rights of occupation.[51] The claimant may be better served by seeking an equitable licence.[52]

Co-existent rights

The various legal rights and remedies are not mutually exclusive. Thus, the result of a claim based on the doctrine of proprietary estoppel may be a beneficial interest under a trust for sale[53] or a lease.[54] Two rights may also co-exist. For example, a claimant may have contributed to the purchase price of the property giving him a beneficial interest under a resulting trust. He may also, as a consequence of representations made by the owner, have an irrevocable licence to remain in occupation of the property arising under the doctrine of proprietary estoppel.[55]

Minimum rights

Even if the conclusion is reached that none of the potential rights and remedies are relevant to the circumstances of the particular claimant, he will still be a bare licensee who is allowed a reasonable time to vacate the property.[56] If the claimant has lent money to the owner, but not in such a way as to give him an interest in the property, the repayment of the loan can be protected by taking a charge on the property under the Charging Orders Act 1979.[57]

Changing law

The law relating to informal land arrangements is prone to change and no solution should be rejected simply because it does not appear to be "popular" at the present time. It may well be, for example, that in the future the courts will impose limitations on the doctrine of proprietary estoppel and show greater interest in the constructive trust. The potential legal rights and remedies should always be considered, therefore, in the context of the most recent decisions of the Court of Appeal.[58]

C. The facts

Relevant information

The facts surrounding an informal arrangement for the sharing of residential accommodation will, inevitably, be confused. Well directed questions can, however, elicit sufficient information to indicate which of the legal rights and remedies is likely to be appropriate. The choice of solution will then dictate the more detailed information which is required. Pertinent questions need to be asked about three separate areas; the original discussions, contributions and living patterns. In addition, any documentary evidence should be considered.

---

[51] See below Chap. 6, Part D1, p. 104.
[52] See below Chap. 2, Part C, p. 35.
[53] *Jones (A.E.)* v. *Jones (F.W.)* [1977] 1 W.L.R. 438.
[54] *Griffiths* v. *Williams* (1978) 248 E.G. 947; see below Chap. 7, Part C1, p. 123.
[55] See *Abbey National Building Society* v. *Cann* (1989) 57 P. & C. R. 381.
[56] See below Chap. 2, Part A2, p. 22.
[57] See below Chap. 8, Part F1, p. 142.
[58] Cases in relation to informal land arrangements rarely go to the House of Lords because of the cost factor.

1. Documents

Clearly, if there is a written agreement setting out the terms on which the property is being shared, that document will provide the basis of all future action. It is the content, and not the form, of the agreement which is important. A document headed "Licence" may well be a lease.[59] Even if there is no **Letters** written agreement, letters written at the time the sharing began may contain important terms of the arrangement. Letters or notes between the parties, written whilst the property was being shared, can be relevant in relation to representations made by the owner for the purposes of proprietary estoppel[60] or refer to the basis on which payments have been made for the purposes of an implied trust.[61] Evidence of payments by the **Payment books** claimant may be available in the form of bank statements, payment books and receipts.

2. Original discussions

The questions relating to the facts surrounding the original discussions are directed to ascertaining whether there was a contract between the parties and the basis on which the move to the property was made.

(a) **What was the relationship between the parties?**
The closer and more amicable the relationship between the parties, whether members of the same family or **Intention to** cohabitees, the less likelihood there is of the court **contract** finding that there was an intention to create legal relations.[62] The nature of the relationship between cohabitants can raise a common intention for the purposes of an implied trust.[63]

(b) **Was there any discussion as to the terms on which the property was to be shared?**
Lack of agreement as to the length of time the sharing would continue, for example, will prevent a contract arising.[64]

(c) **Had the discussions been completed before the claimant moved into the premises?**
Continuing discussion indicates the lack of a concluded contract.[65]

(d) **Did the claimant agree to make any periodic payment to the owner?**
Consideration The existence of periodic payments not only provides consideration for a contract but also provides evidence of an intention to create legal relations.[66]

---

[59] See below Chap. 2, Part G2(a)(iii), p. 55.
[60] See below Chap. 7, Part B1, p. 113.
[61] See below Chap. 6, Part C1(c), p. 93.
[62] See below Chap. 2, Part B2, p. 26, Chap. 3, Part B, p. 40, Chap. 4, Part B, p. 65.
[63] See below Chap. 6, Part C1(c)(v), p. 98.
[64] *Johnson v. Johnson* C.A., unreported, March 11, 1986.
[65] *Maddison v. Alderson* (1883) 3 App. Cas. 467.
[66] *Hardwick v. Johnson* [1978] 1 W.L.R. 683.

Detriment

(e) **Did the claimant give up his own accommodation to go and live with the owner?**
The loss of secure accommodation, such as a protected, statutory or assured tenancy, can provide consideration for a contractual licence,[67] the consideration for a contract to be enforced under the doctrine of part performance,[68] or an act of detriment for the purposes of proprietary estoppel.[69]

Common intention

(f) **Did the claimant receive any encouragement from the owner to move into the premises?**
Statements from the owner at the time of the move can be relevant as, either evidence of a common intention for the purposes of an implied trust[70] or, as acts of encouragement for proprietary estoppel.[71]

(g) **Was there an understanding between the parties that the claimant had some rights in the property?**
Such an understanding can provide evidence of a common intention to give the claimant an interest under an implied trust[72] or as evidence of acquiescence for proprietary estoppel.[73]

Exclusive possession

(h) **Did the parties intend the claimant to have sole use of any particular part of the premises?**
Exclusive possession is essential for a lease.[74]

3. Contributions

Questions relating to contributions are not restricted to financial contributions but extend to work carried out on the premises by the claimant. Periodic contributions of an income nature can be just as relevant as capital contributions.

Financial contributions

(a) **Did the claimant make any financial contribution to the purchase price of the property?**
Payment of part of the purchase price, for example, the deposit, will give rise to an interest under a resulting trust, unless the money was intended as a loan.[75] An initial financial contribution can also be evidence of a common intention for the purposes of an implied trust[76] or an act of part performance.[77]

---

[67] *Tanner* v. *Tanner* [1975] 1 W.L.R. 1346; see below Chap. 2, Part B2, p. 26.
[68] *Kingswood Estate Co. Ltd.* v. *Anderson* [1963] 2 Q.B. 169; see below Chap. 4, Part B, p. 65.
[69] *Watts* v. *Story* (1984) 134 New L.J. 631; see below Chap. 7 , Part B3, p. 118.
[70] *Eves* v. *Eves* [1975] 1 W.L.R. 1338; see below Chap. 6, Part C1(c)(vi), p. 99.
[71] *Pascoe* v. *Turner* [1979] 1 W.L.R. 431; see below Chap. 7, Part B1, p. 113.
[72] See below Chap. 6, Part C1(c)(iv), p. 97.
[73] See below Chap. 7, Part B1, p. 113.
[74] See below Chap. 3, Part G, p. 46.
[75] See below Chap. 6, Part B2, p. 86.
[76] See below Chap. 6, Part C1(c), p. 93.
[77] *Steadman* v. *Steadman* [1976] A.C. 536; see below Chap. 4, Part C, p. 66.

(b) **Did the claimant undertake and pay the whole or part of the mortgage on the property?**
The undertaking of liability for the mortgage will usually give rise to an interest under a resulting trust.[78]

(c) **Did the claimant, in fact, make regular contributions to the mortgage repayments?**
Mortgage repayments are evidence of a common intention that the claimant should have a beneficial interest under an implied trust.[79]

(d) **Did the claimant make regular contributions to the household budget?**
The claimant will only be able to rely on the payment of household expenses as evidence of a common intention under an implied trust if there was a connection between the contributions and the purchase of the property.[80] Payment of living expenses alone does not amount to detriment for the purposes of proprietary estoppel.[81]

(e) **Did the claimant make regular periodic payments to the owner?**
Regular payments may be rent giving rise to a periodic tenancy[82] or a contractual licence[83] but not if they are, in effect, the claimant's share of the living expenses.[84]

(f) **Did the claimant carry out work on the premises?**
Substantial work of improvement or repair, particularly at the time the property was bought, will provide evidence of a common intention for an implied trust.[85]

Work on the premises
Major work can also amount to an act of detriment for proprietary estoppel[86] or an act of part performance.[87] Routine repairs and maintenance are not sufficient for either an implied trust[88] or proprietary estoppel.[89]

4. Living arrangements

The arrangements actually adopted by the parties after the claimant moved into the premises cannot be used to provide evidence of the terms of a lease or a contractual licence because the manner of performance cannot be used to construe a

[78] *Marsh v. von Sternberg* [1986] 1 F.L.R. 526; see below Chap. 6, Part B2, p. 86.
[79] See below Chap. 6, Part C1(c)(i), p. 94.
[80] *Gissing v. Gissing* [1971] A.C. 886; see below Chap. 6, Part C1(c)(ii), p. 95.
[81] *Griffiths v. Williams* (1978) 248 E.G. 947; see below Chap. 7, Part B3, p. 118.
[82] See below Chap. 3, Part C, p. 42.
[83] *Hardwick v. Johnson* [1978] 1 W.L.R. 683; see below Chap. 2, Part B, p. 24.
[84] *Hannaford v. Selby* (1976) 239 E.G. 811.
[85] *Eves v. Eves* [1975] 1 W.L.R. 1338; see below Chap. 6, Part C1(c)(iii), p. 96.
[86] *Pascoe v. Turner* [1979] 1 W.L.R. 431; see below Chap. 7, Part B3, p. 118.
[87] See below Chap. 4, Part C, p. 66.
[88] *Pettitt v. Pettitt* [1970] A.C. 777; see below Chap. 6, Part C1(c)(iii), p. 96.
[89] *Rogers v. Eller* C.A., unreported, May 20, 1986; see below Chap. 7, Part B3, p. 118.

contract.[90] Later events can be relevant, however, for implied trusts, proprietary estoppel and part performance.

(a) **Did the parties treat the property and their other activities as a joint effort?**

Common intention

Joint enterprise between the parties can be evidence of a common intention for the purposes of an implied trust.[91]

(b) **Did the owner say anything to the claimant to indicate that he could remain in the property?**

Proprietary estoppel

Such statements can provide the basis for a claim in proprietary estoppel.[92]

(c) **Did the claimant do work for the owner?**

Unpaid work in looking after either the owner or his business can be acts of detriment for the purposes of proprietary estoppel.[93] Simply looking after the home and family is not sufficient to raise a common intention for an implied trust[94] and will only be an act of detriment for proprietary estoppel in exceptional circumstances.[95]

D. Procedure

The usual way in which disputes relating to informal sharing arrangements come before the court is when the owner or his mortgagee seeks possession. The rights of the sharer are then raised in the defence to the possession action. A sharer need not wait, however, for a possession action to obtain a judicial decision as to his rights to the property; he can bring an action for a declaration. An evicted sharer or an owner may seek an injunction to recover possession. The final form of action which is relevant is an application for an order for sale under section 30 of the Law of Property Act 1925. The reader is referred to the Supreme Court Practice, the County Court Practice and the standard texts[96] for the detailed law of procedure. Certain steps in each of the actions can present problems when the litigation concerns shared residential property and they are examined in detail.

1. Possession actions

Court action

It is generally unlawful for an owner to seek to recover possession other than by an action in court.[97] Whilst physical

---

[90] *Wickman Ltd.* v. *Schuler A.G.* [1974] A.C. 325. See below Chap. 3, Part G2(a), p. 53.

[91] See below Chap. 6, Part C1(c)(iv), p. 97.

[92] *Pascoe* v. *Turner* [1979] 1 W.L.R. 431; see below Chap. 7, Part B1, p. 113.

[93] *Jones* v. *Watkins* C.A., unreported, November 26, 1987; see below Chap. 7, Part B3, p. 118.

[94] *Burns* v. *Burns* [1984] Ch. 317; see below Chap. 6, Part C1(c)(vii), p. 100.

[95] *Grant* v. *Edwards* [1986] Ch. 638, 657 *per* Browne-Wilkinson V.-C.; see below Chap. 7, Part B3, p. 118.

[96] See, for example, Casson and Dennis, *Odgers Principles of Pleading and Practice in Civil Actions in the High Court of Justice* (22nd ed., 1981); Owen, *County Court Litigation* (1988).

[97] Protection from Eviction Act 1977, s.3 as amended by Housing Act 1988, s.30.

repossession is still possible if living accommodation is being shared with the owner,[98] it is not advisable because of the possibility of a claim for damages for trespass, breach of any covenant for quiet enjoyment and the statutory tort of illegal eviction.[99] There is also a danger of prosecution under section 1 of the Protection from Eviction Act 1977 and section 6(1) of the Criminal Law Act 1977.

Determination of licence or lease

Before an action for possession is commenced, the owner must take care to see that any residential licence or tenancy which the sharer has, has been determined. Whilst an oral notice is sufficient to revoke a licence[1], it is preferable for any notice to be in writing. If a licence has not been revoked, or expired by effluxion of time, any possession action will simply be dismissed.[1a] A tenancy will similarly need to be determined by notice to quit unless it is a fixed term tenancy which has expired or been the subject of forfeiture. The tenant's right to remain after the determination of the tenancy will depend upon whether the tenancy comes within any of the regimes of statutory protection.[2] For example, an assured tenant under the Housing Act 1988 will have a periodic tenancy after the expiry of his fixed term tenancy which can only be determined on the grounds, and in accordance with the procedure, laid down in the Act. An unprotected tenant will be the subject of a possession action in the usual way.

The main method available to an owner to recover possession is an ordinary possession proceedings. If the net rateable value of the premises is £1,000 or less, proceedings may be taken in the county court; above that figure proceedings must be brought in the High Court.[3] In certain very limited circumstances summary possession proceedings under R.S.C., Ord. 113 or C.C.R., Ord 24 may be taken.

Summary possession proceedings

Summary possession proceedings[4] should only be used against a licensee who has failed to vacate the premises when his licence has so determined[5] and not against a tenant or former tenant holding over[6] or if any issues relating to the claim or any potential defence are complicated. In cases where there is doubt as to the sharer's rights in the property an ordinary possession action should be used and, if appropriate, then judgment under R.S.C., Ord. 14 once the defence has been served.[7] If summary possession proceedings

---

[98] *Ibid.*, s.3A.
[99] Housing Act 1988, s.27–28.
[1] Unless the licensor is not sharing the premises when four weeks written notice is required, Housing Act 1988, s.32.
[1a] See *Chandler* v. *Kerley* [1978] 1 W.L.R. 693.
[2] For the detailed law relating to security of tenure see Yates and Hawkins, *Landlord and Tenant Law* (2nd ed., 1986); Martin, *Security of Tenure under the Rent Act* (1986); Woodfall, *Landlord and Tenant* (28th ed., 1978). See also Walters and Harris, *Claims to the Possession of Land: The Law and Practice* (1987) Chaps. 10–15.
[3] County Court Act 1984, s.21; Adminstration of Justice Act 1977, Sched. 2; for proceedings under the Rent Act 1977 the jurisdiction in Greater London is £1,500.
[4] More usually used for the removal of "squatters."
[5] *Greater London Council* v. *Jenkins* [1975] 1 W.L.R. 155.
[6] Ord. 113 r. 1 R.S.C.; Ord. 24 r. 1 C.C.R.
[7] See below p. 13.

are commenced[8] and the affidavit in reply reveals a defence[9] or it becomes apparent at the hearing that the owner's claim is not sufficiently clear and straightforward, the judge will direct that the case continue as an ordinary possession action with the affidavits to stand as pleadings.[10-11] He may also direct that the applicant pay the costs of the respondent incurred by the incorrect use of R.S.C., Order 113 or C.C.R., Order 24.

Ordinary possession action

An owner seeking to recover possession from a person sharing his residential property will usually proceed by means of an ordinary possession action. Proceedings in the County Court[12] are fixed date actions commenced in the usual way with particulars of claim. The particulars of claim should specify the plaintiff owner's proprietary interest and set out any tenancy or licence under which the defendant sharer went into possession. The facts establishing the plaintiff's claim to possession should then be detailed, for example, the way in which the licence was revoked. The particulars of claim should also include the net annual value for rating purposes of the premises claimed and any monetary claim for arrears, mesne profits or damages. Actions in the High Court are commenced by writ of summons in the Queens Bench or the Chancery Division and the contents of the statement of claim[13] are the same as for particulars of claim in the county court.

Defence

The defence should, as normal, set out clearly which parts of the particulars, or statement, of claim are being denied and the relevant facts on which the sharer proposes to rely. For example, he may deny that his licence was revoked because sufficient notice was not given in accordance with its terms. The defence also provides the opportunity for the sharer to set out any claims he may have against the owner. Such a counterclaim will usually be in the form of a request for a declaration that the sharer has a particular interest in the property. The facts supporting the counterclaim should be pleaded in the same way as in an originating application for a

Counterclaim

declaration.[14] Thus, a sharer may counterclaim for a declaration that the owner holds the property on trust for himself and the sharer[15] or that the sharer is entitled to an interest arising under the doctrine of proprietary estoppel.[16] If the defendant has several grounds for claiming an interest in the property, each must be separately pleaded; the court will not assume a claim pleaded as a beneficial interest under a trust for sale includes a claim based in proprietary estoppel.[17]

---

[8] See Ord. 113 r. 3 R.S.C.; Ord. 24 r. 2 C.C.R.; for a precedent see Walters and Harris, *Claims to the Possession of Land: The Law and Practice* (1987), p. 442.

[9] If there is a possible defence, affidavit evidence should be filed, *Fryer* v. *Brook* C.A., unreported, July 19, 1984.

[10-11] *Crancour Ltd.* v. *Da Silvesa* (1986) 278 E.G. 618; but see *Henderson* v. *Law* (1985) 17 H.L.R. 237.

[12] For jurisdiction see above, n. 3.

[13] For a precedent see *Atkins Court Forms* (2nd ed., 1985) Vol. 1, p. 287.

[14] See below Part D2, p. 14.

[15] See *Passee* v. *Passee* [1988] 1 F.L.R. 263.

[16] *Pascoe* v. *Turner* [1979] 1 W.L.R. 431.

[17] *Walker* v. *Walker* C.A., unreported, Bound Transcript No. 173, 1984.

Judgment on default of defence

If a defence is served but the owner considers that there is no real defence to the action, he can apply for summary judgment under R.S.C. Ord. 14 in the High Court but not in the County Court. The summons should be supported by an affidavit[18] from the owner. If the defendant's affidavit in reply reveals no defence, judgment for possession will be given by the master or the district registrar. An R.S.C. Ord. 14 summons is appropriate, *inter alia*, where a licensee refuses to leave after a licence granted for a fixed term has expired[19] but generally the use of R.S.C. Ord. 14 will be unusual in the context of sharing residential property because of the potential disputes as to fact.

Summary judgment

Evidence

Before the trial, the plaintiff should ensure that he can prove his title to the property, for example, by producing his land certificate. The plaintiff should also collect together any documents, for example letters,[20] relating to the defendant's occupation of the premises. Consideration should also be given to the oral evidence he wishes to lead at the trial. For example, another member of the family may have been present when the defendant moved in and may be able to give evidence that it was made clear to the defendant that he could only stay for a short while until he found alternative accommodation. The defendant should undertake a similar exercise if he wishes to counterclaim for an interest in the property and ensure, for example, that he has receipts and any other documentary evidence relating to payments made to the owner or work carried out on the premises. If the defendant intends to rely on statements made by the owner as to his continued occupation, the existence of any witnesses to the relevant conversations should be investigated and proofs of evidence taken.[21-23]

Action by mortgagee

If possession proceedings are brought by a mortgagee, he should make any person who may have an interest in the property, other than a tenant or a licensee, a defendant. Notice of the proceedings should be given to a tenant or licensee who can apply to be joined as a defendant. A spouse who has registered her statutory rights under the Matrimonial Homes Act 1983[24] must be given notice of the action[25] and can be made a party even if she has no other rights in the property.[26] The plaintiff mortgagee should be aware of who is in occupation because of the need to include the relevant details in the particulars of claim in the County Court[27] or in the affidavit in support of the originating summons in the Chancery Division.[28] The sharer is then in a position to defend the

---

[18] Ord. 14 r. 2 R.S.C.

[19] *Shell Mex and B.P. Ltd.* v. *Manchester Garages Ltd.* [1971] 1 W.L.R. 613.

[20] See above Part C1, p. 7.

[21-23] For the general law of evidence and the admission of evidence under the Civil Evidence Act 1968 and on affidavit see *Phipson on Evidence* (13th ed., 1982), *Cross on Evidence* (6th ed., 1985).

[24] See below Chap. 8, Part C, p. 138.

[25] Matrimonial Homes Act 1983, s.8(3).

[26] *Ibid.*, s.8(2).

[27] Ord. 6 r. 5(1A) C.R.R.

[28] Ord. 88 r. 5(4) R.S.C.

possession action and counterclaim for a declaration that he or she is entitled to an interest in the property. In addition, the defence will need to allege the way in which the sharer's interest binds the mortgagee. For example, it may be alleged that the sharer's interest is an overriding one and that allegation must be supported by particulars of actual occupation.[29]

2.   Action for a declaration

Jurisdiction

A person sharing residential accommodation may consider that he has an interest in the property beyond a mere licence. In order to determine what his rights are and to gain security, the sharer may bring an action for a declaration. The action may be brought in the County Court[30] if the premises are valued at £30,000 or less. In the High Court the action is usually brought in the Chancery Divison. If the parties are engaged or married, the proceedings may be brought in the Family Division of the High Court or the County Court under section 17 of the Married Women's Property Act 1882.

Summons

If there is no substantial dispute as to the facts and the only question is one of law then the proceedings should be commenced by originating summons[31] in the High Court, or originating application in the County Court.[32] The facts will then appear in the plaintiff's affidavit[33] accompanying the summons and any affidavit the defendant may file in reply. An originating summons or application will be appropriate, for example, where the contributions of both parties towards the property are not in dispute, but a declaration is sought as to whether those contributions are sufficient to give the plaintiff a beneficial interest under a trust for sale.[34] In practice it is comparatively rare for an origination summons to be apposite. Where the facts are in dispute and there is a need to call oral evidence, the action should be commenced by writ of summons in the High Court or as a fixed date action in the County Court. The plaintiff's case will then appear in the statement or particulars of claim.

Resulting or implied trust

If the plaintiff bases his case on a resulting[35] or an implied trust,[36] the originating summons or statement of claim[37] will usually seek a declaration that the defendant owner holds the property on trust for sale for himself and the plaintiff as beneficial joint tenants or tenants in common in specific shares. In the alternative, a declaration will be sought as to the plaintiff's beneficial interest in the property. The affidavit or statement of claim should include particulars of any agreement between the parties as to how the property was to be owned,

---

[29] But see *Lloyds Bank plc* v. *Rossett* [1990] 1 All E.R. 1111. County Court Act 1984, s.22, 23.
[30] County Court Act 1984. s.23.
[31] For a precedent see *Atkins Court Forms* (2nd ed., 1983) Vol. 35 p. 35.
[32] Ord. 5 R. 4 R.S.C.
[33] For a precedent see *Atkins Court Forms* (2nd ed., 1983) Vol. 35 p. 37.
[34] See *Burns* v. *Burns* [1984] Ch. 317.
[35] See below Chap. 6, Part B, p. 83.
[36] See below Chap. 6, Part C, p. 89.
[37] For a precedent see *Atkins Court Forms* (2nd ed., 1986) Vol. 41 p. 88.

together with details of all financial contributions made and work done on the property by the plaintiff.

Proprietary estoppel

Where the claim is based on proprietary estoppel, a declaration will be sought that the plaintiff is entitled to the interest alleged. An order for the defendant to grant the relevant interest to the plaintiff should also be sought.[38] The particulars of the assurances or representations made by the defendant on which the plaintiff relied should be set out in the affidavit or statement of claim. In addition every item of detriment relied upon should be specifically pleaded.[39]

Pleadings

The circumstances of the sharing of the accommodation may be such as to give the plaintiff a potential interest in the property under more than one head. For example, there may have been an initial arrangement giving rise to a contractual licence but later representations by the owner may have given the sharer a further interest under the doctrine of proprietary estoppel. Again, it may not be clear whether work carried out by the plaintiff on the premises was in consequence of a common intention between the parties that he should have a beneficial interest under an implied trust or in reliance on a representation by the owner that he should have an irrevocable licence for life. All possible grounds for the plaintiff's claim must be separately pleaded; the court will not assume any cause of action in addition to those pleaded.[40]

Defence

The defendant owner's affidavit in reply or defence,[41] as well as denying, where appropriate, particulars alleged by the plaintiff, should set out any additional facts which prevent any interest arising. For example, if a beneficial interest under an implied trust is pleaded based on financial contributions, it is a defence if the payments were made as part of the household expenses and not as contributions towards the purchase of the property.[42] If a claim is based on proprietary estoppel it is a defence that the alleged acts of detriment would have taken place in any event and were not done in reliance on the defendant's representation.[43]

Evidence

As in any other action, the evidence either party intends to rely on at trial should be carefully considered. If the plaintiff's claim is based on proprietary estoppel, he should ensure that he can prove all the alleged acts of detriment.[44] For example, if he has alleged that he was obliged to give up secure accommodation to go and live with the defendant, documentary evidence of the sale or the surrender of a tenancy should be available. This may be obtainable from the former landlord; for example, a surrender of a local authority tenancy will usually still be in the housing authority's records. If the plaintiff's claim is based on an implied trust, all the evidence to support a common intention should be explored. For example,

---

[38] For a precedent see *Atkins Court Forms* (2nd ed., 1985) Vol. 18 p. 317.
[39] *Jones* v. *Watkins* C.A., unreported, November 26, 1987.
[40] See *Walker* v. *Walker* C.A., unreported, Bound Transcript No. 173, 1984.
[41] For a precedent for a defence in an action based on proprietary estoppel see *Atkins Court Forms* (2nd ed., 1985) Vol. 18, p. 318.
[42] See below Chap. 6, Part C1(c)(ii), p. 95.
[43] See below Chap. 7, Part B3, p. 118.
[44] *Jones* v. *Watkins* C.A., unreported, November 26, 1987.

if the defendant's statements at the time as to ownership are being relied upon, it may be advisable to take a proof of evidence from the solicitor who did the conveyancing. In relation to a claim based on part performance, any correspondence between the parties at the time the plaintiff moved into the premises will be important.

Court order   The court order declaring the plaintiff's interest in the property should contain sufficient supplementary provision to ensure that the declaration is effective. Thus, a declaration that the plaintiff has an interest arising under the doctrine of proprietary estoppel should be followed by an order that the defendant grant to the relevant interest to the plaintiff, and, in default, the necessary conveyance, transfer or lease to be executed on his behalf by the master or district registrar.[45] A declaration that the plaintiff has a beneficial interest in the property should be supported by an order that the plaintiff be appointed a trustee with the defendant and, if necessary, an order that the property should be sold and for an account.

3. Injunctions

A sharer who has been evicted by the owner may be homeless. The remedy of an injunction[46] allows him to regain possession of the premises. The County Court has jurisdiction over premises with a net rateable value up to, and including £1,000, even if no damages are claimed.[47] It is usual for proceedings to be issued for breach of a covenant of quiet enjoyment or for **Urgent cases**   trespass before any application is made, but in urgent cases application can be made upon an undertaking to file proceedings in either 24 or 48 hours. An injunction may then be applied for either *ex parte*[48] or on notice.[49] The application should be supported by an affidavit setting out the plaintiff's right to be on the premises and the circumstances of the eviction. An interim injunction will not be granted unless the balance of convenience is in favour of an injunction.[50] The order must be served on the owner[51] and enforcement is by means of committal proceedings.[52]

4. Applications for sale

If one or more of the trustees of property held on a trust for sale will not agree to the property being sold, any person interested may apply to the court under section 30 of the Law of Property Act 1925 for an order for sale. An action may be brought by a co-owner or a sharer with a beneficial interest

---

[45] See *Pascoe* v. *Turner* [1979] 1 W.L.R. 431.
[46] For the detailed procedure see Bean, *Injunctions* (4th ed., 1987); Arden and Partington, *Quiet Enjoyment* (2nd ed., 1985).
[47] County Court Act 1984, s.22.
[48] Ord. 29 r. 2 R.S.C.; Ord. 13 r. 6(3) C.C.R.
[49] Ord. 29 r. 1 R.S.C.; Ord. 13 r. 1 C.C.R.
[50] *American Cyanamid Co.* v. *Ethicon Ltd.* [1975] A.C. 396.
[51] Ord.45 r.7 R.S.C.; Ord.29 r.1(2) C.C.R.
[52] Ord. 45 r.5 R.S.C.; Ord. 29 r.1 C.C.R.

Resulting and implied trusts arising under a resulting or an implied trust. The defendant will be the trustee who is refusing to sell. Application is made by originating summons[53] in the Chancery Division of the High Court or by originating application in the County Court.[54] The summons or application must be supported by an affidavit[55] setting out the facts showing that the purpose of the trust has ended.[56] If the terms of the trust for sale are not clear, the summons or application can also seek the court's determination as to the beneficial interests of the parties in the property.[57]

E. Prevention

Many of the problems which arise from the sharing of residential property can be avoided if the parties set out the terms on which they are to live together. Whilst it is unusual for people thinking of sharing property which is already owned by one of the parties to seek advice, a solicitor will usually be involved if the property is being purchased for joint occupation. In addition, legal advice may be sought when the sharing is intended to be on a long term basis. In those situations, there are several steps which can be taken to protect the parties and to clarify the basis on which the property is to be shared.

If property is being purchased in joint names, the **Recording beneficial interests** of each party should be set out in the conveyance or transfer. The point was made forcibly by Griffiths L.J. in *Bernard* v. *Josephs*[58];

> "I wish more heed had been paid to the advice to solicitors given by Bagnall J. in *Cowcher* v. *Cowcher* [1972] 1 W.L.R. 425, 442, in which he pointed out the wisdom of making an express declaration of the beneficial interests in the property at the time it is bought. The home is usually the most valuable asset of any couple living together and if, when they separate, a legal battle is waged with the aid of legal aid over the ownership of their shares in the house the result is that both of them see a large part of their share of the equity disappear in costs into the maw of the legal aid fund, as indeed will happen in this case."

A solicitor who fails to declare the beneficial interests may be liable in negligence.[59]

Many disputes may be avoided if the details of the arrangements between the parties in relation to the property are set out in a separate declaration of trust. The parties' beneficial interests may not be a simple proportion of the proceeds of

---

[53] For a precedent see *Atkins Court Forms* (2nd ed., 1986) Vol. 41, p. 183.
[54] The county court has jurisdiction if the value of the property is £30,000 or less, County Court Act 1984, s.23.
[55] For a precedent see Blackford and Jaque, *Chancery Practice Handbook* (1983) p. 133.
[56] See below Chap. 6, Part D1, p. 104.
[57] For a precedent see *Atkins Court Forms* (2nd ed., 1986) Vol. 41, p. 183.
[58] [1982] Ch. 391, 403.
[59] See *Walker* v. *Hall* [1984] F.L.R. 126, 129 *per* Dillon L.J.

Declaration of trust

sale. For example, if one party was a sitting tenant, the declaration of trust could be in the form that the former tenant, on sale, takes the agreed value of the discount as declared and the remainder of the proceeds of sale, after payment of the mortgage, are to be divided 50/50, or in some other agreed proportion. The nature of the trust for sale is that the normal solution of any dispute between the parties is a sale of the property.[60] Thus, it may be advisable to include a clause that the property is not to be sold without say, six months' notice to the other party. A clause giving one co-owner an option to purchase the other co-owner's beneficial interest at an agreed valuation in the event of the other wishing to sell may save unwelcomed applications to the court. The possibility of dispute as to price could be dealt with by requiring the co-owners to refer the matter to an independent surveyor acting as an expert and not as an arbitrator. In addition, the declaration of trust could set out the liabilities of the individual co-owners for repairs, maintenance and payment of outgoings.

Consent

When property is being purchased in a sole name, the solicitor may become aware that the prospective owner intends to share the property with someone else. If the owner does not intend the sharer to have an interest in the property, it may be possible to get the sharer to sign either a formal declaration or a letter confirming that no beneficial interest is to be acquired.[61] If the sharer has already made, or intends to make, some financial contribution towards the price,[62] the sharer

Separate legal advice

should be advised to seek separate legal advice. The sharer may then be protected by an agreement recording the basis upon which financial contributions are being made or by a contractual licence securing occupation.

Elderly relatives

Additional considerations apply if property is to be shared with an elderly relative. A parent, say, who is contributing to property being purchased with a child and his or her spouse as a joint home should be separately advised. If the parent is to be a joint owner, the conveyance or transfer should record the beneficial interests in the usual way.[63] Alternatively, if the parent's contribution is a loan, it should be recorded as such and the parent given a written licence, revocable only in agreed circumstances, to protect his or her rights of occupation.[64] Usually the child and spouse will provide their portion of the purchase price by means of a mortgage which will mean that a parent who is joint owner will become a joint mortgagor. If the parent is not intended to be liable on the mortgage, a separate declaration of trust and agreement should set out the terms of the arrangement between the parties and give the parent a right of indemnity from the child and spouse for any sums paid to the building society.[64a] It may also be advisable to take an

---

[60] See below Chap. 6, Part D, p. 103.
[61] For precedents see Robin Spon-Smith, "Barring the Mistress's Equity" Law S.G. July 27, 1988.
[62] See below Chap. 6, Parts B and C, pp. 83, 89.
[63] See above, n. 58.
[64] See the arrangement in relation to the bungalow in *Lloyds Bank plc* v. *Rossett* [1989] 1 Ch. 350, 367.
[64a] For a precedent see *Precedents for the Conveyancer* Vol. 2, No. 16–12.

enduring power of attorney so that the property can still be sold or otherwise dealt with if the parent becomes incapable.

Written agreement

If a long-term sharing arrangement is contemplated in property which is already owned by one party, a written agreement should be drawn up to clarify the terms on which joint occupation is to take place and to make it clear that there is an intention to create legal relations.[65] The first decision will be whether there is to be a lease or a licence. This will largely depend upon the way in which the property is to be shared; a sharer who does not have exclusive possession of a particular part of the premises cannot be a tenant.[66] As the owner will be resident in the same premises any tenancy will not be an assured tenancy within the Housing Act 1988.[67] If the parties are to use the premises in common, a contractual licence should deal with such matters as the maximum period of occupation, the notice required for revocation by either party and any sums payable, whether as a fixed sum or as a proportion of the household expenses. The owner may also want to include a clause that the sharer is not intended to acquire any greater interest in the property.

Cohabitees

Cohabitees may wish to enter into a more comprehensive cohabitation agreement[68] dealing with ownership of personal property and liablity for debts and other matters. If the property is being shared by elderly people, it may be advisable for the agreement to deal with the future illness or incapacity of either party.

---

[65] See above Part B, p. 4.
[66] See below Chap. 3, Part G, p. 46.
[67] Housing Act 1988, sched. 1, para. 10.
[68] See Parry, *The Law Relating to Cohabitation*, (2nd ed., 1988) p. 218 *et seq.*

2 LICENCES

Residual claim

A person sharing residential accommodation who is there with the consent of the owner will, at the very least, be a bare licensee; the permission of the owner prevents him being a trespasser. If an intention to create legal relations can be found together with some form of consideration there will be a contractual licence. Neither a bare licence nor a contractual licence gives any rights against third parties[1] but they do give some rights against the owner including limited rights to remain in occupation. Whatever the alternative rights or remedies being pursued, the pleading of a licence should always be considered as, if established, it will leave the claimant with some rights if other claims fail. This can be illustrated by two situations. First, if several unrelated people are sharing a flat and fail to establish that they have a joint lease of the flat because they arrived at different times, they will probably be held to have separate contractual licences.[2] Secondly, if several members of the family are sharing a house and the non-owners fail to establish a beneficial interest in the property because they have not made sufficient contribution to the purchase price, they will be bare licensees.[3]

Equitable licence

The term "equitable licence" has been used in the past[4] as an alternative to a contractual licence where the licence was for an irrevocable right of occupation for a long period of time. This form of contractual licence is now rarely used by the court.[5] If what is sought for the claimant is, in effect a licence for life, the court will require the conditions of proprietary estoppel to be fulfilled[6] before it grants an equitable or estoppel licence. Unlike a bare or a contractual licence, an equitable licence does amount to an interest in the property. Accordingly, the possibility of an equitable licence should always be considered when the claimant is faced with an action for possession by a third party.

A. Bare licences

A bare licence gives the minimum protection to a person sharing residential accommodation.[7] It is a purely personal

---

[1] See below Chap. 8, Part F, 2(a) (b), p. 146.
[2] See below Chap. 3, Part H3, p. 61.
[3] See below Chap. 6, Part B1, p. 85 and Part C1(c), p. 93.
[4] *Hardwick* v. *Johnson* [1987] 1 W.L.R. 683, 688 *per* Lord Denning M.R.
[5] See below Part B4(d), p. 34.
[6] See below Chap. 7, Part B, p. 113.
[7] See Megarry and Wade, *The Law of Real Property*, (5th ed., 1984), p. 799 *et seq.*

Personal right right conferring no interest in the land but it does provide a defence to an action for trespass.[8] If the licence relates to only part of the premises, however, the licencee will have no protection and will be a trespasser if he goes into other parts of the premises.[9]

Gratuitous The licence is not dependent on any contract and is usually a gratuitous permission to occupy the premises. Even if some consideration is present, for example a child contributing to his "keep" or a mistress moving house, there will still only be a bare licence if there was no intention to create legal relations. Bare licences are, therefore, a common feature in family and quasi-family situations.

A bare licence can come into being either expressly or impliedly. Such a licence, however created, is revocable at the will of the licensor but the licensee must be given a reasonable time in which to leave the premises.

1. Creation

As a bare licence neither arises under a contract nor creates an interest in land,[10] it need not be created in writing[11]; most **Oral** express bare licences are, in fact, oral. In the context of sharing residential accommodation, bare licences are more likely to be implied from the circumstances as the parties will not have articulated the terms on which the premises are being shared.

An express bare licence will come into being when an owner gives permission to another to occupy the whole or part **Informal** of his premises without payment on an informal basis. For **permission** example, a bare licence was created in *Booker* v. *Palmer*[12] when the owner allowed an evacuee from the bombing in London to occupy a cottage rent free. It was held that the parties had no intention to create legal relations and, accordingly, no tenancy was created.[13] Similarly, in *David* v. *London Borough of Lewisham*[14] a bare licence was held to have been created when a father gave the keys of a house he owned to his daughter and son-in-law and told them to go and live there for as long as they wanted.

In many cases, particularly if the parties are related, nothing will be said about occupation of the premises and the parties will simply be sharing on a purely informal basis. If no other legal basis for the occupation can be found, the non-owner will be held to have a bare licence. Thus, whilst a wife has both a common law[15] and a statutory[16] right of occupation

---

[8] *Thomas* v. *Sorrell* (1673) Vaugh. 330.
[9] *O'Keeffe* v. *Irish Motor Inns* [1978] I.R. 85.
[10] *Street* v. *Mountford* [1985] A.C. 809, 814 *per* Lord Templeman.
[11] See Law of Property (Miscellaneous Provisions) Act 1989, s.2(1).
[12] [1942] 2 All E.R. 674; see also *Heslop* v. *Burns* [1974] 1 W.L.R. 1241.
[13] See *Street* v. *Mountford* [1985] 1 A.C. 809, 819 *per* Lord Templeman; see below Chap. 3, Part B, p. 40.
[14] (1977) 34 P. & C.R. 112.
[15] *National Provincial Bank Ltd.* v. *Ainsworth* [1965] A.C. 1175.
[16] Matrimonial Homes Act 1983, s.1(1); see Thompson, *Co-ownership* (1988), p. 79 *et seq.*

of the matrimonial home, a *de facto* wife and any children,[17] whether legitimate or illegitimate, have merely a bare licence to remain in the home.

The type of family situation in which the court will imply a bare licence can be seen from *Rogers* v. *Eller*.[18] In that case, the defendant and her husband lived in a house which was owned by her brother who was in the Merchant Navy. Whilst they paid no rent, they did maintain and decorate the property.

Family situations   The basis on which the family shared the property was never discussed. The Court of Appeal held that the defendants could not establish a claim to a beneficial interest in the property under an implied trust[19] nor an interest arising by proprietary estoppel[20] and implied a bare licence. That form of licence was implied because the facts were consistent with an arrangement between the parties that the defendants should be allowed to live in the house rent free without a definite limit of time, but only so long as they and the plaintiff wished. On the same basis in *Hannaford* v. *Selby*,[21] Mr and Mrs Selby were held to have merely a bare licence when they shared a house owned by their daughter and son-in-law as they had only contributed to living expenses and not to the purchase of the property.

Even if the parties are not of the same family, the relationship between them may be such that it is impossible to infer any intention to create legal relations. In those circumstances, if the claimant cannot establish an interest in the property under a resulting or an implied trust or by virtue of proprietary estoppel, the only right he will have is a bare

Cohabitees   licence. For example, in *Horrocks* v. *Forray*[22] a mistress was living in a house owned by her lover and was maintained by him until he died. The parties were on close terms and the Court of Appeal could not find any facts or events from which a contract relating to the mistress' occupation could be inferred.[23] The mistress had, therefore, merely a bare licence which had already terminated. Similarly in *Richards* v. *Dove*,[24] Miss Richards had a bare licence as she could not claim a greater interest in the property; she had only contributed to the household expenses and in no way acted to her detriment. The fact that the parties had been cohabiting did not give Miss Richards any greater right in Mr Dove's House.

2. Termination

A bare licence will terminate automatically on the death of the

---

[17] *Metropolitan Properties Co. Ltd.* v. *Cronan* (1982) 44 P. & C.R. 1; see below Part A.2, p. 23, for the limited power to revoke a child's bare licence.
[18] C.A., unreported, May 20, 1986; see also *Warnes* v. *Hedley* C.A., unreported, January 31, 1984; *cf. Timms* v. *Timms* (1973) 226 E.G. 1565 where the brother and sister did discuss the terms of the joint occupation and a tenancy was held to exist.
[19] See below Chap. 6, Part C, p. 89.
[20] See below Chap. 7.
[21] (1976) 239 E.G. 811.
[22] [1976] 1 W.L.R. 230.
[23] *Cf. Tanner* v. *Tanner* [1975] 1 W.L.R. 1346 where the parties were no longer on good terms; see below Part B, p. 24.
[24] [1974] 1 All E.R. 888; see also *Hoskins* v. *Hoskins* C.A., unreported, December 3, 1981.

Revocable at will licensor or on the assignment of the relevant premises.[25] A licensor may revoke a bare licence at will without the need for a notice to quit[26]; all that is required is a demand for possession. In the case of family and quasi-family disputes, there may be a difficult question of fact as to whether the owner has requested those living with him to leave or whether there was merely an outbreak of argumentative abuse.[27] If the property is jointly owned, one joint tenant can revoke a bare licence without reference to the other joint owner.[28] It would appear that the licence can also be terminated by the licensee without notice.[29]

Children   Whilst, in general, a bare licence can be revoked at any time, the licence of a child to remain in the parental home can only be revoked in limited circumstances. The court will not grant an injunction to exclude even an adult child except in grave circumstances.[30] Circumstances justifying the exclusion of a child from the home include physical assaults on the mother, theft and refusal to contribute to household expenses.[31]

Where a bare licence is revoked, the licensee does not immediately become a trespasser if he remains in occupation.

Packing-up time He is given a reasonable time to leave the premises. This is sometimes called "packing-up time." The revocation, however, takes effect immediately and a notice demanding possession will not be invalid because less than a reasonable period is specified. Thus, in *Minister of Health* v. *Bellott*[32] a notice terminating the defendant's licence to use rooms in an evacuee centre was held to be valid although the defendant was given only a week to leave. The licensor will not be successful in an action for possession until a reasonable time has elapsed.[33]

The length of time the licensee has to leave the premises will depend on the facts of each case. The court will take into account the time needed for the licensee to find alternative accommodation bearing in mind the housing conditions in the area and the particular circumstances of the licensee.[34] On the one hand, if the sharing of accommodation was originally intended to be on a long term basis, a period of six months notice may be considered reasonable for a married couple with no children[35] but a period of up to a year may be allowed if

[25] *Terunnanse* v. *Terunnanse* [1968] A.C. 1086, 1095–1096 *per* Lord Devlin.
[26] *Crane* v. *Morris* [1965] 1 W.L.R. 1104, 1108 *per* Lord Denning M.R.
[27] See for example *Gilham* v. *Breidenbach* [1982] R.T.R. 328 (a police case).
[28] *Annen* v. *Rattee* (1984) 273 E.G. 503 C.A.
[29] *Australian Blue Metal* v. *Hughes* [1963] A.C. 74, 98 *per* Lord Diplock (a contractual licence case); see also Dawson and Pearce, *Licences relating to the occupation or use of land.* (1979), p. 71.
[30] *Metropolitan Properties Co. Ltd.* v. *Cronan* (1982) 44 P. & C.R. 1, 8 *per* May L.J.; see also *Waterhouse* v. *Waterhouse* (1905) 94 L.T. 133; *Stevens* v. *Stevens* (1907) 24 T.L.R. 20.
[31] *Egan* v. *Egan* [1975] Ch. 218.
[32] [1944] 1 K.B. 298.
[33] *Minister of Health* v. *Bellotti* [1944] 1 K.B. 298, 309 *per* Goddard L.J.; see also *Stevens* v. *Stevens* C.A., unreported, March 3, 1989.
[34] *Hannaford* v. *Selby* (1976) 239 E.G. 811, 813 *per* Goulding J.; *E. & L. Berg Homes Ltd.* v. *Grey* (1979) 253 E.G. 473 C.A.
[35] *Hannaford* v. *Selby* (1976) 239 E.G. 811; *Rogers* v. *Eller* C.A., unreported, May 20, 1986.

the licensee has children living with him,[36] On the other hand, if the occupation was intended to be for a very short period whilst alternative accommodation was found, three weeks may be a reasonable period.[37] If the licensor and licensee have argued to such an extent that the continuing joint occupation of the premises is causing a strain on the health of the parties, a shorter period for vacation of the premises may be held to be reasonable.[38]

B. Contractual licences

A contractual licence is permission to be on the land of another which is based on a contract. It has recently been confirmed that such a licence does not give rise to any property interest.[39] A contractual licence may be created either expressly or impliedly. In either case, terms may be implied into the licence by the court. The licence may only be revoked in accordance with the terms of the contract.

Contractual licences are less common in the context of a family sharing residential accommodation because of the need to show an intention to create legal relations. If a contractual licence does not exist, the licensee will have a bare licence.[40] Contractual licences are important in those cases where the parties, whilst intending to contract, fail to establish a lease, for example, because exclusive possession of the premises has not been given.[41]

1. Personal right

History

Until 1952, it was always considered that a contractual licence did not create any estate or interest in the land and that it was a purely personal right.[42] Then, in the case of *Errington* v. *Errington and Woods*[43] Lord Denning, after considering that equity would intervene to prevent the revocation of a licence in breach of contract[44] said[45];

> "This infusion of equity means that contractual licences now have a force and validity of their own and cannot be revoked in breach of contract. Neither the licensor nor

---

[36] *Warnes* v. *Hedley* C.A., unreported, January 31, 1984.
[37] *Patel* v. *Patel* C.A., unreported, June 30, 1983 (a contractual licence case).
[38] *Hannaford* v. *Selby* (1976) 239 E.G. 811.
[39] *Ashburn Anstalt* v. *Arnold* [1989] 1 Ch. 1, 24 *per* Fox L.J.
[40] See above Part A1, p. 21.
[41] See below Chap. 3, Part G, p. 46.
[42] *King* v. *David Allen and Sons (Billposting) Ltd.* [1916] 2 A.C. 54; *Clore* v. *Theatrical Properties Ltd.* [1936] 3 All E.R. 483.
[43] [1952] 1 K.B. 290; see the text at n. 24 below for the facts of this case.
[44] See below Part 4, p. 30.
[45] [1952] 1 K.B. 290, 299; Wade, "Licences and Third Parties" (1954) 68 L.Q.R. 337.

anyone who claims through him can disregard the contract except a purchaser for value without notice."

Despite adverse comments by the House of Lords[46] on his decision in *Errington* v. *Errington and Woods*,[47] Lord Denning continued to hold that a contractual licence gave rise to an equitable interest which bound third parties.[48] This view was also adopted by other members of the judiciary.[49] These moves to elevate a contractual licence into an interest in land were clearly an attempt to protect licensees against third parties.[50] The Court of Appeal, however, has recently been less sympathetic and has returned the law to its original position.

Two recent cases have confirmed that a contractual licensee does not have any interest in the property. In *Patel* v. *Patel*[51] Slade L.J. said[52];

No property interest

"But with respect to [the judge] I think it would be a heresy to suggest that the mere fact that a licence to occupy land has been given for consideration renders it irrevocable or confers any interest in the land on the licensee. As I understand it, the general rule is that a mere licence to occupy land, albeit of a contractual nature, as opposed to a lease, does not confer any interest on the licensee in the land."

After a very careful consideration of all the authorities, Fox L.J. in *Ashburn Anstalt* v. *Arnold*[53] reached the following conclusion[54];

"Before *Errington* the law appears to have been clear and well understood. It rested on an important and intelligible distinction between contractual obligations which gave rise to no estate or interest in the land and proprietary rights which, by definition did. The far-reaching statement of principle in *Errington* was not supported by authority, not necessary for the decision of the case and *per incuriam* in the sense that it was made without reference to authorities which, if they would not have compelled, would surely have persuaded the court to adopt a different ratio."

Whilst the confirmation that a contractual licensee has no interest in the land presents few problems for a licencee intending to stay only a few weeks, it can provide considerable problems where a long period of secure accommodation is contemplated. In the latter situation, the court is now more

---

[46] *National Provincial Bank Ltd.* v. *Ainsworth* [1965] A.C. 1175, 1224 *per* Lord Hodson, 1251 *per* Lord Wilberforce.
[47] [1952] 1 K.B. 290.
[48] *Binions* v. *Evans* [1972] Ch. 359, 367; *D.H.N. Food Distributors Ltd.* v. *Tower Hamlets London Borough Council* [1976] 1 W.L.R. 852, 859.
[49] *Midland Bank Ltd.* v. *Farmpride Hatcheries Ltd.* (1980) 260 E.G. 493; *Pennine Raceway Ltd.* v. *Kirklees Metropolitan Council* [1983] Q.B. 382.
[50] See Briggs, "Licences: Back to Basics" [1981] Conv. 212, 216.
[51] C.A., unreported, June 30, 1983.
[52] Quoting from the transcript.
[53] [1989] 1 Ch. 1.
[54] *Ibid.*, 22.

likely to treat any licence as an equitable one arising under the doctrine of proprietary estoppel.[55]

2. Creation

The necessary elements for the creation of a contractual licence were set out by Megaw L.J. in *Horrocks* v. *Forray*[56];

Basic conditions

"Now in order to establish a contract, whether it be express or implied by law, there has to be shown a meeting of the minds of the parties with a definition of the contractual terms reasonably clearly made out and with an intention to affect the legal relationship, that is, that the agreement that is made is one which is properly regarded as being enforceable by the court if one or the other fails to comply with it; and it still remains a part of the law of this country, though many people think that it is time that it was changed to some other criterion, that there must be consideration moving in order to establish a contract."

Provided that the above conditions are satisfied, the licence does not have to be any particular form and may be written or oral.[57]

Intention to create legal relations

The requirement of an intention to create legal relations may prevent the formation of a contractual licence if the parties are on close terms, for example, a couple cohabiting in amity[58] or related.[59] If the parties do actually discuss the terms on which the property is to be occupied, however, the court may find an intention to create legal relations.[60] The consideration moving from the licensee need not consist of periodic payments but can comprise such matters as giving up accommodation with security of tenure to go and live with the licensor.[61]

Definition of terms

The need to define the contractual terms can cause difficulty where property is being shared on an informal basis and is a particular problem in relation to implied licences. This can be seen from *Johnson* v. *Johnson*[62] where the claimant and her two children were sharing a flat with the owner who was the father of one of the children. There was no evidence as to the period the parties contemplated that the claimant would remain in the flat and she failed to establish a contractual licence to remain there. By comparison, in *Tanner* v. *Tanner*[63] there was evidence that the parties contemplated that the

---

[55] See below Part C, p. 35.
[56] [1976] 1 W.L.R. 230, 236.
[57] Law of Property (Miscellaneous Provisions) Act 1989, s.2 does not apply as a contractual licence is not an interest in land.
[58] *Horrocks* v. *Forray* [1976] 1 W.L.R. 230, see the text at n. 22 above for the facts of this case.
[59] *Rogers* v. *Eller* C.A., unreported, May 20, 1986, see the text at n. 18 above for the facts of this case.
[60] *Timms* v. *Timms* (1973) 226 E.G. 1565 see also *Nunn* v. *Dalrymple* (1989) 21 H.L.R. 569.
[61] See *Tanner* v. *Tanner* [1975] 1 W.L.R. 1346.
[62] C.A., unreported, March 11, 1986.
[63] [1975] 1 W.L.R. 1346.

claimant would remain in the house until the children left school and on that basis a contractual licence was implied.

Express licence

An express contractual licence is created when the licensor and the licensee agree the terms of the licensee's occupation of the premises for a consideration but all the conditions necessary to create a lease are not fulfilled. Thus, a lodger has a contractual licence[64] as does a service occupant.[65] A contractual licence will also be created when several people have separate agreements to share flat and no joint tenancy is created.[66]

Implied licence

The court will imply a contractual licence if the conditions set out in *Horrocks* v. *Forrays*[67] are satisfied. The test to be applied is whether there are "events or facts from which the inference could fairly be drawn, on the balance of probability, that there was a contract such as suggested."[68] The courts have varied over the years as to the strictness with which they have applied the test and the basic requirements for a contractual licence.

Examples of implied licences

Three cases illustrate the court's inference of a contractual licence. First, in *Tanner* v. *Tanner*[69] the claimant left her rent controlled flat and moved into a house bought by the defendant after she bore him twin daughters. The Court of Appeal implied that she had a contractual licence to remain in the house until the girls finished school. Secondly, in *Hardwick* v. *Johnson*[70] a contractual licence was implied where a mother permitted her son and his second wife to live in a house she had purchased. There was an understanding that the couple would pay her £28 a month, although few payments were actually made. The third case is *Chandler* v. *Kerley*[71] where the plaintiff purchased the former matrimonial home of the defendant and her husband at an undervalue. The plaintiff lived with the defendant and her children in the house for about six weeks and then left and claimed possession. The Court of Appeal held that the defendant had a contractual licence to remain in the house terminable on reasonable notice which would give her ample opportunity to re-house herself and her children.

No implication

The courts have not always been so willing to infer a contractual licence and in other cases have taken a far stricter approach in family and quasi-family situations. For example, in *Horrocks* v. *Forray*[72] the Court of Appeal refused to imply a contractual licence on the grounds that there was neither

---

[64] See below Chap. 3, Part G1(a), p. 47.
[65] See below Chap. 3, Part G1(c), p. 49.
[66] *A.G. Securities* v. *Vaughan* [1988] 3 W.L.R. 1205; see below Chap. 3, Part H, p. 59.
[67] [1976] 1 W.L.R. 230; see the text at n. 56.
[68] *Horrocks* v. *Forray* [1976] 1 W.L.R. 230, 238 *per* Megaw L.J.
[69] [1975] 1 W.L.R. 1346.
[70] [1978] 1 W.L.R. 683, Roskill and Browne L.JJ. considered it to be a contractual licence whereas Lord Denning M.R. termed it an 'equitable' licence; see below Part C1, p. 35.
[71] [1978] 1 W.L.R. 693.
[72] *Ante*, see also *Coombes* v. *Smith* [1986] 1 W.L.R. 808, see below Chap. 7, Part B3, p. 118.

consideration nor an intention to create legal relations. The courts also refused to infer a contractual licence between a man and his mistress in *Johnson* v. *Johnson*[73] but, in that case, on the grounds that there was no certainty as to the terms on which the licence was to take effect.

Alternative remedy

In view of the courts' ambivalent approach to the inference of a contractual licence in informal family and quasi-family sharing arrangements, proprietary estoppel[74] should always be considered in such situations. Although action to detriment on the part of the claimant will have to be proved, there is no necessity to show an intention to create legal relations between the parties.[75]

3. Terms

The terms of a contractual licence may be express or implied. Express terms are those specifically agreed between the parties in an express licence. An express licence, however, may also have obligations imposed on the parties by the court. In the case of an implied licence, all the terms will be implied by the court; one area of difficulty being the term as to duration of occupation.

Express terms

Express terms may deal with such matters as the licensee's obligation to pay a periodic sum, to share common facilities and not to cause damage to the premises.[76] Terms may also include an obligation on the part of the licensor to keep the property in repair[77] and reserve to him a right of entry. If the obligations of the parties are spelt out in too great detail, particularly if the terms are similar to those found in a tenancy agreement, the court may hold that there is a lease and not a licence.[78]

Implied terms

A contractual licence for occupation of residential premises may well contain an implied undertaking by the licensor for quiet enjoyment. In *Smith* v. *Nottinghamshire County Council*[79] the Court of Appeal implied such a term into a student's contractual licence for his room in a hall of residence. The term was implied in that case because of the student's need of reasonable quietude for study.

It is now clear that the courts will imply a term into a contractual licence that the premises are fit for the purposes of the licensee.[80] Except in relation to safety, however, such a term will only be implied[81] on the basis of the test in *The*

---

[73] C.A., unreported, March 11, 1986, see the text at n. 62 above for the facts of this case.
[74] See below Chap. 7.
[75] *Jones* v. *Watkins* C.A. unreported, November 26, 1987; see below Chap. 7, Part B1, p. 113.
[76] For the terms of a typical flat sharing licence see *A.G. Securities* v. *Vaughan* [1988] 3 W.L.R. 1205, 1210.
[77] See *Binions* v. *Evans* [1972] Ch. 359.
[78] *Addiscombe Garden Estates Ltd.* v. *Crabbe* [1958] 1 Q.B. 513; see below Chap. 3, Part G2(a)(iii), p. 55.
[79] *The Times*, November 7, 1981, H.L.
[80] *Wettern Electric Ltd.* v. *Welsh Development Agency* [1983] 1 Q.B. 796.
[81] *Ibid.*, 808 *per* Judge John Newey Q.C.

Moorcock.[82] On this basis, there is an implied term in a contractual licence for the occupation of a room in a hotel that the premises are as safe as reasonable care and skill on the part of anyone can make them with a proviso that the licensor is not responsible for defects which could not have been discovered by reasonable care.[83]

The courts have not imposed any implied obligations on contractual licensees of residential premises. By analogy with leases,[84] the licensee may be under an implied obligation not to cause damage and to use the premises "in a licence-like manner."[85]

Length of licence

An important term in any licence is the period for which it is to last. In *Tanner* v. *Tanner*[86] the Court of Appeal implied a contractual licence for the licensee to occupy the premises for so long as her children were of school age and such accommodation was reasonably required for her and the children. A long period of occupation was also implied in *Broughall* v. *Hunt*[87] where a mother had contributed £1,000 towards the cost of an extension to the house of daughter and son-in-law when she went to live with them. Michael Wheeler Q.C., sitting as a deputy judge of the Chancery Division, held that she had a contractual licence to live in the house for as long as she wished.

Long licences

Terms implied into a contractual licence for a long period of undisturbed occupation are problematic for two reasons. First, it is not clear when the period of occupation will in fact terminate. For example, in *Hardwick* v. *Johnson*[88] where a wife was held to have a contractual licence to remain in a house owned by her mother-in-law provided she made payment of £7 a week, Brown L.J. said[89];

> "I should add that I am not saying that the wife is necessarily entitled to stay in the house indefinitely so long as she makes these payments: circumstances might arise in the future which might entitle the plaintiff to determine the licence, but it is not necessary to consider on this appeal what those circumstances might be."

Secondly, the relationship between the licensor and licensee may change, particularly if the relationship was initially close, and a long period of joint occupation then becomes impracticable.

These problems have been recognised by the courts and there now appears to be considerable reluctance to imply a term into a contractual licence for a long period of settled

---

[82] (1889) 14 P.D. 64; see Treitel, *The Law of Contract* (7th ed. 1987), p. 164.
[83] *Maclenan* v. *Segar* [1917] 2 K.B. 325.
[84] See, for example, *Warren* v. *Keen* [1954] 1 Q.B. 15.
[85] See Dawson and Pearce, *Licences relating to the occupation or use of land* (1979), pp. 109–110.
[86] [1975] 1 W.L.R. 1346.
[87] Ch.D., unreported, February 1, 1983; see Gypps, "Living-in Relatives: Some Legal Consequences" (1983) 80 L.S.Gaz. 2198.
[88] [1978] 1 W.L.R. 683; see the text at n. 70 above for the facts of this case.
[89] *Ibid.*, 692.

residence by the licensee. For example, in *Rogers* v. *Eller*[90]
Slade L.J. said[91];

> "However, I find myself quite unable to impute to the
> parties an intention . . . that to all intents and purposes
> Mrs Eller should have a perpetual licence to occupy this
> property for the rest of her life. This would really mean
> imputing, not only to this defendant but also to the
> plaintiff, the intention that he should grant her the right to
> remain there for the rest of her life however soured or
> acrimonious the relationship between them might
> thereafter become."

Similarly, in *Chandler* v. *Kerley*[92] the Court of Appeal held that
the plaintiff had merely a licence terminable on reasonable
notice. The court's approach was set out by Scarman L.J.[93];

**Terminable on
reasonable notice**

> "I agree with the judge that it is not possible to imply a
> licence to the defendant to occupy the house for her life.
> The plaintiff had invested £10,000 in the house and, in the
> absence of express stipulation, cannot be supposed in the
> circumstances to have frozen his capital for as long as the
> defendant pleased or for the duration of her life. On the
> other hand, the plaintiff was well aware that the defendant
> wanted the house as a home for her children as well as
> herself. It would be wrong, however, to infer, in the
> absence of an express promise, that the plaintiff was
> assuming the burden of housing another man's wife and
> children indefinitely, and long after his relationship with
> them had ended. The balance of these factors leads me to
> the conclusion that the defendant's contractual licence was
> terminable upon reasonable notice, and that the notice
> must be such as to give the defendant ample opportunity
> to re-house herself and her children without disruption."

Alternatively, the court may imply a term that the licence
should terminate on the licensee's unreasonable behaviour.

4. Termination

For a long time, it was considered that a licensor could revoke
a contractual licence at will, even if he was in breach of
contract in so doing.[94] The only remedy available to the
licensee was damages.[95] This precarious position of the licensee
arose because the licence was considered to be a separate entity
and, in law, licences could always be revoked at will.

The basis of the present law is to be found in *Winter
Garden Theatre (London) Ltd.* v. *Millennium Productions Ltd.*[96]
which laid down that a contractual licence is an inherent part of

---

[90] C.A., unreported, May 20, 1986.
[91] Quoting from the transcript.
[92] [1978] 1 W.L.R. 693; see the text at n. 71 above for the facts of this case.
[93] *Ibid.*, 698.
[94] *Wood* v. *Leadbitter* (1845) 13 M. & W. 838; see Dawson and Pearce,
   Licences relating to the occupation or use of land. (1979), p. 73 *et seq.*
[95] *Booker* v. *Palmer* [1942] 2 All E.R. 674, 677 *per* Lord Greene M.R.
[96] [1948] A.C. 173.

the contract which brings it into being. The basic position emerges clearly from the judgment of Lord Greene M.R. in the Court of Appeal[97];

Basic position

"A licence created by contract is not an interest. It creates a contractual right to do certain things which otherwise would be a trespass. It seems to me that, in considering the nature of such a licence and the mutual rights and obligations which arise under it, the first thing to do is to construe the contract according to ordinary principles. There is the question whether or not the particular licence is revocable at all and, if so, whether by both parties or by only one. There is the question whether it is revocable immediately or only after the giving of some notice. Those are questions of construction of the contract. It seems to me quite inadmissible to say that the question whether a licence is revocable at all can be, so to speak, segregated and treated by itself, leaving only the other questions to be decided by reference to the true construction of the contract."

(a) Revocation by the licensor It is now clear that a licensor has no right to revoke a licence in breach of contract. Thus a contractual licensee does not become a trespasser after a purported revocation as long as his contract entitles him to remain on the premises. That is so whether the contract is specifically enforceable or not.[98] In any event, if the licensor is not resident in the premises, four weeks written notice must be given under section 5(1A) of the Protection from Eviction Act 1977.

A licensee faced with a wrongful revocation can use equitable remedies to enforce his licence. The courts' approach was set out by Lord Uthwatt in *Winter Garden Theatre (London) Ltd.* v. *Millennium Productions Ltd.*[99]

Equitable remedies

"The settled practice of the courts of equity is to do what they can by an injunction to preserve the sanctity of a bargain. To my mind, as at present advised, a licensee who has refused to accept the wrongful repudiation of the bargain which is involved in an unauthorised revocation of the licence is as much entitled to the protection of an injunction as a licensee who has not received any notice of revocation; and if the remedy of injunction is properly available in the latter case against unauthorised interference by the licensor, it is also available in the former case."

Equitable remedies are available regardless of the period for which the contractual licence was intended to last; a licence for

---

[97] *Millennium Productions Ltd.* v. *Winter Garden Theatre (London) Ltd.* [1946] 1 All E.R. 678, 680, although the decision of the Court of Appeal was reversed by the House of Lords, Lord Greene M.R.'s statement of the law was accepted, see [1948] A.C. 173, 202 *per* Lord Uthwatt.
[98] *Hounslow London Borough Council* v. *Twickenham Garden Developments Ltd.* [1971] Ch. 233, 255 *per* Megarry J.
[99] [1948] A.C. 173, 202–203.

a day will be enforced if necessary.[1] If the licence is repudiated before the licensee has gone into possession, a grant of specific performance may be made requiring the licensor to grant the licence.[2]

The legal rights of the licensee granted by the contract are, therefore, supported by equity.[3] If the contract does not contain an express obligation not to revoke the licence during the currency of the contract, the court will imply such an obligation.[4] That obligation can then be enforced by the grant of an injunction. The period for which revocation will be restrained will depend upon the construction of the contract. If the licence was granted for a specific purpose or for a specified period of time, revocation will be restrained until the purpose has been carried out[5] or the time elapsed.[6] In other cases, the length of the licence and the protection afforded by equity will depend upon the implied intention of the parties.[7]

An example of an express revocation clause can be seen in *A. G. Securities* v. *Vaughan*[8] where the licence was made terminable on one months notice. In that situation, if the **Notice period** licensor sought to revoke the licence without notice, he would be restrained by injunction from revoking until the one month period of notice had expired. If no period is specified, the court will usually infer that the licence is revocable on reasonable notice.[9] What is reasonable notice will depend on the facts of each case. Three weeks notice has been held to be sufficient where the contractual licence was intended to provide short term accommodation while the licencees looked for a new permanent residence.[10] By comparison, in *Chandler* v. *Kerley*[11] the Court of Appeal held that 12 months was reasonable notice for a mistress to vacate her former matrimonial home. In the event of a wrongful revocation of such a licence, an injunction would be granted restraining the licensor from interfering with the licensee's occupation of the premises until the relevant period of notice had expired.

Injunction and specific performance are equitable remedies and, thus, available only at the discretion of the court. If the **Licensee's** licensee has been guilty of serious misconduct, for example by **misconduct** causing damage to the licensor's property, the court may refuse to grant an injunction.[12] The court may also refuse equitable

---

[1] *Verrall* v. *Great Yarmouth Borough Council* [1981] 1 Q.B. 202, 209 *per* Watkins J.; noted [1981] Conv. 212 (A. Briggs).

[2] *Ibid.*

[3] See *Chandler* v. *Kerley* [1978] 1 W.L.R. 693, 697 *per* Scarman L.J.

[4] *Hounslow London Borough Council* v. *Twickenham Garden Developments Ltd.* [1971] Ch. 233, 247 *per* Megarry J.; see also Briggs, "Contractual Licences, a Reply" [1983] Conv. 285, 287.

[5] See *Hurst* v. *Picture Theatres Ltd.* [1915] 1 K.B. 1.

[6] See *Foster* v. *Robinson* [1951] 1 K.B. 149, 156 *per* Lord Evershed M.R., an express licence to a former employee to occupy a cottage rent free until he died.

[7] See above Part B3, p. 28.

[8] [1988] 3 W.L.R. 1205, 1211.

[9] See below Part B4(d), p. 34.

[10] *Patel* v. *Patel* C.A., unreported, June 30, 1983.

[11] [1978] 1 W.L.R. 693; see the text at n. 71 above for the facts of this case.

[12] See *Thompson* v. *Park* [1944] K.B. 408.

relief if the arrangements are such that the licensor and licensee have to share common facilities. The point was made by Megarry J. in *Hounslow London Borough Council* v. *Twickenham Garden Developments Ltd.*[13];

> "If the courts sought to enforce a licence to share, a multitude of practical problems would arise which would be absent if the licence was for exclusive occupation."

The remedy of injunction will also not be available if the revocation has, in fact, become effective before any application is made to the court.[14] In the case of a service occupancy, it would appear that the licensee will not be granted equitable relief to allow him to remain in possession once the contract of employment has been terminated, even if that termination was wrongful.[15]

Damages   The common law remedy of damages is always available in the event of a wrongful revocation of a contractual licence, even if the equitable remedies are not. Damages are the appropriate remedy when the licensee has already left the premises and has no wish to return. The level of damages should depend upon the benefits lost under the particular contract but there are no judicial guidelines as to the assessment of damages. Indeed, in *Broughall* v. *Hunt*[16] the judge considered that he was in the position of having to "pluck a figure off the wall." In that case the mother was awarded damages of £1,500 for the wrongful revocation of her contractual licence for life. A mistress was awarded £2,000 for the loss of a licence to occupy a house until her children left school in *Tanner* v. *Tanner.*[17] By comparison, in *Ivory* v. *Palmer*[18] an employee was awarded only £200 when he lost his service occupancy on the wrongful termination of his contract of employment.

(b)   Termination by the licensee   If there is an express contractual provision governing termination by the licensee[19] requiring a specific period of notice to be given, the licensee will be in breach of contract if he fails to give the stipulated notice. If the licence is silent as to notice, a term requiring the licensee to give reasonable notice would probably be implied by **Notice period**   the court.[20] If consideration for the licence is a periodic sum, reasonable notice for the licensee may be the period of payment; *i.e.* a weekly payment requires a week's notice.[21]

---

[13] [1971] Ch. 233, 250.
[14] See *Tanner* v. *Tanner* [1975] 1 W.L.R. 1346, 1351 *per* Lord Denning M.R.
[15] See *Ivory* v. *Palmer* (1976) 237 E.G. 411, 415 *per* Roskill L.J.; see also *Whitbread West Pennines* v. *Reedy* [1988] I.C.R. 807.
[16] Ch.D., unreported, February 1, 1983; see the text at n. 87 above for the facts of this case.
[17] [1975] 1 W.L.R. 1346.
[18] (1976) 237 E.G. 411.
[19] See *A.G. Securities* v. *Vaughan* [1988] 3 W.L.R. 1205, 1211.
[20] See *Australian Blue Metal Ltd.* v. *Hughes* [1963] A.C.74, 99 *per* Lord Devlin; see also Dawson and Pearce, *Licences relating to the occupation or use of land.* (1979), p. 94 *et seq.*
[21] See *Winter Garden Theatre (London) Ltd.* v. *Millennium Productions Ltd.* [1948] A.C. 173, 195 *per* Lord Porter.

(c) **Termination by expiry** If a contractual licence is for a fixed period, it terminates on the expiry of that period. The licensor will be entitled to summary judgment for possession under Order 14 of the Rules of the Supreme Court if the licensee does not vacate the premises.[22]

(d) **Irrevocable licences** In several cases[23] particularly in family or quasi-family situations, a person sharing residential accommodation has been held by the court to have an irrevocable licence for life or until children leave home. For example in *Errington* v. *Errington and Woods*[24] a father promised his son and daughter-in-law that, if they continued in occupation of a house he had purchased and paid the mortgage instalments, he would transfer the property to them. In the course of his judgment Lord Denning M.R. said[25];

> "The father's promise was a unilateral contract—a promise of the house in return for their act of paying the instalments. It could not be revoked by him once the couple entered on performance of the act, but it would cease to bind him if they left it incomplete or unperformed, which they have not done."

Any trend towards irrevocable contractual licences in family, or other, sharing arrangements would now appear to have gone into reverse. As already noted,[26] the courts are showing increasing reluctance to imply a term for a long period of secure occupation into a contractual licence. Also the courts are now more likely to imply a term into a licence that it is revocable on reasonable notice.[27] The courts' present approach can be seen from the judgment of Slade L.J. in *Patel* v. *Patel*[28];

Revocable on reasonable notice

> "Furthermore, the general rule is that the question of whether a contractual licence is revocable or not must depend on the express or implied terms of the contract. Of course, in some circumstances the implicit terms of a contractual licence will render it irrevocable, as was the case in the particular circumstances of *Hardwick* v. *Johnson* [1978] 2 All E.R. 935, [1978] 1 W.L.R. 683, to which we have been referred. In the present case, nothing was expressly said between the parties about the termination of the licence. As to implied terms, as I read the evidence and indeed the judge's judgment, all the implications are that it must have been always intended and contemplated by both parties, that these temporary arrangements made, as the judge said, by the plaintiffs 'as

---

[22] *Shell-Mex and B.P. Ltd.* v. *Manchester Garages Ltd.* [1971] 1 W.L.R. 612.
[23] See *Binions* v. *Evans* [1972] Ch. 359, 367 *per* Lord Denning M.R.; *Hardwick* v. *Johnson* [1978] 1 W.L.R. 683; *Broughall* v. *Hunt* Ch.D., unreported, February 1, 1983.
[24] [1952] 1 K.B. 290.
[25] *Ibid.*, 295.
[26] See above Part B3, p. 29, and *Rogers* v. *Eller* C.A., unreported, May 20, 1986.
[27] See *Chandler* v. *Kerley* [1978] 1 W.L.R. 693.
[28] C.A., unreported, June 30, 1983.

a favour to fellow countrymen,' should be determinable on reasonable notice."

Thus, whilst it is still possible that the court will find that a contractual licensee has an irrevocable licence for life or until children cease to attend school, the court will require clear evidence that the parties intended a long period of secure joint occupation. Lord Porter's dicta in *Winter Garden Theatre (London) Ltd.* v. *Millennium Productions Ltd.*.[29] that "prima facie licences are revocable" again provides the starting point for the courts' construction of the contract between the parties.

C. Equitable licences

The first problem in relation to equitable licences is one of definition. Despite earlier views that some contractual licences were also equitable licences, it is now reasonably clear that the term "equitable licence" should be restricted to those licences arising under the doctrine of proprietary estoppel. The second problem is whether equitable licences, as so defined, amount to an interest in land.

1. Definition

In *Hardwick* v. *Johnson*[30] Lord Denning M.R. held that the daughter's licence arising from the family arrangement was an equitable one; the other members of the Court of Appeal considered it to be a contractual one. This judgment echoed his earlier views in *Binions* v. *Evans*[31] that a contractual licence for **Not a** life gave rise to an equitable interest.[32] This confusion **contractual** between contractual and equitable licences was resolved by **licence** Lord Scarman in *Chandler* v. *Kerley*[33] when he pointed out that the availability of equitable remedies to enforce a contractual licence does not convert such a licence into an equitable one or give rise to an equitable interest. The role of equity was purely to support and supplement the contractual agreement.[34] This division between contractual licences which can be enforced by means of equitable remedies and equitable licences which may give rise to an equitable interest has now been accepted by the Court of Appeal in *Patel* v. *Patel*[35] and *Ashburn Anstalt* v. *Arnold*.[36] It was also considered at one time that a contractual licence gave rise to an equitable interest

[29] [1948] A.C. 173, 195; see also below Part C.
[30] [1978] 1 W.L.R. 683, 688; see the text at n. 70 above for the facts of this case.
[31] [1972] Ch. 359, 367.
[32] See above Part B1, p. 24.
[33] [1978] 1 W.L.R. 693.
[34] *Ibid.*, 697.
[35] C.A., unreported, June 30, 1983.
[36] [1989] 1 Ch. 1; see above Part B1, p. 25.

under a construction trust[37] but this view has similarly been rejected.[38]

Proprietary estoppel

Thus the term "equitable licence" would now appear to be restricted to those licences which arise under the doctrine of proprietary estoppel where all the conditions for the operation of that doctrine are complied with.[39] It is not easy to differentiate the circumstances in which the court will hold there is an equitable rather than a contractual licence, particularly in the context of permission for a long period of secure accommodation. In the case of family and quasi-family arrangements, the courts show reluctance to infer an intention to create legal relations or to find sufficient certainty of terms both of which are essential for a contractual licence.[40] The courts are now similarly reluctant to infer a term into a contractual licence that it should be irrevocable for a long period.[41] On balance, therefore, an informal arrangement for sharing residential accommodation for a long period is now less likely to be a contractual licence but to be either an equitable licence, if the conditions for proprietary estoppel are satisfied, or a bare licence.[42]

Theoretical distinctions between "promises" and "representations"[43] to determine whether there is a contractual or an equitable licence are extremely difficult to apply in practice. It is also possible that the same set of facts can give rise to both a contractual and an equitable licence.[44] Heretical[45] though it may sound, this area would appear to be one in which the court works backwards, *i.e.* it looks for the result it wishes to achieve and then finds the form of licence most appropriate to provide that result. Thus, if the licensee merely requires damages as a remedy because alternative

Courts approach

accommodation has been found, the court is more likely to find that there is a contractual licence even though there is evidence which would support the finding of an equitable licence.[46] If the claimant needs to be protected against a third party, however, the court is more likely to find that there is an equitable licence.[47] Accordingly, whenever the licensee is faced

---

[37] *D.H.N. Food Distributors Ltd.* v. *Tower Hamlets London Borough Council* [1976] 1 W.L.R. 852, 859 *per* Lord Denning M.R.; *Re Sharpe (A Bankrupt)* [1980] 1 W.L.R. 219, 225 *per* Browne-Wilkinson J.

[38] *Ashburn Anstalt* v. *Arnold* [1989] 1 Ch. 1, 24 *per* Fox L.J.; see below Chap. 5, Part B4, p. 77.

[39] See below Chap. 7, Part B, p. 113.

[40] See above Part B.2, p. 26; see also Todd, "Estoppel Licences and Third Party Rights" [1981] Conv. 347.

[41] See above Part B4(d), p. 34.

[42] See above Part A, p. 20.

[43] See Briggs, "Licences: Back to Basics" [1981] Conv. 212.

[44] See for example, *Errington* v. *Errington and Woods* [1952] 1 K.B. 290; *Tanner* v. *Tanner* [1975] 1 W.L.R. 1346; Thompson, "Licences: Questioning the Basics" [1983] Conv. 50; Moriarty, "Licences and Land Law: Legal Principles and Public Policies" (1984) 100 L.Q.R. 376.

[45] The author is not a lone heretic, see Dewar, "Licences and Land Law: An Alternative View" (1986) 49 M.L.R. 741.

[46] See *Tanner* v. *Tanner* [1975] 1 W.L.R. 1346.

[47] See below Chap. 7, Part C1, p. 123; *Re Sharpe (A Bankrupt)* [1980] 1 W.L.R. 219.

with an action for possession by a third party, all possible evidence of representation, reliance and detriment should be made available to the court to provide grounds for a finding of an equitable licence arising under proprietary estoppel.[48]

Form of licence   The form of the licence awarded by the court to satisfy the equity[49] raised by proprietary estoppel can vary from a licence to occupy the premises rent free for life[50] to a right to remain until money previously paid to the licensor is repaid.[51] One specific problem in relation to an irrevocable licence for life is whether it amounts to a tenancy for life under the Settled Land Act 1925.[52] The solution adopted by the court, to prevent the licensee obtaining greater powers over the land than the parties intended, is to require the owner to grant to the claimant a long lease determinable on the claimant's death at a nominal rent, subject to an absolute covenant against assignment.[53]

2. Interest in land

The precise status in law of an equitable licence arising by proprietary estoppel is still open to doubt.[54] Clearly, if the court grants the claimant a non-assignable lease[55] he will have a legal estate in the usual way. Similarly, if the court satisfies the equity by granting the claimant a contractual licence for a limited period he will have no interest in the land.[56] The problem occurs when the court declares the claimant to have an irrevocable licence for life or until money is repaid. The courts appear to have accepted that the licensee has some interest greater than a personal one which is binding on third parties.[57]

Lesser property   For example, in *Bristol and West Building Society* v. *Henning*[58]
right   Browne-Wilkinson L.J. regarded an irrevocable licence as being "some lesser property right."[59]

Third parties   The interest of an equitable licensee would appear to be less than a full equitable interest in the property.[60] Personal representatives have been held to be bound by a licence to remain in occupation as long as the claimant desired arising from representations made by the deceased[61] and an equitable

---

[48] See below Chap. 7, Part B, p. 113.
[49] See below Chap. 7, Part C1, p. 123.
[50] See for example *Greasley* v. *Cooke* [1980] 1 W.L.R. 1306; see also Chap. 7, Part C1, p. 123.
[51] See for example *Dodsworth* v. *Dodsworth* (1973) 228 E.G. 1115.
[52] See Martin, "Contractual Licensee or Tenant for Life" [1972] Conv. 266; see below Chap. 7, Part C1, p. 123.
[53] *Griffiths* v. *Williams* (1977) 248 E.G. 947.
[54] See Todd, "Estoppel Licences and Third Party Rights" [1981] Conv. 347; for the position of the claimant before the courts decision as to his precise remedy see below Chap. 8, Part F7, p. 156.
[55] See above the text at n. 53.
[56] See above Part B1, p. 24.
[57] *Inwards* v. *Baker* [1965] 2 Q.B. 29; *Williams* v. *Staite* [1979] Ch. 291 where the point was assumed; *Re Sharpe (A Bankrupt)* [1980] 1 W.L.R. 219.
[58] [1985] 1 W.L.R. 778.
[59] *Ibid.*, 782.
[60] See Everton, "Towards A Concept of 'Quasi-Property'?" [1982] Conv. 118 and 177.
[61] *Inwards* v. *Baker* [1965] 2 Q.B. 29.

licence has been held to bind a trustee in bankruptcy.[62] However, in *Re Sharpe (A Bankrupt)*[63] Brown-Wilkinson J. voiced doubts as to whether an equitable licence would bind a purchaser without express notice.

3. Revocation

Revocation of an equitable licence depends initially on the terms of the order made by the court when satisfying the equity raised by proprietary estoppel.[64] If the licence granted is an irrevocable one, it is unlikely that it will be terminated by subsequent misconduct by the licensee.[65] Certainly, far more serious misconduct is required to revoke an equitable licence once it has been granted than would have prevented the establishment of the equitable licence in the first place.[66]

---

[62] *Re Sharpe (A Bankrupt)* [1980] 1 W.L.R. 219.
[63] *Ibid.*, 226.
[64] See Dawson and Pearce, *Licences relating to the occupation or use of land.* (1979) p. 99.
[65] *Williams* v. *Staite* [1979] Ch. 291; Thompson, "Estoppel and Clean Hands" [1986] Conv. 406.
[66] *Willis (J.) & Son* v. *Willis* (1986) 277 E.G. 1133; see below Chap. 7, Part B4, p. 120.

3 LEASES

The aim of many people sharing residential accommodation will be to establish the existence of a lease, as a lease is the key to several forms of security and protection. Security stems from the fact that a lessee acquires a legal estate which is enforceable against third parties regardless of notice[1]; nor will the lessee's interest terminate on the death of his landlord. A contractual licence, by comparison, is a purely personal right.[2] Further, the law implies covenants into leases, for example, the covenant for quiet enjoyment[3] and, in some cases, a covenant for repair[4] which allows a lessee to enjoy the full benefits of his lease.

A major reason for seeking to establish a lease, or tenancy, is to gain the protection given to tenants of residential property by statute. The level of protection, however, has been

Statutory protection
considerably reduced by the Housing Act 1988.[5] A private sector landlord of a tenant who is a statutory or protected tenant under the old regime of the Rent Act 1977 will only be granted possession if he can satisfy one of the grounds under that Act,[6] for example, non-payment of rent or nuisance. Such tenants also have the right to apply to the local rent officer for the registration of a fair rent in respect of the premises subject to the tenancy.[7] An assured tenant under the Housing Act 1988 has security of tenure but the number of mandatory, as opposed to discretionary, grounds for possession has been increased.[8] The fair rent procedure does not apply and subsequent increases in rent are subject to only limited control.[9]

If a tenant has exclusive occupation of some living accommodation, the fact that he has to share other living accommodation, for example a bathroom, with persons other than the landlord will not prevent him having security of tenure under either the Rent Act 1977[10] or the Housing Act 1988.[11] Where the landlord resides in part of the same

[1] See below Chap. 8, Part F.3, p. 148.
[2] See above Chap. 2, Part B.1, p. 24; see below Chap. 8, Part F.2(b), p. 146.
[3] *Budd-Scott* v. *Daniell* [1902] 2 K.B. 351; *Markam* v. *Paget* [1908] 1 Ch. 697.
[4] Landlord and Tenant Act 1985, ss.11–15.
[5] See Rodgers, Housing; *The New Law* (1989).
[6] Section 98 and Sched. 15, Part 1. For the detailed law relating to security of tenure under the 1977 Act see Yates and Hawkins, *Landlord and Tenant Law* (2nd. ed., 1986); Martin, *Security of Tenure under the Rent Act* (1986); Woodfall, *Landlord and Tenant*; Megarry, *The Rent Acts* (11th ed., 1988).
[7] Rent Act 1977, s.67(1).
[8] Housing Act 1988, s.7(1), Sched. 2.
[9] *Ibid.*, ss.13–14.
[10] Rent Act 1977, s.22.
[11] Housing Act 1988, s.3.

building as his only or principal home, however, the tenant has no protection under the Housing Act 1988.[12] Tenants under restricted contracts[13] with a resident or sharing landlord[14] entered into prior to the commencement of the 1988 Act can apply for the registration of a reasonable rent[15] but they have very little security of tenure following the Housing Act 1980. Even such limited security is not available if the landlord provides "board"[16] and the provision of continental breakfast is sufficient for these purposes.[17]

Basic conditions A tenancy will only come into existence if certain conditions are satisfied. The parties must have an intention to create legal relations and the owner must have the capacity to grant a lease. In addition, the term granted must be for a fixed or ascertainable period. The recent House of Lords decision in *A. G. Securities* v. *Vaughan*[18] has confirmed the enjoyment of exclusive possession as the hallmark of a tenancy, as opposed to a licence. The same conditions apply when determining whether a lease is held by joint tenants. If there are several people sharing the accommodation, the problem is to determine whether they are joint tenants of a lease or a licence or whether each of them has an individual lease or licence.[19]

A. Definition

The Law of Property Act, 1925, section 1(1)(*b*) provides that a term of years absolute granted by a lease is one of the two legal estates in land. "Term of years absolute" is defined in section 205(1)(xxvii) to include a term for less than a year but to **Judicial definition** exclude any term determinable on death. In the leading case of *Street* v. *Mountford*[20] a judicial definition was given by Lord Templeman when he said;

> "To constitute a tenancy the occupier must be granted exclusive possession for a fixed or periodic term certain in consideration of a premium or periodical payments."

B. Intention to create legal relations

A lease is essentially a contract which creates a legal estate in land. Accordingly, if the parties have no intention of creating legal relations, *i.e.* of entering into a contract, there cannot be a lease. This initial question is completely separate from any question as to the parties' intention in relation to exclusive

[12] *Ibid.*, s.1(2), Sched. 1, para. 10.
[13] Rent Act 1977, s.19.
[14] *Ibid.*, s.12.
[15] *Ibid.*, s.77(1).
[16] Rent Act 1977, ss. 7(1) and 19(5)(*c*).
[17] *Otter* v. *Norman* [1988] 3 W.L.R. 321.
[18] [1988] 3 W.L.R. 1205.
[19] See below Part H, p. 59.
[20] [1985] A.C. 809, 818.

possession,[21] which can only arise once it is established that there is a contract of some form between the parties.

The two most common situations where the law is unlikely to impute an intention to create legal relations are family arrangements and acts of generosity.[22] A loose informal arrangement between members of the same family or quasi–family will probably not give rise to a lease or contractual licence without some evidence of intention to create legal relations, for example, written documentation or regular payments. Again, spontaneous acts of generosity in the provision of accommodation by non-family members are unlikely to give rise to a lease in the absence of further evidence. Occupiers in such cases are far more likely to succeed, if at all, under the heading of proprietary estoppel.[23]

Family arrangements

Acts of generosity

An illustration of an act of generosity failing to give rise to a lease can be seen in the case of *Booker* v. *Palmer*.[24] In that case the owner of a cottage permitted a friend to install an evacuee in the cottage rent free for the rest of the war. The law was summarised by Lord Greene M.R.[25];

"To suggest there is an intention there to create a relationship of landlord and tenant appears to me to be quite impossible. There is one golden rule which is of very general application, namely, that the law does not impute intention to enter legal relationships where the circumstances and conduct of the parties negatives any intention of the kind. It seems to me that this is a clear example of the application of that rule."

Examples

Modern day Samaritans are still protected by that principle. In *Sharp* v. *McArthur*[26] the owner of a flat took pity on the defendant who was in urgent need of accommodation and allowed him to move into possession until the flat was sold. The Court of Appeal held that there was no intention to create legal relations despite the fact that the defendant was given a rent book to show to the Department of Health and Social Security. Similarly, in *Heslop* v. *Burns*[27] the Court of Appeal refused to infer an intention to create legal relations where a cottage was provided for a couple by the wife's employer out of sympathy for their conditions. There was no arrangement as to terms and the owner visited the cottage regularly for meals. The Court of Appeal refused to imply a tenancy at will and indicated[28] that such a tenancy was probably now only applicable where there was a holding over or an entry prior to purchase.

The fact that a landlord is motivated by feelings of generosity or friendship to grant possession of premises will not

---

[21] See below Part G1(e), p. 50.
[22] See *Facchini* v. *Bryson* [1952] 1 T.L.R. 1386, 1389–90 *per* Denning L.J.
[23] See below Chap. 7.
[24] [1942] 2 All E.R. 674.
[25] *Ibid.*, 677; see also *Isaac* v. *Hotel de Paris Ltd.* [1960] 1 All E.R. 348, 352.
[26] (1987) 19 H.L.R. 364; see also *Marcroft Wagons Ltd.* v. *Smith* [1951] 2 K.B. 496.
[27] [1974] 1 W.L.R. 1241.
[28] *Ibid.*, 1253 *per* Scarman L.J.

prevent there being a tenancy if there is a clear intention to create legal relations. This will be so even though the rent is low and there is a "gentleman's agreement" by the occupier to give up possession at short notice.[29]

Family arrangement   A family arrangement failing to give rise to legal relations and, thus, to a tenancy can be seen in *Cobb* v. *Lane*.[30] In that case the owner let her brother live in her house rent free. The Court of Appeal held that he had no interest which survived his sister's death. Most family informal sharing arrangements are unlikely to create legal relations and any non-owner will have merely a bare licence.[31] If a member of a family was involved in any way at the time of purchase and subsequently makes payments beyond mere contributions to joint living expenses, the possibility of an equitable interest under a trust for sale should be considered.[32]

Lord Templeman in *Street* v. *Mountford*[33] accepted cases such as *Booker* v. *Palmer*[34] as examples of cases where the parties did not intend to enter legal relations. It has been argued that these cases ought to be considered as creating mere licences because the occupier was not truly invested with exclusive possession.[35] It has also been argued that many of the cases can be treated as cases where the parties real intention was to create purely a licence.[36] If cases of genuine family arrangements and acts of generosity are kept outside the field of contract by treating them as cases in which there is no intention to create legal relations, any potential injustice could be removed by invoking the doctrine of proprietary estoppel.[37]

Alternative remedy   An example of a situation in which proprietary estoppel should have been used is *Barnes* v. *Barratt*.[38] That case concerned a married couple who moved into a widower's house in order to look after him and were given exclusive possession of three rooms in return for domestic services and paying some of the household bills. This was held to be akin to a family arrangement and to create purely a personal licence to occupy.

C.   Formalities

The Law of Property Act 1925[39] requires all interests in land to be created by deed. Such formalities, however, do not apply to leases taking effect in possession for a term not exceeding

---

[29] *Sopwith* v. *Stutchbury* (1983) 17 H.L.R. 50, C.A.
[30] [1952] 1 All E.R. 1199; see also *Errington* v. *Errington and Woods* [1952] 1 All E.R. 149, 154.
[31] *David* v. *London Borough of Lewisham* (1977) 34 P. & C.R. 112; *c.f. Nunn* v. *Dalrymple*, (1989) 21 H.L.R. 569; see above Chap. 2, Part A, p. 20.
[32] See *Grant* v. *Edwards* [1986] Ch. 638; see below Chap. 6, Part G, p. 89.
[33] [1985] A.C. 809, 820–821.
[34] [1942] 2 All E.R. 674.
[35] Gray, *Elements of Land Law* (1987), p. 460.
[36] Yates and Hawkins, *Landlord and Tenant Law* (2nd ed., 1986), p. 25; see below Part G.1(*e*), p. 50, for a discussion of the relevance of the parties' intention.
[37] See below Chap. 7.
[38] [1970] 2 Q.B. 657.
[39] S.52(1).

three years at the best rent which can reasonably be obtained
Less than three without taking a fine.[40] Thus leases for less than three years
years can be created informally and will be valid even if oral. If only
a token rent is payable, the lease will take effect at will only.[41]

Periodic tenancy Periodic tenancies can take effect orally[42] as they are
regarded as being for less than three years although the tenancy
may, in fact, ultimately exceed three years. There is a common
law presumption that the payment and acceptance of rent on a
periodic basis by an occupier in possession with the owner's
consent will give rise to a periodic tenancy. The presumption,
however, is capable of rebuttal by clear evidence of the parties'
contrary intention.[43]

D. Competent lessor

If the person purporting to grant a lease has no estate or
interest in the relevant premises, a lease will not be created and
the occupier will have a licence, or at most, a tenancy by
estoppel.[44] Thus a squatter cannot grant a co–squatter a lease
which will bind third parties. Similarly, a person sharing a
house will not be able to gain a lease from the apparent owner
occupiers if the house is, in fact, owned by a company, for
example a family company or the husband's employer.[45] The
converse applies equally, a company cannot grant a lease of a
house owned by one of its directors.[46]

Company lessors Even though a company is the owner of property, it may
still not be able to grant a lease if it does not have the specific
power to grant leases in its memorandum and articles of
association; any tenancy would be *ultra vires* the powers of the
company.[47] If such a company did purport to grant a lease, a
term of years may be created, however, if the prospective
tenant was not aware that the powers of the company were
limited. This follows from section 35 of the Companies Act
1985, which provides, in favour of a person dealing with the
company in good faith, that any transaction decided on by the
directors is deemed to be within the powers of the company
and the powers of the directors are deemed to be free of any
limitation under the memorandum and articles of association. A
company which only has power to grant licences should make
that fact clear to any prospective licensee, otherwise a tenancy
binding on the company may be created if the prospective
licensee is given exclusive possession. Once section 108 of the

---

[40] Ss.54(2) and 52(2)(*d*); Law of Property (Miscellaneous Provisions) Act 1989,
s.2(5).
[41] S.54(1).
[42] *Kushner* v. *Law Society* [1952] 1 K.B. 264.
[43] *Cardiothoracic Institute* v. *Shrewdcrest Ltd.* [1986] 1 W.L.R. 368, 378; see also
Javid v. *Aqil, The Times*, May 29, 1990.
[44] See Pettit, "Judge-Proof Licences" [1980] Conv. 112; see below Chap. 8,
Part F3, p. 148.
[45] For an example of other problems caused by company owned houses see
Winkworth v. *Baron (Edward) Developments Co. Ltd.* [1987] 1 All E.R. 114.
[46] *Torbett* v. *Faulkner* [1952] 2 T.L.R. 659.
[47] See the old cases on limited powers of requisitioning authorities—*Ministry of
Agriculture and Fisheries* v. *Matthews* [1950] 1 K.B. 148; *Lewisham Borough
Council* v. *Roberts* [1949] 2 K.B. 608; *Finbow* v. *Air Ministry* [1963] 1
W.L.R.

Companies Act 1989 comes into force in November or
December 1990, amending section 35, the *ultra vires* rule will
be abolished; after that date a lease will bind any company
regardless of its actual powers.

E. Certainty of time

A lease, to be valid must be for a period of time which is
certain and certainty of time comprises two elements,

Commencement commencement and duration. The time of commencement of a
lease must either be fixed by the parties or be readily
ascertainable. In the case of many sharing arrangements there
will have been no discussion of the date of commencement but
that is not fatal to the grant of a lease. The law will assume
that the term began on the taking of possession, provided it is
clear when that occurred.[48]

Duration There is no restriction on the length of the term of a lease,
a week is just as acceptable as 999 years.[49] A period of time of
less than a day, however, is likely to be treated as a licence.[50]
The period of time need not be continous. An agreement to
occupy for a set number of weeks a year for, say 80 years, can
be a lease.[51] Holiday time shares are capable, therefore, of
being leases.

The length of the term granted, however, must either be
for a certain maximum duration or the length of the term must
be ascertainable by reference to a certain event or events. The
classic illustration is the case of *Lace* v. *Chantler*[52] which
concerned the grant of a right of occupation "for the duration
of the war." It was held that the term was completely uncertain
and no lease took effect.[53] Thus, a simple permission for
someone to reside in premises rent free "until they can find
somewhere else" will not create a lease.

Certainty by The requirement of certainty of term has been eased by
notice the recent case of *Ashburn Anstalt* v. *Arnold*.[54] It has long been
accepted that a periodic tenancy satisfies the requirement of
certainty of term although the maximum duration of the total
term is not known at its commencement.[55] That principle has
been applied even though either parties' power to determine
the periodic tenancy is dependant on the happening of an
outside event whose occurrence is not certain.[56] The Court of
Appeal in *Ashburn Anstalt* v. *Arnold*[57] took the argument one

---

[48] *James* v. *Lock* (1977) 246 E.G. 395.
[49] See Law of Property Act 1925, s.205(1)(xxvii).
[50] *Krell* v. *Henry* [1903] 2 K.B. 740; *Winter Garden Theatre (London) Ltd.* v.
Millennium Productions Ltd. [1948] A.C. 173.
[51] *Cottage Holiday Associates Ltd.* v. *Customs and Excise Commissioners* [1983]
Q.B. 735.
[52] [1944] K.B. 368.
[53] But see the Validation of War-time Leases Act, 1944.
[54] [1989] 1 Ch. 1.
[55] *Re Midland Railway Co's Agreement* [1971] Ch. 725.
[56] *Ibid.*
[57] [1989] 1 Ch. 1.

stage further and held that an open ended grant determinable by one party on the happening of an event which may or may not occur was sufficiently certain. The particular grant was to allow the defendants to remain in possession until the landlords gave three months notice certifying that they were ready to proceed with redevelopments. This liberal approach to certainty of term was expressed by Fox L.J. as follows[58];

Ashburn Anstalt
v. Arnold

> "The result, in our opinion, is that the arrangement could be brought to an end by both parties in circumstances which are free from uncertainty in the sense that there would be no doubt whether the determining event had occured. The vice of uncertainty in relation to the duration of the term is that the parties do not know where they stand. Put another way, the court does not know what to enforce. That is not the position here. It seems to us therefore, that, as in the *Midland Railway Co.'s Agreement*[59] there is no reason why the court should not hold the parties to their agreement. That is so even though the tenancy is not (or may not be) an ordinary periodic tenancy. The rights of the parties are no more subject to uncertainty than those in the *Midland Railway Co.'s Agreement* case. We do not see why the mere absence of a formula referring to a periodic tenancy or occupancy should alter the position."

It would now seem, following *Ashburn Anstalt* v. *Arnold*[60] that any reference to the parties being able to determine the tenancy will serve to ward off the vice of uncertainty. Such phrases as "a months notice after you find somewhere else to live" in the agreement should ensure that the lease is valid.

Lease for life

Section 205(1)(xxvii) specifically excludes from the definition of a lease any term which is determined by reference to life. Thus, the common agreement to allow someone to live in premises rent free for the rest of their life cannot amount to a legal lease. Such an agreement may fall within the Settled Land Act 1925.[61] If a lease for life is granted at a rent, or in consideration of a fine, however, the lease is converted into a term for 90 years which is determinable on the death of the original lessee by the giving of one month's notice[62]

F. Rent

Lord Templeman's definition of a lease in *Street* v. *Mountford*,[63] reiterated in *A. G. Securities* v. *Vaughan*[64] seems to indicate that the payment of a rent or premium is essential

---

[58] *Ibid.*, 12.
[59] [1971] Ch. 725.
[60] [1989] 1 Ch. 1.
[61] See *Binions* v. *Evans* [1972] Ch. 359 but see the criticisms in *Griffiths* v. *Williams* (1977) 248 E.G. 947, 949–950 *per* Goff L.J.; see above Chap. 2, Part C.1, p. 37.
[62] Law of Property Act 1925, s.149(6).
[63] [1985] A.C. 809, 818.
[64] [1988] 3 W.L.R. 1205, 1212.

before there can be a tenancy. Section 205(1)(xxvii), however, refers to "whether or not at a rent." The Court of Appeal in *Ashburn Anstalt* v. *Arnold*[65] have now confirmed that the reservation of a rent is not essential for the creation of a tenancy.

Evidence of intent

This does not mean that the payment of rent or other monetary payments are irrelevant. On the one hand, the absence of rent is evidence that no more than a mere licence has been created.[66] On the other hand, payments may be evidence of intention to create legal relations[67] or, if the payments are regular, raise a presumption of a periodic tenancy.[68] If rent is reserved, it should be certain or capable of being calculated with certainty, for example the payment of specific outgoings.[69] The court will not, on the usual contractual principles, enquire into the adequacy of any rent reserved.[70]

G.   Exclusive possession

The final requirement for a lease is that the occupier should have exclusive possession of the premises. Indeed, it can be said that this is the most important requirement because without exclusive possession there can never be a tenancy. The concept of exclusive possession and its importance for differentiating a licence from a lease was set out by Lord Templeman in the leading case of *Street* v. *Mountford*[71];

Basic condition

"The traditional view that the grant of exclusive possession for a term at a rent creates a tenancy is consistent with the elevation of a tenancy into an estate in land. The tenant possessing exclusive possession is able to exercise the rights of an owner of land, which is in the real sense his land albeit temporary and subject to certain restrictions. A tenant armed with exclusive possession can keep out strangers and keep out the landlord unless the landlord is exercising limited rights reserved to him by the tenancy agreement to enter and view or repair. A licensee lacking exclusive posession can in no sense call the land his own and cannot be said to own any estate in the land. The licence does not create an estate in the land to which it relates but only makes an act lawful which would otherwise be unlawful."

The importance of exclusive possession was confirmed recently by the House of Lords in *A. G. Securities* v. *Vaughan.*[72]

---

[65] [1989] 1 Ch. 1, 9; noted Thompson [1988] Conv. 201.
[66] *Soldiers', Sailors' and Airmen's Families Association* v. *Merton London Borough Council* [1967] 1 W.L.R. 736.
[67] See above Part B, p. 40.
[68] See above Part C, p. 42.
[69] *Bretherton* v. *Paton* (1986) 18 H.L.R. 257; *Phillips* v. *Wilde* C.A., unreported, November 3, 1986.
[70] *Royal Philanthropic Society* v. *County* (1985) 276 E.G. 1068, 1072.
[71] [1985] A.C. 809, 816.
[72] [1988] 3 W.L.R. 1205, 1212 *per* Lord Templeman, noted [1989] Conv. 128 (P. F. Smith).

1. Concept of exclusive possession

It is thus the degree of control possessed by the occupier which determines whether he is a tenant or a licensee. A person may be the sole occupant of his particular part of a house but if the landlord has a free right of entry, for example, as in a hotel, there can be no tenancy. In *Street* v. *Mountford*[73] Lord Templeman stated;

> "An occupier of residential accommodation at a rent is either a lodger or a tenant."

This statement is too simplistic as it stands and indeed, Lord Templeman qualified it later in his speech.[74] It is clear that there can be other categories of occupier besides lodgers who are not tenants.[75] A person occupying premises under a contract of sale or a contract of employment is a licensee as is a person occupying under certain charitable arrangements. An occupier will not be a licensee, however, simply because both parties intend that relationship to result.

(a) **Lodgers**   A lodger will always be a licensee and never a tenant. A useful starting point for identifying a lodger is Lord Templeman's statement in *Street* v. *Mountford*[76];

Definition
> "The occupier is a lodger if the landlord provides attendance or services which require the landlord or his servants to exercise unrestricted access to and use of the premises. A lodger is entitled to live in the premises but cannot call the place his own."

Thus, there will be a lodging agreement, and not a tenancy, where the landlord retains control over access to the occupier's room.[77] The retention of a key alone by the landlord is not sufficient; there will only be a lodging agreement if the key is retained to enable the landlord to provide services.[78]

Examples   The hallmarks of a lodging arrangement, rather than a tenancy, can be seen in *Appah* v. *Parncliffe Investments Ltd.*[79] In that case, whilst occupiers had individual rooms which locked, the management were responsible for cleaning, bed–making and laundry. Further, occupiers could not have

---

[73] [1985] A.C. 809, 817.
[74] *Ibid.*, 826–827; see also *Facchini* v. *Bryson* [1952] 1 T.L.R. 1386, 1389 *per* Denning L.J.
[75] *Brooker Settled Estates Ltd.* v. *Ayres* (1987) 54 P. & C.R. 165, 168 *per* O'Connor L.J.; see below Part G1(b)–(e), p. 48 *et seq.*
[76] [1985] A.C. 809, 818; see *Allan* v. *Liverpool Overseers* (1874) L.R. 9 Q.B. 180, 190–192 *per* Blackburn J.; *A. G. Securities* v. *Vaughan* [1988] 3 W.L.R. 1205, 1213 *per* Lord Templeman.
[77] *Bradley* v. *Baylis* (1881) 8 Q.B.D. 195, 218 *per* Sir George Jessel M.R.; *Westminster Council* v. *Southern Railway Co.* [1936] A.C. 511, 530; *Soldiers', Sailors' and Airmen's Families Association* v. *Merton London Borough Council* [1967] 1 W.L.R. 736.
[78] *Aslan* v. *Murphy* [1989] 3 All E.R. 130; *Family Housing Association* v. *Jones* [1990] 1 All E.R. 385.
[79] [1964] 1 W.L.R. 1064; see also *Luganda* v. *Services Hotels Ltd.* [1969] 2 Ch. 209.

unauthorised guests at all or visitors in their rooms after
l0.30pm.

Marchant v. *Charters*[80] provides a further illustration of a
lodging arrangement. In that case, occupiers had individual
rooms but a housekeeper cleaned daily and provided clean linen
weekly. Lord Denning M.R. summed up the test for the
distinction between a lodging agreement and a tenancy as
follows[81];

> "Eventually the answer depends upon the nature and
> quality of the occupancy. Was it intended that the
> occupier should have a stake in the room or did he have
> only permission for himself personally to occupy the room,
> whether under contract or not, in which case he is a
> licensee."

A more recent illustration of a failure to give the occupier
a "stake in the room" is the case of *Markou* v. *Da Silvaesa*.[82]
By the terms of the agreement, the occupiers had to leave the
premises between 10.30 am. and noon each day, the owner
retained keys and reserved an absolute right of entry at all
times. The occupier could also be moved to other premises
under the terms of the agreement and cleaning, rubbish
collection and laundry was provided by a housekeeper. The
Court of Appeal held that if the written agreement accurately
reflected the agreement between the parties the occupants were
lodgers.[83]

Need for access   The provision of services is not sufficient, on its own, to
convert what would otherwise be a tenancy into lodgings. The
services must require the landlord to have unrestricted access to
the premises. For example, in *Guppys (Bridport) Ltd.* v.
Brookling[84] some services such as clean linen were provided
but there was no access by the landlord to the individual
rooms; the tenants collected clean linen and did their own
cleaning. In those circumstances the Court of Appeal held that
the occupiers had tenancies.

(b) Contract of sale If the exclusive occupation of premises
is referable to a contract for the sale of the premises, there will
not be a tenancy.[85] It is now clear that if a person goes into
occupation before sale, a tenancy will only be excluded if the
contract of sale actually exists at the time occupation
commences; negotiations for sale are not sufficient.[86]

**Requirement of
contract**   In *Bretherton* v. *Paton*,[87] Mrs Paton was let into possession
of a house in bad condition on payment of rates and £1.20 a
week for insurance. The idea was that Mrs Paton would put

---

[80] [1977] 1 W.L.R. 1181.
[81] *Ibid.*, 1185.
[82] (1986) 52 P. & C.R. 204.
[83] See below Part G2, p. 52 for the construction of such agreements.
[84] (1984) 269 E.G. 846.
[85] *Street v. Mountford* [1985] A.C. 809, 827 *per* Lord Templeman.
[86] *Bhattacharya v. Raising* C.A., unreported, March 25, 1987.
[87] (1986) 18 H.L.R. 257.

the house into repair and then purchase it with the aid of a mortgage within two years. It was held that Mrs Paton had a tenancy of the house as she had exclusive possession for a periodic term at a rent. There was no other contract in existence to which possession could be refered as, for example, the purchase price had not been agreed. A tenancy was also held to exist in *Bhattacharya* v. *Raising*[88] where the occupiers remained in possession pending negotiations as to the purchase of the flat. A person with exclusive possession may also be held to be a licensee if he is in occupation awaiting the grant of a lease and he does not have an agreement for a lease.[89]

(c) Service occupancy Where the grant is made by an employer and the occupier is required to occupy the premises for the better performance of his duties as an employee, there will be a licence and not a tenancy.[90] This exceptional case will only apply where the occupation is necessary for the performance of the services provided by the employee. The occupation must be strictly ancillary to the performance of the employee's duties.[91] On this basis living accomodation provided on the premises for household staff such as a housekeeper, chauffeur or gardener will be held to be a licence and not a tenancy.[92]

Necessary occupation   If the occupation is not necessary for the performance of the employee's duties, the fact that the accommodation is provided by the employer and it is more convenient for the employee to live at the relevant premises will not turn what would otherwise be a tenancy into a licence. This can be seen from *Royal Philanthropic Society* v. *County*[93] where a teacher was held to have a tenancy of a school house. None of the teacher's duties required him to live in the house and it was irrelevant that his contract required him to leave the house at the termination of his employment and that the rent was very low.

(d) Charity The final exceptional case mentioned by Lord Templeman in *Street* v. *Mountford*[94] where exclusive possession does not denote a tenancy, is an occupier who is an object of charity. Some of the cases under this head can also be explained as instances where the occupier does not truly have exclusive possession, but not all.

Examples   In *Abbeyfield (Harpenden) Society Ltd.* v. *Woods*[95] the occupant of a room in an old peoples' home was held to be a licensee and not a tenant. This decision can be explained by saying that the occupant was a lodger,[96] particularly in view of

---

[88] C.A., unreported, March 25, 1987.
[89] *Sopwith* v. *Stutchbury* (1983) 17 H.L.R. 50.
[90] *Street* v. *Mountford* [1985] A.C. 809, 818 *per* Lord Templeman.
[91] *Smith* v. *Seghill Overseers* (1875) L.R. 10 Q.B. 422, 428 *per* Mellor J.
[92] *Ramsbottom v Snelson* [1948] 1 K.B. 473, 477.
[93] (1985) 276 E.G. 1068.
[94] [1985] A.C. 809, 818 *per* Lord Templeman.
[95] [1968] 1 W.L.R. 374; see also Housing Act 1985, Sched. 1, para. 12 in relation to a licence to occupy an almshouse.
[96] See above Part G1(a), p. 47.

the meals and other housekeeping services provided. The licence of a Y.W.C.A. hostel resident can be explained on the same grounds.[97]

There is no explanation, other than the charity exception, for the decision in *Trustees of the Alcoholic Recovery Project* v. *Farrell*.[98] In this case, the occupier of a self–contained bed–sitting room in a rehabilitation hostel for former alcoholics was held to be a licensee even though no services were provided. The exception is construed narrowly, however, and does not extend to a housing association providing temporary accommodation for a homeless person; such a person will be held to have a tenancy.[98a]

(e) **Intentional licences**   The question remains as to whether there are any other circumstances in which a person may have exclusive possession of premises and yet be granted a licence rather than a lease. The one possibility which is re-emerging is where both of the parties intend only a licence.

The traditional view of the distinction between a lease and a licence was that the existence of exclusive possession by the occupier was conclusive of the existence of a tenancy.[99] From the mid 1970s onwards, however, the intention of the parties became increasingly important. The courts began to support licences of residential accommodation entered into to avoid the effects of the Rent Acts.

Relevance of intention

The high water mark of the "intentional" licence came with the decision of the Court of Appeal in *Somma* v. *Hazelhurst*.[1] In that case a young unmarried couple occupied a double bed–sitting room for which they each paid a weekly rent. They entered into two separate residential occupation licences which reserved the right for the owner to require either licensee to share the room with someone else. Despite the fact that the couple clearly had exclusive possession of the room, it was held that they were each licensees as that was the form of arrangement which both parties intended and that was the written agreement which they had entered into.

Intention irrelevant?

The pendulum swung completely in the opposite direction with the decision of the House of Lords in *Street* v. *Mountford*.[2] In the words of Lord Templeman[3];

> "My Lords, the only intention which is relevant is the intention demonstrated by the agreement to grant exclusive possession for a term at a rent."

In particular the House of Lords disapproved of the decision in *Somma* v. *Hazelhurst*[4] holding that[5] the room was

---

[97] *R.* v. *South Middlesex Rent Tribunal, ex p. Beswick* (1976) 32 P. & C.R. 67.
[98] [1976] L.A.G. Bulletin 259; see also *Carr Gomm Society* v. *Hawkins* [1990] 4 C.L. 244.
[98a] *Family Housing Association* v. *Jones* [1990] 1 All E.R. 385.
[99] See Gray, *Elements of Land Law* (1987), p. 445.
[1] [1978] 1 W.L.R. 1014.
[2] [1985] A.C. 809.
[3] *Ibid.*, 826; see also *A. G. Securities* v. *Vaughan* [1988] 3 W.L.R. 1205, 1217 *per* Lord Templeman.
[4] [1978] 1 W.L.R. 1014.
[5] [1985] A.C. 809, 825 *per* Lord Templeman.

let and taken as residential accommodation with exclusive possession in order that the defendants could cohabit. The agreements signed by the defendants constituted a grant to them jointly of exclusive possession at a rent for a term for the purposes for which the room was taken and the grant, thus, created a tenancy. Until recently this decision has been interpreted to mean that if exclusive possession had been granted to the occupier, unless it fell within one of the exceptional cases set out above, there was a tenancy[6]; the intentions of the parties being irrelevant. Landlords' views totally ignored have included an intention to grant a licence until sale of the property[7] and an intention to grant a licence for only so long as the occupier remained employed as a teacher.[8]

Recent cases indicate that the courts may be taking a more flexible approach and, in certain circumstances, having regard to the intentions of the parties. A distinction appears to be emerging between those cases where the property is suitable for, and physically capable of, being shared with others and those where it is not. In the latter situation, the occupier or occupiers will be held to have a tenancy regardless of any stated intention by either them or the landlord as to future sharing. The House of Lords[9] made this clear when reversing the Court of Appeal's decision in *Antoniades* v. *Villiers*.[10] In that case, a young unmarried couple entered into two separate residential licences, paying separate rents for a flat which was not suitable for occupation by more than one couple, save on a very temporary basis. A clause permitting the landlord and others to share the flat with the occupiers was dismissed as a pretence[11] and the occupiers held to be tenants. This approach was followed by the Court of Appeal in *Aslan* v. *Murphy*[12] where an occupier of a room 4 feet 3 inches by 12 feet 6 inches was held to be a tenant although there was an express provision in the agreement for sharing with others.

Nature of the premises

If the premises are suitable for multiple occupation, the courts appear to have regard to the intentions of the parties when considering the agreement of an individual occupier. In *A. G. Securities* v. *Vaughan*,[13] a large flat was occupied by four people under separate agreements entered into at different times. The House of Lords accepted that the purpose and intention of both parties to each agreement was that the occupier should have permissive enjoyment of the flat with an obligation to share that occupation with up to three other people. On that basis, each occupier was held to have an individual licence and there was no joint tenancy.[14] A similar

[6] *Markou* v. *Da Silvaesa* (1986) 52 P.& C.R. 204, 219 *per* Ralph Gibson L.J.
[7] *Bretherton* v. *Paton* (1986) 18 H.L.R. 257.
[8] *Royal Philanthropic Society* v. *County* (1985) 276 E.G. 1068.
[9] Reported with *A. G. Securities* v. *Vaughan* [1988] 3 W.L.R. 1205.
[10] [1988] 3 W.L.R. 139.
[11] See below Part G2(a)(ii), p. 54.
[12] [1989] 3 All E.R. 130; noted by Evans [1990] J.S.W.L. 128.
[13] [1988] 3 W.L.R. 1205.
[14] See below Part H, p. 59.

approach was taken by the Court of Appeal in *Stribling* v. *Wickham*[15] where each of three occupiers sharing a house was held to have an individual licence. In confirming the existence of a series of licences rather than a tenancy, Parker L.J. said of the agreements setting out the parties' intention that possession should be shared[16];

> "They represent the realities of the transaction and a genuine and sensible arrangement for the benefit of both sides."

Lessor's intention

In contrast, if the landlord does not truly intend to exercise his power to introduce a further person into the premises, the occupiers will have a tenancy even if sharing with others is physically possible.[17] Thus in *Duke* v. *Wynne*[18] Mr. and Mrs. Wynne were held to be tenants of a three bedroomed house because Mrs. Duke did not seriously intend to exercise her power in the agreement to place other occupiers in the house.

Temporary accommodation

The case of *Ogwr Borough Council* v. *Dykes*[19] raised the possibility that the intentions of the parties to create a licence could be relevant where the circumstances in which the right to exclusive occupation was granted negatived any intention to create a tenancy. In that case, the Court of Appeal held that a local authority exercising its duty under the Housing Act 1985 in relation to homeless persons granted a licence and not a tenancy. It is now clear that the courts will not have regard to the parties' mutual intentions in any circumstances if the property is not suitable for sharing. In *Family Housing Association* v. *Jones*[20] exclusive occupation of a two roomed self-contained flat was granted by the Association to the defendant and her son when they were homeless. The Court of Appeal held that the defendant had a tenancy of the flat although both parties intended the accommodation to be purely temporary. Slade L.J. recognised, however, that the finding of a tenancy in such situations would restrict the ways in which bodies like the plaintiffs could deal with their property and may not be for the benefit of homeless people as a whole.

2. Identifying exclusive possession

The main criterion for determining whether there is a lease or a licence is the enjoyment of exclusive possession by the occupier. The courts' approach to the identification of exclusive possession depends upon whether there is a written agreement in existence and whether that agreement or part of it is a sham or a pretence. The recent cases are not free from conflict. This is partly explained by the fact that the exclusive possession

---

[15] [1989] 27 E.G. 81.
[16] *Ibid.*, 86.
[17] See *Nicolaou* v. *Pitt* [1989] 21 E.G. 71.
[18] [1989] 3 All E.R. 130.
[19] [1989] 1 W.L.R. 295 C.A.
[20] [1990] 1 All E.R. 385.

Lack of guidance

point was conceded in *Street* v. *Mountford*[21] and, therefore, Lord Templeman's speech has been found to lack guidance in relation to the determination of exclusive possession in complex factual situations.[22] Whilst the House of Lords in *A. G. Securities* v. *Vaughan*[23] clarified the position as to exclusive possession in the two factual situations before them, their Lordships offered no general guidance beyond the need to seek the true nature of the bargain.

(a) **Written agreements** The courts' approach to the construction of a written agreement and the determination of whether an occupier has exclusive possession was summarised by Lord Oliver in *A. G. Securities* v. *Vaughan*[24] as follows;

True nature of the agreement

"The critical question, however, in every case is not simply how the agreement is presented to the outside world in the relevant documentation, but what is the true nature of the agreement."

Three stages procedure

There are three stages in finding the true nature of the bargain between the parties. First, it should be considered whether the whole agreement is a sham. If it is not, the second stage is to consider whether any individual clauses in the agreement are pretences. The final stage is to construe the agreement, disregarding any clauses which have been held to be pretences.[25]

(i) Shams

Deceit

A sham is an agreement which is deliberately framed with the object of deceiving third parties as to the true nature and effect of legal relations between the parties.[26] If an agreement is found to be a sham it will be ineffective and the occupier's status as tenant or licensee will depend upon the court's construction of the original oral agreement.

Example

An example of a licence being declared to be a sham can be seen from *Demuren* v. *Seal Estates Ltd.*[27] In that case, two separate licences were entered into by two men who were to occupy a flat. The licences were in terms that each would occupy bedroom No. 1 and share the rest of the flat in common. They were also required to make immediate payment of all monthly instalments by post-dated cheques. Despite the pre-payment, the licences reserved to the licensor a unilateral right to terminate the licences at any time on one weeks notice. There was evidence from the two occupiers from which the trial judge concluded that there was a mutual concurrent

---

[21] [1985] A.C. 809, 816.
[22] *A. G. Securities* v. *Vaughan* [1988] 3 W.L.R. 1205, 1225 *per* Lord Jauncey; *Hadjiloucas* v. *Crean* [1987] 3 All E.R. 1008, 1014.
[23] [1988] 3 W.L.R. 1205; see Sparkes, "Breaking Flat Sharing Licences" [1989] J.S.W.L. 293.
[24] [1988] 3 W.L.R. 1205, 1219; see also *Stribling* v. *Wickham* [1989] 27 E.G. 81, 85 *per* Parker L.J.
[25] *Aslan* v. *Murphy* [1989] 3 All E.R. 130.
[26] See *Snook* v. *London and West Riding Investments Ltd.* [1967] 2 Q.B. 786; *Hadjiloucas* v. *Crean* [1987] 3 All E.R. 1008, 1014 *per* Mustill L.J.
[27] (1978) 249 E.G. 440.

intention at the time that the agreement was made that the two occupiers should together have and enjoy exclusive occupation of the whole flat. The Court of Appeal had no difficulty in finding that the licences were shams and that the occupiers were joint tenants with Rent Act protection.

Less important

Lord Templeman in *Street* v. *Mountford*[28] was of the view that the agreements in *Somma* v. *Hazelhurst*[29] were also shams. In *A. G. Securities* v. *Vaughan*,[30] however, Lord Templeman indicated that he preferred the use of the word "pretence" rather than "sham device" or "artificial transcation." The courts now appear less likely to declare an entire transaction a sham[31] but to disregard individual clauses as pretences when construing the written agreement.[32]

(ii) Pretences

A pretence is a clause in an agreement which is not a true statement of the rights intended between the parties. The nature and effect of pretences was set out by Lord Donaldson

Definition

M.R. in *Aslan* v. *Murphy*[33];

> 'Quite apart from labelling, parties may succumb to the temptation to agree to pretend to have particular rights and duties which are not in fact any part of the true bargain. Prima facie the parties must be taken to mean what they say, but given the pressures on both parties to pretend, albeit for different reasons, the courts would be acting unrealistically if they did not keep a weather eye open for pretences, taking due account of how the parties have acted in performance of their apparent bargain. This identification and exposure of such pretences does not necessarily lead to the conclusion that their agreement is a sham, but only to the conclusion that the terms of the true bargain are not wholly the same as the bargain appearing on the face of the agreement. It is the true rather than the apparent bargain which determines the question: tenant or lodger?'

Examples

In *Aslan* v. *Murphy*[34] itself, a clause requiring the occupier to share a room measuring 4 feet 3 inches by 12 feet 6 inches was held to be a pretence as was a clause requiring the occupier to vacate the room for 90 minutes each day. A further example of an agreement containing clauses which were pretences appears in *Markou* v. *Da Silvaesa*.[35] In that case a clause allowing occupation between midnight and 10.30 am. and between noon and midnight only and a clause permitting the licensor to remove furniture were held to be ineffective.[36]

---

[28] [1985] A.C. 809, 825.
[29] [1978] 1 W.L.R. 1014; see above p. 50 for the facts of the case.
[30] [1988] 3 W.L.R. 1205, 1216.
[31] See *Hilton* v. *Plustitle Ltd.* [1988] 3 All E.R. 1051.
[32] See *Aslan* v. *Murphy* [1989] 3 All E.R. 130.
[33] [1989] 3 All E.R. 130, 133; see also *A. G. Securities* v. *Vaughan* [1988] 3 W.L.R. 1205, 1218 *per* Lord Templeman.
[34] *Ibid.*
[35] (1986) 52 P. & C.R. 204.
[36] *Ibid.*, 216 *per* Ralph Gibson L.J.

Surrounding circumstances

The court determines whether a particular clause is a pretence by looking at both the surrounding circumstances at the time the agreement was made and the subsequent acts of the parties.[37] Thus the choice of a double bed rather than two single beds by joint applicants for a flat is an indication that a clause in the agreement requiring the occupiers to share with others is a pretence.[38] It is also relevant when considering a sharing clause to have regard to the steps the landlord took to find other occupiers.[39]

Lord Templeman in *Street* v. *Mountford*[40] said that the courts should be astute to detect and frustrate any devices which were intended to disguise the grant of a tenancy. The courts approach does not now appear to be quite so vigorous or acute. A more accurate view appears in the following extract from Sir Denys Buckley's judgment in *Stribling* v. *Wickham*[41];

Even-handed approach

"The question whether there is a sham device, an artificial transaction or a pretence involved in the transaction under consideration must be approached even-handedly. Only if an even-handed approach to all relevant considerations leads to the conclusion that some feature of the transaction in question is in fact a pretence can the court proceed to consider whether that constitutes a ground for holding that that feature amounts to an attempt to evade the Rent Acts."

Effect

If a clause is held to be a pretence, it is ignored and the remainder of the agreement is then construed in the usual way.[42] Thus a finding that a clause is a pretence does not automatically mean that an occupier has a tenancy and not a licence.[43] In an summary action for possession under R.S.C. Order 113,[44] the existence of clauses which are clearly pretences will be sufficient to prevent the court ordering possession and for the case to be remitted for further investigation.[45]

(iii) Method of construction

The aim of the court, when construing one or more documents for the purpose of determining whether there is a tenancy or a lease, is to find the substance and reality of the agreement entered into by the parties.[46] The cases establish that there are certain matters to which the court cannot have regard when construing an agreement. It is also possible to extract from the cases particular circumstances and types of clause which are relevant to the court's decision.

Irrelevant and relevant factors

[37] *A. G. Securities* v. *Vaughan* [1988] 3 W.L.R. 1205, 1219 *per* Lord Oliver.
[38] *Ibid.*, 1220.
[39] *Duke* v. *Wynne* [1989] 3 All E.R. 130.
[40] [1985] A.C. 809, 825.
[41] [1989] 27 E.G. 81, 89.
[42] *A. G. Securities* v. *Vaughan* [1988] 3 W.L.R. 1205, 1229 *per* Lord Jauncey.
[43] *Hadjiloucas* v. *Crean* [1987] 3 All E.R. 1008, 1023 *per* Mustill L.J.
[44] See above Chap. 1, Part D1, p. 10.
[45] *Markou* v. *Da Silvaesa* (1986) 52 P. & C.R. 204.
[46] *A. G. Securities* v. *Vaughan* [1988] 3 W.L.R. 1205, 1219 *per* Lord Ackner.

Manner of
performance

The first irrelevant consideration stems from the basic rule of contract that contracts cannot be construed by reference to their manner of performance.[47] Thus the court should not refer to anything said or done by the parties after the agreement was made. There is also the practical reason that the parties later actions may be based on a misunderstanding of the true meaning of the agreement.[48] The parties' subsequent actions are only relevant for the finding of a sham or pretence.[49]

Skill of draftsman

The second irrelevant matter is the skill, or otherwise, of the draftsman of the agreement.[50] The courts will not draw up a "shopping list" of clauses or award prizes for draftmanship.[51] Thus a rigorous judicial analysis of every clause of the agreement is unlikely. In particular, references to money payments as rent is not decisive. The courts accept that the word "rent" is not used in any technical sense by non-lawyers. Accordingly, references to rent in an agreement has not prevented the finding of a licence where there was no exclusive possession.[52]

Effect of Rent Acts

The third matter ignored by the courts is the effect of the Rent Acts.[53] The point was made by Ralph Gibson L.J. in *Markou* v. *Da Silvaesa*[54];

> "The principle that the Rent Acts must not be allowed to influence the construction of an agreement which was re-asserted in *Street* v. *Mountford* means, of course, that it is not open to the court to dismiss as 'sham' a term in an agreement merely because it is either effective in demonstrating that the agreement does not grant exclusive possession or, taken with other terms, contributes to that result."

As it has been pointed out, it is not a crime or contrary to public policy to grant to occupiers of residential property a licence rather than a tenancy.[55]

Label

The label the parties place on their agreement is the fourth factor which cannot affect the substance of the agreement.[56] Thus in *Street* v. *Mountford*[57] a tenancy was held to exist even though the relevant document was headed "licence agreement." The point was made by Lord Templeman when he said[58];

---

[47] *Wickman Machine Tool Sales Ltd.* v. *Schuler* [1974] A.C. 325; *Chitty on Contracts*, (25th ed., 1983) Vol. 1, para. 825; *A. G. Securities* v. *Vaughan* [1988] 3 W.L.R. 1205, 1221 *per* Lord Oliver.
[48] *Hadjiloucas* v. *Crean* [1987] 3 All E.R. 1008, 1023 *per* Mustill L.J.
[49] *A. G. Securities* v. *Vaughan* [1988] 3 W.L.R. 1205, 1221 *per* Lord Oliver; see above, Part G2(a)(i) and (ii), pp. 53 *et seq.*
[50] *Street* v. *Mountford* [1985] A.C. 809, 826 *per* Lord Templeman.
[51] *Markou* v. *Da Silvaesa* (1986) 52 P. & C.R. 204, 230 *per* Purchas L.J.
[52] *Soldiers' Sailors' and Airmen's Families Association* v. *Merton London Borough Council* [1966] 1 W.L.R. 736.
[53] *Street* v. *Mountford* [1985] A.C. 809, 819 *per* Lord Templeman.
[54] (1986) 52 P. & C.R. 204, 214.
[55] *Hilton* v. *Plustitle Ltd.* [1988] 3 All E.R. 1051, 1053 *per* Croom-Johnson L.J.; *Aslan* v. *Murphy* [1989] 3 All E.R. 130, 135 *per* Lord Donaldson M.R.
[56] *A. G. Securities* v. *Vaughan* [1988] 3 W.L.R. 1205, 1219 *per* Lord Oliver.
[57] [1985] A.C. 805.
[58] *Ibid.*, 819.

"If the agreement satisfied all the requirements of a tenancy, then the agreement produced a tenancy and the parties cannot alter the effect of the agreement by insisting that they only created a licence. The manufacture of a five-pronged implement for manual digging results in a fork even if the manufacturer, unfamiliar with the English language, insists that he intended to make and has made a spade."

Several other matters are accepted as being irrelevant to the question of whether there is a tenancy or a licence. The passing of time cannot convert a licence into a tenancy if there is no exclusive possession. The duration of the agreement is, therefore, irrelevant to the question of exclusive possession.[59] Whether or not furniture is provided is also irrelevant.[60] Provided that the relevant provisions are not pretences,[61] it is not of decisive importance that certain terms of the agreement are not performed.[62] A term in an agreement in relation to the provision of services may well indicate a licence even if the services are not provided because the occupier has a contractual right to call for those services.

Duration
Provisions of
furniture
Performance of
terms

Subjective
intention

It was said very forcibly in *Street* v. *Mountford*[63] that the subjective intention of the parties is irrelevant and that view was reiterated by the House of Lords in *A. G. Securities* v. *Vaughan*.[64] Where the terms of the agreement show a clear intention to grant exclusive possession, any contrary subjective intention on the part of either party is irrelevant. If it is not apparent, however, from the usual construction of the agreement whether exclusive possession is to be given, it now appears that the court will have regard to the intentions of the parties. For example, if a clause permits sharing with persons other than the parties to the agreement and sharing is practically possible in those premises, the court will have regard to the intentions of either party to determine whether sharing was truly part of the bargain.[65]

The relevant factors which the court will take into account include both the surrounding circumstances at the time the agreement was entered into and specific clauses of that agreement. The courts have never set out an exhaustive list and particular factors will have different weight in different cases.[66] It is highly unlikely that one particular factor will be decisive; the court looks to the effect of the combination of the relevant factors.[67]

Wide variety of
factors

Particular circumstances at the time the agreement was made which are of relevance include the relationship between the prospective occupiers and the course of the negotiations.

Relationship
between parties

---

[59] *Marchant* v. *Charters* [1977] 1 W.L.R. 1181, 1185.
[60] *Ibid.*
[61] See above Part G2(a)(ii), p. 54.
[62] *Markou* v. *Da Silvaesa* (1986) 52 P. & C.R. 204, 230 *per* Purchas L.J.
[63] [1985] A.C. 809, 819 *per* Lord Templeman.
[64] [1988] 3 W.L.R. 1205, 1217 *per* Lord Templeman.
[65] *Stribling* v. *Wickham* [1989] 27 E.G. 81; see above Part G1(e), p. 50.
[66] *Ibid.*, 85 *per* Parker L.J.
[67] *Aslan* v. *Murphy* [1989] 3 All E.R. 130.

Type of accommodation

The court will also have regard to the nature and extent of the accommodation and the intended and actual mode of occupation of that accommodation[68]; for example, is the property physically suitable for sharing with other occupiers?[69]

The court will construe two or more documents together where they have been entered into in respect of the same premises.[70] A highly relevant clause in relation to the question of exclusive possession is one reserving to the owner a right to put another occupier in the premises. A valid sharing clause

Particular clauses

defeats exclusive possession.[71] Other clauses which are particularly relevant include those making provision for attendance and service requiring unrestricted access to the premises.[72] Examples would be cleaning at the owner's convenience and the changing and laundering of linen. Equally relevant are terms requiring the premises to be left vacant at certain times of the day[73] and reserving to the owner the right to refuse entry to visitors or to restrict the hours guests may be on the premises.[74] A term permitting the removal of an occupier from one room to another in residential premises is not, by itself, conclusive that there was no grant of exclusive possession but it is still relevant.[75]

Rights of entry

The reservation by the owner of a right to enter and inspect the premises is an indication of a lease because if the occupier had not been granted exclusive possession there would be no need to reserve the right of entry.[76] The point was made by Lord Templeman in *Street* v *Mountford*[77];

> "Any express reservation to the landlord of limited rights to enter and view the state of the premises and to repair and maintain the premises only serves to emphasise the fact that the grantee is entitled to exclusive possession and is a tenant."

Obligation to repair

A term imposing on the occupier an obligation to repair, wider than merely remedying damage caused by his own act or default, is an indication of a tenancy rather than a licence.[78] Any reference to the occupier's right to transfer his interest is highly relevant because only if the occupier has exclusive

[68] *A. G. Securities* v. *Vaughan* [1988] 3 W.L.R. 1205, 1212 *per* Lord Templeman; see also *Mikeover Ltd.* v. *Brady* [1989] 3 All E.R. 618.
[69] *Ibid.*, 1219 *per* Lord Oliver.
[70] *Ibid.*, 1212 *per* Lord Templeman.
[71] *A. G. Securities* v. *Vaughan* [1988] 3 W.L.R. 1205, 1208 *per* Lord Templeman; see also *Brooker Settled Estates Ltd.* v. *Ayres* (1987) 54 P. & C.R. 166.
[72] *Markou* v. *Da Silvaesa* (1986) 52 P. & C.R. 204, 212 *per* Ralph Gibson L.J.; see above Part G1(a), p. 47.
[73] *Ibid.*
[74] *Soldiers' Sailors' and Airmen's Families Association* v. *Merton London Borough Council* [1966] 1 W.L.R. 736; *cf. Guppys (Bridport) Ltd.* v. *Brookling* (1984) 269 E.G. 846.
[75] *Markou* v. *Da Silvaesa* (1986) 52 P. & C.R. 204, 212 *per* Ralph Gibson L.J. See also *Dresden Estates Ltd.* v. *Collinson* (1988) 55 P. & C. R. 47.
[76] *Addiscombe Garden Estates Ltd.* v. *Crabbe* [1958] 1 Q.B. 513, 524.
[77] [1985] A.C. 809, 818.
[78] *Addiscombe Garden Estates Ltd.* v. *Crabbe* above; *Walsh* v. *Griffiths-Jones and Durant* [1978] 2 All E.R. 1002, 1009.

possession will he have any interest to transfer. A term
forbidding transfer can be equally relevant as such a term
presupposes that the occupier has some alienable right.[79]

(b) Unwritten agreements If there is no written agreement
the court will consider the surrounding circumstances to see if
Relevant the occupier has exclusive possession. Relevant questions are
questions directed to the degree of control exercised by either party over
the premises and include;

> Did the owner ask permission before entering?
> Did the landlord provide services which required his
> entry into the premises?
> Did the occupier have friends to stay?
> Was the occupier moved to other premises?

The ultimate question can be summarised by asking—did the
occupier have a stake in the room?[80]

H. Joint tenancy

The question of whether a lease exists has so far been
considered largely in the context of only one occupier of the
relevant premises. Further difficulties arise if there are several
occupiers sharing residential property. The problems were
recognised by Mustill L.J. in *Hadjiloucas* v. *Crean*[81] when he
said that the court had to make a choice not simply between
Options licence and tenancy, but rather a threefold choice between a
licence and two different kinds of tenancy; the first kind being
parallel tenancies, each between the landlord and one tenant, in
relation to an identifiable separate portion of the premises and
the second being a single tenancy for the whole of the
premises, with the two occupiers as joint tenants of the whole.
The task was rendered more difficult when, as often occured,
the document was embodied in a standard form ill adapted to
the special needs of the letting.
    To Mustill L.J.'s three options of a licence, joint tenancy
and parallel tenancies must be added a fourth option of parallel
licences. If it is clear that only one of the occupiers is the
tenant of the whole of the relevant premises, the remaining
occupiers are probably licensees. There is unlikely to be
separate legal possession of different parts of the premises to
support a sub-tenancy and payment of rent alone will not raise
an equitable interest under a trust of the lease.[82]
    Before a joint tenancy of a lease by several occupiers can
be established, they will have to show, not only that they have
exclusive possession of the premises, but also that they satisfy
the legal requirements of a holding as joint tenants. If a lease is
established, the joint tenants are in the same position as any

---

[79] *Lewis* v. *Bell* [1985] 1 N.S.W.L.R. 73.
[80] See *Marchant* v. *Charters* [1977] 1 W.L.R. 1181, 1185.
[81] [1987] 3 All E.R. 1008, 1022.
[82] *Savage* v. *Dunningham* [1974] Ch. 181.

Effect of joint tenancy other tenant and enjoy the same protection. Although joint tenants must usually act together, a tenancy may be determined by one joint tenant acting alone.[83] If one joint statutory tenant leaves the premises, however, the joint tenants left in occupation remain as statutory tenants.[84] On the death of a joint tenant, the remaining tenants become entitled to the lease and responsible for the rent[85] but if the joint tenants were protected under the Rent Act 1977 or the Housing Act 1988 a sole remaining tenant should be resident.

1.   Exclusive possession

The courts approach to the question of exclusive possession is the same as in the case of single occupation; in the absence of a sham, the agreement is construed in the context of the relevant factual circumstances, ignoring any clauses which are pretences.[86] Whilst the factual matrix against which the agreement was made is likely to be more complex, the courts task is still the same—to determine the reality of the transaction.

It may be thought from Lord Templeman's comments in *Street* v. *Mountford*[87] on cases like *Somma* v. *Hazelhurst*[88] that the courts were more likely to find that an agreement was a
Shams sham in the case of multiple occupancy. It is now clear that the courts do not take such a rigid view. Only if the premises are physically unsuitable for sharing will any clause permitting the landlord to introduce further occupiers be ignored without any regard to the intentions of the parties.[89] Thus in *Stribling* v. *Wickham*[90] the Court of Appeal held that three friends sharing a large two-bedroomed flat had separate licences and not a joint tenancy. The terms of each individual agreement represented the realities of the transaction and no clauses were ignored as pretences.
Pretences Even if a clause is ignored as a pretence, a tenancy does not follow automatically. The warning was sounded by Mustill L.J. in *Hadjiloucas* v. *Crean*[91];

> "It would not however appear to follow inevitably that if a clause of this kind is disregarded it will necessarily be revealed that the true intent of all the parties was to bind themselves jointly for a lease of the whole flat for the whole rent. Such an intention would have to be derived from the whole of the circumstances."

For example, a clause permitting the landlord to share the premises may be dismissed as a pretence but a clause requiring

---

[83] *Leek and Moorlands Building Society* v. *Clark* [1952] 2 Q.B. 788; *Greenwich London Borough Council* v. *McGrady* (1982) 46 P. & C.R. 223.
[84] *Lloyd* v. *Sadler* [1978] Q.B. 774; Housing Act 1988, s.1(1)(*b*).
[85] *Cunningham-Reid* v. *Public Trustee* [1944] K.B. 602.
[86] *A. G. Securities* v. *Vaughan* [1988] 3 W.L.R. 1205; see above Part G2, p. 52.
[87] [1985] A.C. 809, 825–826.
[88] [1978] 2 All E.R. 1011.
[89] See above Part G1(e), p. 50 and Part G2(a)(iii), p. 55.
[90] [1989] 27 E.G. 81.
[91] [1987] 3 All E.R. 1008, 1023.

the occupants to accept a new occupier if one should leave and
other circumstances may lead to a licence.[92]

In the case of joint occupancy, when construing the
agreement, the court is looking to see whether there is a joint
Joint exclusive right to exclusive possession of the whole premises. The fact
possession that individual occupiers have exclusive possession of parts of
the premises, with rights in common over the rest of the
premises, will not be sufficient. Thus, on the one hand, the
granting of individual bed-sitting rooms in a flat to individual
occupiers with common use of kitchen and bathroom looks like
a series of parallel tenancies.[93] On the other hand, the grant of
a three bed-roomed flat to three people together who decide
themselves who is to have which room, looks far more like a
joint tenancy.[94]

2. Rent

It was at one time thought that there could not be a lease held
by joint tenants if they were not all jointly and severally liable
Joint liability for the whole rent. A tenant being liable for only half the rent
was regarded as "creating a logical inconsistency."[95] The
House of Lords in *A. G. Securities* v. *Vaughan*[96] has now held
that an agreement to pay only part of the total rent is not a bar
to the creation of a joint tenancy, but a clause genuinely
intended to impose liability for only a portion of the total rent
will still lead the court to find a licence.[97] Lack of joint and
several liability for the total rent is likely to cause less problem
where the landlord has a right to nominate a new occupier in
the event of a departure. In that case the landlord can preserve
the total number of occupiers and claim the full rent.[98]

3. Joint tenancy

Four unities Before a joint tenancy can be created the four unities must be
present; unity of possession, unity of interest, unity of title and
unity of time.[99] This applies equally to joint holdings of leases
as it does to freeholds. If the alleged joint tenancy began on the
same day and each occupier holds for the same term and at the
same rent, the requirement of the four unities is unlikely to
present any problems. Even if separate licences were used, they
can be read together as one document.

The requirement of the four unities can cause considerable
problems if occupation started at different times, particularly if

---

[92] *Hadjiloucas* v. *Crean* [1987] 3 All E.R. 1008, 1016; see also *A. G. Securities*
v. *Vaughan* [1988] 3 W.L.R. 1205, 1214 *per* Lord Templeman.
[93] See *A. G. Securities* v. *Vaughan* [1988] 3 W.L.R. 1205, 1214 *per* Lord
Templeman.
[94] *Stribling* v. *Wickham* [1989] 27 E.G. 81; *Walsh* v. *Griffiths-Jones and Durant*
[1978] 2 All E.R. 1002.
[95] *Aldrington Garages Ltd.* v. *Fielder* (1978) 37 P. & C.R. 461; *Somma* v.
Hazelhurst [1978] 1 W.L.R. 1014; *Sturolson & Co.* v. *Weniz* (1984) 272 E.G.
326.
[96] [1988] 3 W.L.R. 1205, 1214 *per* Lord Templeman.
[97] See *Mikeover Ltd.* v. *Brady* [1989] 3 All E.R. 618.
[98] *Demuren* v. *Seal Estates Ltd.* (1978) 249 E.G. 440, 444.
[99] See Thompson, *Co-ownership* (1988), p. 12.

each occupier, as a result, is paying a different rent. Thus, in
A.G. Securities v. *Vaughan*[1] it was held that there was a series
of licences where each of the four occupiers had arrived at
different times and agreed to pay a different sum for the shared
use of the flat. Even if the agreements under consideration were
all entered into at the same time, the court is not likely to find
a joint tenancy if those agreements were replacements for
earlier agreements which were entered into separately.[2]

Grant to one occupier   If there is a clear written grant of a tenancy to one named
occupier, the other occupiers will have to show that this was a
sham if they are to establish a joint tenancy. There will have to
be evidence of an intention that all were intended to be tenants,
for example, by showing that all took part in the negotiations,
that the landlord took up references on all occupiers and that
he accepted initial payments from other than the named tenant.

4.   Relevant considerations

Relevant questions   The following[3] are relevant questions when considering
whether joint occupancy amounts to a joint tenancy, a licence,
parallel licences or parallel tenancies.

(a)   Was a joint approach made to the landlord and who
      conducted negotiations?

(b)   Who was liable for the rent and how much?

(c)   Was there any provision for the rights *inter se* of the
      occupants?

(d)   Was there any provision for change of occupiers?

(e)   Was there any provision for any or all of the occupiers
      to terminate the agreement?

(f)   If there was a change of occupier, what happened?

(g)   If one occupier left, would the remaining occupiers
      have paid his part of the rent?

(h)   Was the occupation of individual rooms designated by
      the landlord or decided by the occupiers?

The finding that there is a joint tenancy of premises will
give the occupiers security of tenure. That must be balanced
against two factors. First, the remaining occupiers may well
become liable for the whole of the rent if one occupier leaves or
defaults. Secondly, a joint tenant who terminates the agreement
and leaves will still remain liable for the full rent if those
Realistic licence   remaining in occupation default.[4] In the case of fairly short
term flat sharing arrangements the courts may conclude that
there was a series of individual licences simply because of the
flexibility clearly intended. Thus Lord Bridge concluded that
the separate licences arrangement in *A. G. Securities* v.
Vaughan[5];

---

[1] [1988] 3 W.L.R. 1205.
[2] *Stribling* v. *Wickham* [1989] 27 E.G. 81, 85 *per* Parker L.J.
[3] See *Hadjiloucas* v. *Crean* [1987] 3 All E.R. 1008, 1017; *Stribling* v. *Wickham*
    [1989] 27 E.G. 81, 86 *per* Parker L.J.
[4] *Aldrington Garages Ltd.* v. *Fielder* (1978) 37 P. & C.R. 461, 472.
[5] [1988] 3 W.L.R. 1205, 1206–1207.

"Seems to have been a sensible and realistic one to provide accommodation for a shifting population of individuals who were genuinely prepared to share the flat with others introduced from time to time who would, initially, be strangers to them."

4 PART PERFORMANCE

The doctrine of part performance[1] is a possible solution to the situation where there has been a sharing of residential accommodation following an oral agreement that the owner should transfer the property to the sharer or grant him a lease. If the owner fails to carry out the promised transfer or lease of the property, the doctrine of part performance allows the contract to be enforced and requires the owner to grant the relevant estate to the sharer. As the sharing of the premises has usually come about in direct response to the owner's promise to transfer or lease the property, the doctrine overlaps with that of proprietary estoppel[2] to a certain extent.

Before 27.9.89   Section 2 of the Law of Property (Miscellaneous Provisions) Act 1989 provides that, after September 27, 1989, a contract for the sale or other disposition of an interest in land can only be made in writing. Section 40 of the Law of Property Act 1925, however, continues to apply to agreements made before that date.[3] Thus, the doctrine will only be a potential solution where the claimant began sharing the accommodation before September 27, 1989.

A. The doctrine

Section 40 of the Law of Property Act 1925 provides that no action shall be brought upon any contract for the sale of land unless the agreement, or some memorandum of it, is in writing. An oral agreement will be enforced, however, if there is a sufficient act of part performance. This exception to the requirement of writing for contracts relating to land stems from equity's reluctance to allow a statute to be used as an instrument of fraud.[4]

Basic doctrine   If a party to an oral contract for the sale or lease of land has acted to his detriment by carrying out acts in performance of the contract this will raise equities in his favour.[5] The incurring of expenditure or the prejudicing of position on the faith of the agreement amounts to fraud[6] in its older and less precise sense and this allows parol evidence of the agreement for sale or lease to be given. Equity's remedy is to grant a decree of specific performance of the contract.

---

[1] For the detailed law see Jones and Goodhart, 'Specific Performance,' (1986), p. 96 *et seq.*
[2] See below Chap. 7.
[3] Law of Property (Miscellaneous Provisions) Act 1989, s.2(7).
[4] *Maddison* v. *Alderson* (1883) 8 App.Cas. 467, 474.
[5] *Ibid.*, 475.
[6] *Steadman* v. *Steadman* [1976] A.C. 536, 540.

The remedy of part performance will only be available if two conditions are satisfied. First, there must be a contract which is otherwise enforceable apart from the lack of writing and, secondly, there must be a sufficient act of part performance.

B. Contract

There is no restriction on the type of contract which may be enforced by the doctrine of part performance. It can be bilateral or unilateral[7] and the contract can include matters other than the disposition of land.[8] The burden of proof is on the plaintiff although the acts of both plaintiff and defendant are admissible to prove the contract.[9] Evidence other than the plaintiff's acts cannot be led, however, until sufficient acts of part performance by the plaintiff have been established. Lord Reid in *Steadman* v. *Steadman*[10] said

Evidence of contract

> "You must not first look at the oral contract and then see whether the alleged acts of part performance are consistent with it. You must first look at the alleged acts of part performance to see whether they prove that there must have been a contract and it is only if they do so prove that you can bring in the oral contract."

There will be no contract to enforce by means of the doctrine of part performance if the parties had no intention to enter into legal relations. This is a particular problem where the parties are related. The claim failed for this reason in *In re Gonin dec'd.*[11] Here a daughter returned home to look after her parents after they had promised to leave her the house and its contents when they died. Walton J. set out the problem as follows[12];

Intention to contract

> "I then come to the final consideration . . . , namely that in any family situation of this nature one would not expect to find any strict contractual bond between parents and daughter, the whole resting much more on the good faith of each side without there being any intention on either side to enter into strict legal relationship. I am inclined to think that this is in fact a correct way to view the matter. Would her parents have stood in her way by threatening to sue her for damages for breach of contract, which could have been very heavy, if she had left the house? I think not."[13]

The court will infer an intention to create legal relations between members of the same family if they are acting at arm's

[7] *Daulia Ltd.* v. *Four Millbank Nominees Ltd.* [1978] Ch. 231; see also *Errington* v. *Errington and Woods* [1952] 1 All E.R. 149, 153.
[8] *Steadman* v *Steadman* [1976] A.C. 536.
[9] *Dickinson* v. *Barrow* [1904] 2 Ch. 339; *Brough* v. *Nettleton* [1921] 2 Ch. 25.
[10] [1976] A.C. 536, 541; see also *Daulia Ltd.* v. *Four Millbank Nominees Ltd.* [1978] Ch. 231.
[11] [1979] 1 Ch. 16.
[12] *Ibid.*, 33.
[13] *C.f. Wakeham* v. *Mackenzie* [1968] 1 W.L.R. 1175, 1178, for a similar situation between unrelated parties.

Family situations length or on a business like basis. Accordingly, a contract for the transfer of a house entered into by an estranged husband and wife has been enforced by acts of part performance.[14] The courts have also indicated that a unilateral contract to transfer a house from a father to his children on completion of detailed specified payments would be enforced.[15]

Negotiations Apparent acts of part performance will not assist a party if there is no definite and concluded contract. The existence of negotiations or mere inducements is not sufficient; there must be an agreement before the alleged acts of part performance take place.[16] Thus in *Maddison v. Alderson*,[17] a resident housekeeper failed to establish an oral contract for the transfer of her employer's house when she remained in service without wages after her employer had said that he would leave her a life interest in the house. By comparison, in *Wakeham v. Mackenzie*[18] an oral contract for the transfer of a house to the housekeeper was established where the housekeeper did not move into the house until the terms on which she was to live in the house with the employer were agreed. In the former situation the remedy of proprietary estoppel should be considered.[19]

C.   Acts of part performance

Referable to some contract
Originally, the plaintiff had to show acts of part performance which were unequivocally referable to the oral agreement alleged.[20] The requirements for a relevant act of part performance were considerably relaxed in the case of *Kingswood Estate Co. Ltd. v. Anderson*[21] so that the acts now only need be referable to some contract which is consistent with the contract alleged. The change was approved by the House of Lords in *Steadman v. Steadman*.[22] Lord Simon of Glaisdale summarised the present position as follows[23]

> "I am therefore of the opinion not only that the facts relied on to prove acts of part performance must be established merely on a balance of probabilities, but that it is sufficient if it can be shown that it was more likely than not that those acts were in performance of some contract to which the defendant was a party."

If there is more than one act, the acts need not be looked at in isolation but can be considered together to see if they refer to a contract.[24]

---

[14] *Re Windle* [1975] 1 W.L.R. 1628.
[15] *Errington v Errington and Woods* [1952] 1 K.B. 290.
[16] See *Kingswood Estate Co. Ltd. v. Anderson* [1963] 2 Q.B. 169, 188.
[17] (1883) 8 App.Cas. 467.
[18] [1968] 1 W.L.R. 1175.
[19] See below Chap. 7.
[20] *Maddison v. Alderson* (1883) 8 App.Cas. 467, 479.
[21] [1963] 2 Q.B. 169, 189 *per* Upjohn L.J.
[22] [1976] A.C. 536.
[23] *Ibid.*, 564.
[24] *Ibid.*

Taking possession

The classic example of an act of part performance is the taking of possession of the defendant's premises at his request or with his consent.[25] Thus in *Kingswood Estate Co. Ltd.* v. *Anderson*[26] where a widow gave up her Rent Act protected tenancy and moved into a new flat it was held that there was a sufficient act of part performance to enforce an oral agreement that there should be a tenancy of the new flat for the joint lives of the widow and her invalid son and for the life of the survivor. As Willmer L.J. said in that case[27];

> "Where the question is whether there was an agreement for a tenancy, I cannot imagine any better evidence of part performance than the fact of the tenant going into actual occupation."

If the plaintiff is already in possession when the agreement is entered into, continuing in possession, by itself, is not a sufficient act of part performance. Some further act is required, for example, carrying out improvements on the premises if the alleged contract is one of sale or paying the higher rent if the alleged contract is for a new lease.[28]

Steps in conveyancing

Steps in the conveyancing procedure may be sufficient acts of part performance. In *Steadman* v. *Steadman*[29] the preparation and sending of a deed of transfer was held to be a sufficient act of part peformance. Earlier acts in the conveyancing process have previously been held not to be acts of part performance[30] but in *Re Windle*[31] the giving of instructions by a wife to her solicitors to prepare the conveyance and the payment of costs and disbursements were held to be sufficient acts of part performance of an oral agreement with her husband for the transfer of the matrimonial home to her. Acts preparatory to entering a contract are not sufficient, for example, tendering the purchaser's part of the written contract.[32]

Payment of money

It was once considered that the payment of money could never amount to an act of part performance.[33] A far less rigid view was taken in *Steadman* v. *Steadman* where Lord Reid said[34];

> "But to make a general rule that payment of money can never be part performance would seem to defeat the whole purpose of the doctrine and I do not think that we are compelled by authority to do that."

The mere payment of money is still not a sufficient act of part performance but payment together with the circumstances

---

[25] *Morphett* v. *Jones* (1818) 1 Swan. 172; *Brough* v. *Nettleton* [1921] 2 Ch. 25; *Kingswood Estate Co. Ltd.* v. *Anderson* [1963] 2 Q.B. 169.
[26] [1963] 2 Q.B. 169.
[27] *Ibid.*, 181.
[28] *Nunn* v. *Fabian* (1865) 1 Ch.App. 35.
[29] [1976] A.C. 536.
[30] See, for example, *Phillips* v. *Edwards* (1864) 33 Beav. 440.
[31] [1975] 1 W.L.R. 1628.
[32] *Daulia Ltd.* v. *Four Millbank Nominees Ltd.* [1978] Ch. 231.
[33] *Thursby* v. *Eccles* (1900) 49 W.R. 281; *Chaproniere* v. *Lambert* [1917] 2 Ch. 356.
[34] [1976] A.C. 536, 541.

surrounding the payment may be an act of part performance. The limitations were set out by Lord Salmon in *Steadman* v. *Steadman*[35];

> "Nevertheless the circumstances surrounding a payment may be such that the payment becomes evidence not only of the existence of the contract under which it was being made but also of the nature of the contract. What the payment proves in the light of its surrounding circumstances is not a matter of law but a matter of fact. There is no rule of law which excludes evidence of the relevant circumstances surrounding the payment—save parole evidence of the contract on behalf of the person seeking to enforce the contract under which the payment is alleged to have been made."

Thus the full payment of the purchase price to a defendant who is unable to repay is probably a sufficient act of part performance.[36]

D.   Practical considerations

The major limitation on the remedy of part performance is that there must be in existence a contract which is enforceable apart from the lack of writing. The remedy is unlikely to be available where there is a family agreement or the sharing of the accommodation commenced during extended negotiations.[37] The remedy will be available even between members of the same family if the terms on which the sharing of accommodation was to take place were clearly agreed beforehand.

Following the decision in *Steadman* v. *Steadman*[38] the range of acts which can amount to part performance is very wide and need only be referable to some contract and not necessarily the particular contract alleged.[39] Accordingly, all acts following the alleged contract should be considered as potential acts of part performance, including the payment of money.

Applications   Particular situations in which the remedy of part performance should be considered are first, where an elderly person has given up her home to go and live with a friend on the basis that the friend will leave her the house in her will[40] and, secondly, where a person has been induced to give up secure rented accommodation and to move into another house or flat after agreement that he is to have a lease of the new premises for the rest of his life.[41] The remedy may also be relevant where cohabitees have separated after agreeing, *inter alia*, that the premises are to be transferred by the owner to the other cohabitee, the second cohabitee remaining in possession

---

[35] *Ibid.*, 570.
[36] *Steadman* v. *Steadman* [1976] A.C. 536, 571 *per* Lord Salmon.
[37] See above Part B, p. 65.
[38] [1976] A.C. 536.
[39] See above Part C, p. 66.
[40] See *Wakeham* v. *Mackenzie* [1968] 1 W.L.R. 1175.
[41] See *Kingswood Estate Co Ltd.* v. *Anderson* [1963] 2 Q.B. 169.

and improving the premises or setting in train the conveyancing procedure.[42]

---

[42] See for example, *Re Windle* [1975] 1 W.L.R. 1628.

5 EXPRESS AND CONSTRUCTIVE TRUSTS

A person sharing residential property may be protected by being granted a beneficial interest under a trust. The clearest evidence of such a trust is a written declaration of trust of the property in question. Such an express trust will always be enforced by the courts. Indeed, a written express trust will prevail, in the absence of fraud or mistake, over any contrary presumptions from contributions to the purchase price.[1] The point was made by Slade L.J. in *Goodman v. Gallant*[2];

> **Express declaration**
>
> "If, however, the relevant conveyance contains an express declaration of trust which comprehensively declares the beneficial interests in the property or its proceeds of sale, there is no room for the application of the doctrine of resulting, implied or constructive trusts unless and until the conveyance is set aside or rectified; until that event the declaration contained in the document speaks for itself."

The express trust will be enforced even if the parties have not read the declaration of trust.[3]

Oral declaration An oral declaration of trust, however clear and unambiguous, is ineffective by virtue of section 53(1)(*b*) of the Law of Property Act 1925 which renders a declaration of trust not evidenced in writing unenforceable. Equity will not allow a statute to be used as an instrument of fraud, however, and in certain circumstances an oral declaration will be enforced by the courts. If the declaration forms part of an agreement for consideration, the trust may be enforced under the doctrine of part performance.[4] Alternatively, the trust may be enforced under the rule in *Rochefoucauld v. Boustead*.[5] The trust enforced under the later rule can be regarded as either the original express trust which becomes enforceable on the non-application of section 53(1)(*b*)[6] or a new constructive trust imposed to enforce the oral undertaking.[7]

---

[1] *Pariser v. Wilson* (1973) 229 E.G. 786; *Brykiert v. Jones* (1981) 2 F.L.R. 373; *Goodman v. Gallant* [1986] Fam. 106; but only against a person who is party to the deed, see *City of London Building Society v. Flegg* [1988] A.C. 54.

[2] [1986] Fam. 106, 110–111; for the effect of an unsigned declaration on a transfer of registered property see *Re Gorman (a bankrupt)* [1990] 1 All E.R. 717.

[3] *Pink v. Lawrence* (1978) 36 P. & C.R. 98.

[4] *Cowcher v. Cowcher* [1972] 1 W.L.R. 425, 430–431, 435, 436 *per* Bagnall J.; see also above Chap. 4.

[5] [1879] 1 Ch. 196; see also below Part A, p. 71.

[6] *Hodgson v. Marks* [1971] Ch. 892, 909 *per* Ungoed-Thomas J.

[7] *Bannister v. Bannister* [1948] 2 All E.R. 133, 135.

Constructive trusts

In the absence of an express declaration of trust, the courts have, from time to time, sought to impose a constructive trust on the legal owner of property where it would be inequitable for him to ignore the rights of a non-owner.[8] Such constructive trusts are sometimes called 'new model' constructive trusts[9] and imposed as a remedial device. Constructive trusts of this nature clearly have considerable advantages for non-owners sharing residential property who are relying merely on the justice of their case. The use of this type of trust, however, creates uncertainty and problems for third parties, particularly on bankruptcy. The courts in recent years have, therefore, discouraged their use.

A.   Oral declarations of trust

If property is conveyed following an oral undertaking or agreement that the new owner will hold that property, wholly or partly, on trust for another, the owner will not be allowed to go back on his undertaking simply because the declaration was oral. This rule has particular application where property is conveyed specifically subject to the right of an existing occupier to remain in the premises and no mention of that undertaking appears in either the written contract or the conveyance.

1.   The rule

The rule was set out by Lindley L.J. in *Rochefoucauld v. Boustead*[10];

Rochefoucauld v. Boustead

"It is further established by a series of cases, the propriety of which cannot now be questioned, that the Statute of Frauds does not prevent the proof of a fraud; and that it is a fraud on the part of a person to whom land is conveyed as a trustee, and who knows it was so conveyed, to deny that trust and claim the land himself. Consequently, notwithstanding the statute, it is competent for a person claiming land conveyed to another to prove by parol evidence that it was so conveyed upon trust for the claimant, and that the grantee, knowing the facts, is denying the trust and relying upon the form of conveyance and the statute, in order to keep the land himself."

Any beneficiary

The rule will only apply where the declaration of trust was made before the legal title to the property was acquired; the trust to take effect on acquisition of the legal title. It is irrelevant, however, whether the legal title is acquired from the potential beneficiary or a third party.[11] Apparently, it is also irrelevant whether the potential beneficiary has provided any consideration for the declaration of trust.[12] On balance, it

---

[8] See Oakley, *Constructive Trusts* 2nd ed., (1987), p. 36 *et seq.*
[9] *Eves* v. *Eves* [1975] 1 W.L.R. 1338, 1341 *per* Lord Denning M.R.
[10] [1879] 1 Ch. 196, 206.
[11] *Chattock* v. *Muller* (1878) 8 Ch.D. 177, 181; *Pallant* v. *Morgan* [1953] Ch. 43, 48.
[12] See Youdan, 'Formalities for Trusts of Land, and the Doctrine in Rochfoucauld v. Boustead.' (1984) 43 C.L.J. 306, 331.

would appear that the rule can be invoked by a potential
beneficiary who was not a party to the undertaking or
agreement giving rise to the trust.[13] There is no restriction on
the type of beneficial interest which can be in whole or part of
the property.[14]

2.   Applications of the rule

The rule has been applied in a variety of situations to enforce
oral undertakings, even where that has involved the
circumvention of the rules of registration.[15] Of particular
relevance is the case of *Bannister* v. *Bannister*[16] where the rule
was used to protect a widow's occupation of her cottage. The
widow owned two adjoining cottages which she sold to her
brother-in-law (the plaintiff) at an undervalue after he agreed
that she could remain in possession of one of them, rent free,
for the rest of her life. The widow moved into the downstairs
room of her cottage to allow the plaintiff and his wife to occupy
the rest of the cottage. The plaintiff then claimed possession of
that room. The Court of Appeal held that the widow was
entitled to a declaration that the plaintiff held that cottage on
trust during her life to permit her to occupy it for so long as
she wished and accordingly refused to order possession.

The grounds for the court's intervention were stated by
Scott L.J.[17] as follows;

Bannister v.
Bannister

"The fraud which brings the principle into play arises as
soon as the absolute character of the conveyance is set up
for the purpose of defeating the beneficial interest, and
that is the fraud to cover which the Statute of Frauds or
the corresponding provisions of the Law of Property Act
1925, cannot be called in aid in cases in which no written
evidence of the real bargain is available. Nor is it, in our
opinion, necessary that the bargain on which the absolute
conveyance is made should include any express stipulation
that the grantee is in so many words to hold as a trustee.
It is enough that the bargain should have included a
stipulation under which some sufficiently defined beneficial
interest in the property was to be taken by another."

The effect of the trust was to make the widow a tenant for
life under the Settled Land Act 1925.[18] This interest would
appear to be larger than that contemplated by the parties as

---

[13] Oakley, *Constructive Trusts* 2nd ed., (1987), p. 33; *Neale* v. *Willis* (1986) 19
P. & C.R. 39; Youdan, 'Formalities for Trusts of Land, and the Doctrine in
Rochfoucauld v. Boustead.' (1984) 43 C.L.J. 306, 335–336; Youdan,
'Informal Trusts and Third Parties: A Response.' [1988] Conv. 267; *c.f.*
Feltham, 'Informal Trusts and Third Parties.' [1987] Conv. 246.

[14] *Bannister* v. *Bannister* [1948] 2 All E.R. 133, 136 *per* Scott L.J.

[15] See *Peffer* v. *Rigg* [1977] 1 W.L.R. 285; *Lyus* v. *Prowsa Developments Ltd.*
[1982] 1 W.L.R. 1044.

[16] [1948] 2 All E.R. 133.

[17] *Ibid.*, 136.

[18] See Oakley, 'Has the Constructive Trust Become a General Equitable
Remedy?' [1973] C.L.P. 17, 24–25; R. J. Smith, 'Licences and Constructive
Trusts—"The Law is what it Ought to be." ' [1973] C.L.J. 123, 139–141.

they are unlikely to have intended that the widow should retain power to deal with the legal estate. *Bannister* v. *Bannister*[19] was applied, albeit with reluctance, by Megaw and Stephenson LL.J. in *Binions* v. *Evans*[20] to make Mrs Evans a tenant for life of her cottage. In that case the Tredegar Estate had entered into a written agreement with the defendant, who was the widow of a former employee, that she was to be allowed to reside in her Estate cottage, rent free, for the rest of her life. The Estate then sold the cottage to the plaintiffs at a reduced price, expressly subject to the defendant's interest.

Settled Land Act 1925

Lord Denning M.R. decided the case on a different basis, holding that the widow had a contractual licence which the court would protect by imposing a constructive trust on the plaintiffs as it would be inequitable for the plaintiffs to evict the defendant contrary to the agreement subject to which they took the premises.[21]

A declaration of trust in favour of a third party was enforced in *Neale* v. *Willis*.[22] In that case, a husband borrowed £50 towards the purchase of a house from his mother-in-law. On enquiry, he assured her that the house would be placed in the joint names of himself and his wife. In fact, the house was conveyed into his name alone. The Court of Appeal, on the wife's application, held that the house was held by the husband upon trust for himself and his wife by application of *Bannister* v. *Bannister*.[23]

Common intention

It has been argued[24] that the rule applies whenever the beneficial interest in property, the legal title to which is held by one person, is shared as a result of a common intention, because what is being enforced is an actual agreement between the parties. This is probably too wide an application of the rule and the better view is to treat all such common intention cases as resulting or implied trusts.[25] Where, however, the legal owner has in fact made an oral declaration of trust at the time of purchase, there is no reason why the non-owning party should not be protected by the imposition of a trust under the rule in *Rochefoucauld* v. *Boustead*.[26] A case such as *Eves* v. *Eves*,[27] where the plaintiff worked on the house after the defendant declared that the house was to be theirs as a home for themselves and their children but that it would be conveyed to him alone because she was under 21 years of age, can be regarded as an instance of an express trust unenforceable for want of writing. A similar view could be taken of *Grant* v.

[19] [1948] 2 All E.R. 133.
[20] [1972] Ch. 359; Martin, 'Contractual Licensee or Tenant for Life?' (1972) 36 Conv.(N.S.) 266; also noted at (1972) 36 Conv.(N.S.) 277 (D. J. Hayton); (1972) 88 L.Q.R. 336 (P. V. Baker).
[21] See below Part B4, p. 77.
[22] (1968) 19 P. & C.R. 839.
[23] [1948] 2 All E.R. 133.
[24] *Re Densham* [1975] 1 W.L.R. 1519, 1525 *per* Goff J.
[25] See above Chap. 6, Part A1, p. 80.
[26] [1879] 1 Ch. 196.
[27] [1975] 1 W.L.R. 1338; see below Chap. 6, Part C1(c)(vi), p. 99 for the facts of this case.

Edwards[28] but in either case a liberal approach would have to be made as to the words necessary for an effective declaration of trust. If the present rule is used, it is the terms of the declaration that are important, not the amount of any contribution made by the non-owning party.

In the above cases, a trust was imposed because the holder of the legal estate sought to escape from an obligation which had been freely undertaken before the property was conveyed to him. These cases, whether classified as express or constructive trusts, are very different from constructive trusts imposed on the grounds of inequitable conduct which rely as much on both the owner's and the non-owner's conduct during the holding of the property as on initial declarations or undertakings.

B. New model constructive trusts

Definition

New model constructive trusts are true constructive trusts[29] in that they satisfy the definition propounded in Snell's, *Principles of Equity*,[30] *i.e.* they are trusts imposed by equity in order to satisfy the demands of justice and good conscience without reference to any express or presumed intention of the parties.

There are many instances of sharing residential property where the factual circumstances fail to fit neatly within existing land law concepts and where it is very difficult, if not impossible, to discover the intentions of the parties. For example, there may have been no direct or indirect contribution to the purchase of the property but contributions to the running of the household over a number of years. Further, to apply the existing concepts in such situations can lead to hardship.

1. The basic doctrine

Remedial device

In order to remedy the injustice created, the courts, in particular Lord Denning M.R. in the Court of Appeal, began to impose a constructive trust on the owner of the property in question. The basis of the courts' wider use of a constructive trust as a remedial device[31] was confirmed by Lord Denning M.R. in *Eves* v. *Eves*[32] when he said;

> "Such is the strict law. And a few years ago even equity would not have helped her. But things have altered now. Equity is not past the age of child bearing. One of her latest progeny is a constructive trust of a new model."

[28] [1986] Ch. 638; see below Chap. 6, Part C1(c)(vi), p. 99 for the facts of this case.
[29] See below Chap 6, Part A1, p. 81.
[30] 28th ed., (1984), p. 192 cited with approval in *Carl Zeiss Stiftung* v. *Smith (Herbert) & Co.* No. 2 [1969] 2 Ch. 276, 301 *per* Edmund Davies L.J.
[31] American practice is sometimes relied on as justification for this form of constructive trust—see *Beatty* v. *Guggenheim Exploration Co.* (1919) 225 N.Y. 380, 386 *per* Cardoza J.; see also Oakley, *Constructive Trusts.* 2nd ed., (1987), p. 10; Gray, *Elements of Land Law* (1987), p. 812 *et seq.*
[32] [1975] 1 W.L.R. 1338, 1341.

**New model
constructive trust**

The circumstances in which a new model constructive trust could be imposed were set out in *Hussey* v. *Palmer*[33]

"It is a trust imposed by law whenever justice and good conscience require it. It is a liberal process, founded upon large principles of equity, to be applied in cases where the legal owner cannot conscientiously keep the property for himself alone, but ought to allow another to have the property or the benefit of it or a share in it."

New model constructive trusts were used in the 1970's in three areas; to grant beneficial interests without strict reference to financial contributions, to give lenders security and to protect contractual licensees. More recent court decisions have rejected the use of constructive trusts in these areas, either directly or by implication, and insisted on the creation of interests in land only in accordance with settled concepts and procedures.

2. Beneficial interests

A non-owner sharing residential property will normally only be held to have a beneficial interest in that property if the conditions necessary for a resulting trust are satisfied or if there is a common intention that the beneficial interest is to be shared.[34] On the principles laid down in *Gissing* v. *Gissing*,[35] the court is unlikely to find a common intention in the absence of some form of financial contribution to the purchase. To avoid injustice to a spouse or cohabitee who had either contributed to household expenses as opposed to the purchase price of the property[36] or who had helped with substantial work on the property[37] the Court of Appeal imposed a constructive trust to give the non-owner a beneficial interest. For example, in *Davis* v. *Vale*[38] the Court of Appeal granted a wife a half share in the beneficial interest in a house the legal title to which was held by her husband. The husband had paid the mortgage but she had paid for some improvements and paid part of the family expenses. The approach of the Court of Appeal appears from the judgment of Lord Denning M.R.[39];

"According to that broad consensus of judicial opinion, if both parties contribute, directly or indirectly in money or money's worth to the initial deposit or to the mortgage instalments, the court imposes or confers a trust whereby the legal owner holds the house on trust for them both, giving to each a beneficial interest of such an extent as may in all the circumstances seem just."

[33] [1972] 1 W.L.R. 1286, 1289 *per* Lord Denning M.R.
[34] See below Chap. 6.
[35] [1971] A.C. 886; see also below Chap. 6, Part C, p. 89.
[36] *Falconer* v. *Falconer* [1970] 1 W.L.R. 1333; *Davis* v. *Vale* [1971] 1 W.L.R. 1022; *Hargreaves* v. *Newton* [1971] 1 W.L.R. 1611; *Hazell* v. *Hazell* [1972] 1 W.L.R. 301; noted at (1972) 88 L.Q.R. 333 (J. M. Eekelaar).
[37] *Cooke* v. *Head* [1972] 1 W.L.R. 518; *Eves* v. *Eves* [1975] 1 W.L.R. 1338 *per* Lord Denning M.R.; *c.f.* Browne L.J. and Brightman J.
[38] [1971] 1 W.L.R. 1022.
[39] *Ibid.*, 1026.

On the same basis in *Cooke* v. *Head*,[40] the Court of Appeal granted a mistress a one third share in the equity of a house to which she had made a small financial contribution but also helped to build.

After earlier criticism by Bagnall J. in *Cowcher* v. *Cowcher*,[41] the Court of Appeal in recent cases has refused to follow the previous liberal approach to the granting of beneficial interests by the use of a constructive trust based on inequitable conduct and has returned to a more formal and rigid approach to the question of contribution and common **Restrictions** intention. Thus, in *Midland Bank plc* v. *Dobson*[42] the Court of Appeal refused to grant a beneficial interest in the matrimonial home to a wife who had made no direct contributions to the acquisition of the house. Although she had used her income for household expenses, such payments were not made in pursuance of an agreement that she was to have a beneficial interest in the property. Again, in *Burns* v. *Burns*[43] the Court of Appeal held that a non-owner sharing residential property was not entitled to a beneficial interest unless there was payment by the non-owner referable to the acquisition of the house. Lord Denning M.R.'s dicta in *Hall* v. *Hall*[44] that account could be taken of contributions in the form of house-keeping and looking after children was held to be wrong.[45] The use of a new model constructive trust was specifically rejected by the Court of Appeal in *Grant* v. *Edwards*.[46] In that case, Nourse L.J. said[47] that the grounds for Lord Denning M.R.'s decision in *Eves* v. *Eves*[48] was at variance with the principles stated in *Gissing* v. *Gissing*[49]; the House of Lords in that case having stated that a common intention could be inferred from the parties' conduct but that a deemed common intention could not be imputed to them. *Grant* v. *Edwards* shows a rigid analytical approach[50] to the question of the acquisition of a beneficial interest in property by a non-owner and indicates that it is highly unlikely that a constructive trust based purely on inequitable conduct will be used again in this area.[51]

3. Loans

The second area in which a new model constructive trust has been used to protect a non-owner sharing residential property is

[40] [1972] 1 W.L.R. 518.
[41] [1972] 1 W.L.R. 425, 430.
[42] [1986] 1 F.L.R. 171.
[43] [1984] Ch. 317.
[44] (1981) 3 F.L.R. 379.
[45] [1984] Ch. 317, 342 *per* May L.J.
[46] [1986] Ch. 638.
[47] *Ibid.*, 647.
[48] [1975] 1 W.L.R. 1338.
[49] [1971] A.C. 886.
[50] [1986] Ch. 638, 647 *per* Nourse L.J., 656 *per* Browne-Wilkinson V.-C. and in particular 651–652 *per* Mustill L.J.; see also *Lloyds Bank plc* v. *Rosset* [1990] 1 All E.R. 1111 (H.L.).
[51] By comparison, a remedial or new model constructive trust has been used by the High Court of Australia in *Baumgarten* v. *Baumgarten* (1988) 62 A.L.J. 29; Hayton, 'Remedial Constructive Trusts of Homes: An Overseas View.' [1988] Conv. 259.

Hussey v. Palmer

that of loans. In *Hussey* v. *Palmer*[52] the plaintiff went to live with her daughter and son-in-law and paid £607 for an extension to be built to the house to provide her with a bedroom. When she later left, she claimed repayment of the £607. The Court of Appeal held that it was against conscience for the son-in-law to retain the benefit of the payment and imposed a constructive trust under which the plaintiff was to have an interest in the property proportionate to the sum paid. Cairns L.J., dissenting, held that the transaction was one of loan which gave rise to no interest in the property.

Limitations

The approach of Cairns L.J. was followed in *Re Sharpe (A Bankrupt)*[53] where an aunt lent her nephew £12,000 to purchase a maisonette and shop. There was an arrangement that she would live in the premises with the nephew and his wife. When the nephew was declared bankrupt, Browne-Wilkinson J. held that the £12,000 was advanced by way of loan which conferred no interest in the property on the aunt under a trust.[54] It appears unlikely, therefore, that a new model constructive trust will be imposed in the future to grant a beneficial interest where there was purely a loan, as opposed to a contribution to the purchase of the property.[55]

4. Contractual licences

In *Binions* v. *Evans*[56] Lord Denning M.R. imposed a constructive trust to protect the widow's right of occupation as follows;

> "In these circumstances, this court will impose on the plaintiffs a constructive trust for her benefit: for the simple reason that it would be utterly inequitable for the plaintiffs to turn the defendant out contrary to the stipulation subject to which they took the premises."

This approach was followed in *Re Sharpe (A Bankrupt)*[57] where it was held that the aunt's right to live in the premises until her loan was repaid was protected by the imposition of a constructive trust on the nephew's trustee in bankruptcy.

Considerable doubt was thrown on this use of a constructive trust in *Ashburn Anstalt* v. *Arnold*[58] where Fox L.J. held that a contractual licence was not an interest in land.[59] He then went on to say[60];

> "The court will not impose a constructive trust unless it is satisfied that the conscience of the estate owner is affected. The mere fact that land is expressed to be conveyed

---

[52] [1972] 1 W.L.R. 1286.
[53] [1980] 1 W.L.R. 219.
[54] *Ibid.*, 223.
[55] See below Chap. 8, Part F1, p. 142 for the desirability of securing such loans by means of a charging order under the Charging Orders Act 1979.
[56] [1972] Ch. 359, 368; see above the text at n. 20 for the facts of this case.
[57] [1980] 1 W.L.R. 219, 225; see also *D. H. N. Food Distributors Ltd.* v. *Tower Hamlets London Borough* [1976] 1 W.L.R. 852.
[58] [1989] Ch. 1; noted (1988) 51 M.L.R. 226 (J. Hills), [1988] Conv. 201 (M. P. Thompson).
[59] *Ibid.*, 22.
[60] *Ibid.* 25–26.

Limited circumstances

'subject to' a contract does not necessarily imply that the grantee is to be under an obligation, not otherwise existing, to give effect to the provisions of the contract. The fact that the conveyance is expressed to be subject to the contract may often, for the reason indicated by Dillon J. in *Lyus* v. *Prowsa Developments Ltd.*[61] be at least as consistent with an intention merely to protect the grantor against claims by the grantee as an intention to impose an obligation on the grantee. The words 'subject to' will, of course, impose notice. But notice is not enough to impose on somebody an obligation to give effect to a contract into which he did not enter."

Thus it would appear that a 'constructive' trust will not be imposed to protect a contractual licence except where there is in effect a declaration of trust of the type in *Bannister* v. *Bannister*.[62]

5. Alternative rights and remedies

The courts are showing increasing reluctance to use a new model constructive trust to assist a non-owner of property. There are, however, various potential alternative rights and remedies available. If there is not sufficient contribution to establish a beneficial interest under a resulting or implied trust, proprietary estoppel[63] should be considered,[64] particularly where the plaintiff has lived in the premises for some time. In the case of breach of a contractual licence after the premises have been conveyed by the grantor, a claim for damages for breach of contract against the grantor should be considered together with a possible action against the present owner for the tort of interference with contractual rights.[65]

---

[61] [1982] 1 W.L.R. 1044.
[62] [1948] 2 All E.R. 133; see above Part A2, p. 72; Underhill and Hayton, *Law of Trusts and Trustees* 14th ed., (1987), p. 327 *et seq.*
[63] See below Chap. 7.
[64] *Grant* v. *Edwards* [1986] Ch. 638, 656 *per* Browne-Wilkinson V.-C.
[65] *Binions* v *Evans* [1972] Ch. 359, 371 *per* Megaw L.J.; see also R. J. Smith, 'Licences and Constructive Trusts—"The Law is what it Ought to be." ' [1973] C.L.J. 123, 136; Briggs, 'Contractual Licences: A Reply' [1983] Conv. 285, 290.

6 RESULTING AND IMPLIED TRUSTS

When property is being shared on more than a casual basis, and in particular where it is being regarded by all concerned as the family home, the non-owner will expect to have more than a mere right of occupation and to have some interest in the property itself. The best way in which effect can be given to those expectations is for the non-owner to have a beneficial interest in the property. A beneficial interest gives the party without a legal interest an equitable interest under a trust for sale which is enforceable against third parties,[1] a share in the proceeds of sale[2] and limited rights of occupation until the property is sold.[3] Throughout this chapter it is assumed that the claimant to a beneficial interest is not named on the title deeds unless the contrary is stated.

No express declaration If there is no express written declaration of trust at the time of purchase, the non-owner will have to rely on the doctrine of resulting and implied trusts. The court will use the doctrine to find an equitable interest where there has been some contribution to the purchase of the property by the non-owner or where the parties have had a common intention, usually from the beginning, that the property is to be treated as jointly owned. Regrettably, the law in this area is not clear; in particular the precise nature of the trust being used as the basis for the equitable interest is the subject of disagreement. The way in which the courts approach the finding of an equitable interest can be seen with reasonable clarity, however, and factors leading to the imposition of a trust can be isolated and assessed. In certain factual situations, for example, if the financial contributions of the non-owner are small and reliance is being placed on an oral declaration by the owner or the non-owner is relying solely on contributions made after the property was purchased, the unsettled state of the law makes it desirable to consider the additional remedy of proprietary estoppel.[4]

The only interest which can be granted to the non-owner under a resulting or implied trust is a beneficial interest in the property. If the facts do not support the finding of an equitable interest, the claim will fail. Thus if there is doubt about the case, alternative solutions, particularly that of a contractual licence,[5] should always be considered.

---

[1] See below Chap. 8, Part F6, p. 150.
[2] See below Part D2, p. 105.
[3] See below Part D1, p. 104.
[4] See below Chap. 7.
[5] See below Chap. 2, Part B, p. 24.

A. Basic principles

Trusts

Any claim to a beneficial interest in property held by another must be made under the law of trusts. It is now settled that a claim cannot be made based on the law of contract even if the court is, in effect, giving effect to an agreement between the parties.[6] Accordingly, the interest granted is an equitable one and takes effect behind a trust for sale.[7]

Actual intention

It is now clear that the court does not have a broad discretion to make such order as it thinks fair between the parties. What is relevant is the parties' actual intention; the court has no power to impute an intention to the parties in the absence of any evidence to that effect.[8] Moves by the Court of Appeal to impose a constructive trust to such an extent as was just, unrelated to the intentions of the parties, have now been rejected.[9] The following statement by Goff J. in *Re Densham (A Bankrupt)*[10] still represents the law;

> "If the parties have not in fact agreed about the ownership, the court cannot make an agreement for them and give them such interest as it feels they would have determined upon had they thought about it, or which the court thinks fair in all the circumstance. On the other hand, the court may infer from the circumstances and the conduct of the parties, including subsequent conduct, that there was an agreement, and if it does the court will give effect to that agreement."

The basis of the law in this area was laid down by the House of Lords in *Pettitt* v. *Pettitt*[11] and *Gissing* v. *Gissing*.[12] The following extract from the speech of Lord Diplock in *Gissing* v. *Gissing*[13] has been referred to in later cases[14];

Basic criteria

> "A resulting, implied or constructive trust—and it is unnecessary for present purposes to distinguish between these three classes of trust—is created by a transaction between the trustee and *cestui que trust* in connection with the acquisition by the trustee of a legal estate in land, whenever the trustee has so conducted himself that it would be inequitable to allow him to deny to the *cestui que trust* a beneficial interest in the land acquired. And he will

---

[6] *Gissing* v. *Gissing* [1971] A.C. 886, 896 *per* Lord Reid, 902 *per* Lord Diplock; *Bernard* v. *Josephs* [1982] Ch. 391, 401 *per* Griffiths L.J.; *Grant* v. *Edwards* [1986] Ch. 638, 651 *per* Mustill L.J.
[7] *Bull* v. *Bull* [1955] 1 Q.B. 234, approved in *Williams & Glyn's Bank Ltd.* v. *Boland* [1981] A.C. 487; see also Thompson, *Co-ownership* (1988), pp. 15–16.
[8] *Gissing* v. *Gissing* [1971] A.C. 886, 898 *per* Lord Morris of Borth-y-Gest, 900 *per* Viscount Dilhorne.
[9] See above Chap. 5, Part B2, p. 75.
[10] [1975] 1 W.L.R. 1519, 1524.
[11] [1970] A.C. 777.
[12] [1971] A.C. 886.
[13] *Ibid.*, 905.
[14] See for example *Grant* v. *Edwards* [1986] Ch. 638.

be held so to have conducted himself if by his conduct he has induced the *cestui que trust* to act to his detriment in the reasonable belief that by so acting he was acquiring a beneficial interest in the land."

The court's approach was summarised by Fox L.J. in *Burns* v. *Burns*[15] when he said;

"For present purposes I think that such a trust could only arise (a) by express declaration or agreement or (b) by way of resulting trust where the claimant has directly provided part of the purchase price or (c) from the common intention of the parties."

1. Form of trust

Whilst it is clear that any interest acquired by the non-owner will be under a trust, the courts and commentators do not agree on the type of trust concerned. Trusts based on the common intention of the parties have been classified at various times as express trusts,[16] resulting trusts,[17] implied trusts[18] and constructive trusts.[19] Some judges have refused to classify the trust and referred simply—if compendiously—to 'resulting, implied or constructive trust.'[20] The distinction is not merely an academic one as the classification of the trust not only affects the factors to be considered when determining the parties' beneficial interests but can also affect the extent to which the beneficial interest is enforceable against third parties.

Express trust   An express trust occurs when ever there is an express declaration of trust in writing. Although the settlor need not use the words 'on trust' he must use equivalent words which are clear. The words 'The money is as much yours as mine' have been held[21] to be a declaration of trust but it was regarded as a borderline case.[22] This type of trust does not arise, therefore, where there has been no declaration or statement by the owner and the parties common intention is being inferred from their conduct. Even if the owner has made

---

[15] [1984] Ch. 317, 326 noted (1984) 47 M.L.R. 735 (J. Dewar), [1984] Conv. 381 (S. Coneys).

[16] *Re Densham (A Bankrupt)* [1975] 1 W.L.R. 1519, 1525 *per* Goff J.; *Allen* v. *Snyder* [1977] 2 N.S.W.L.R. 685, 692 *per* Glass J.A.

[17] *Gissing* v. *Gissing* [1971] A.C. 886, 902 *per* Lord Pearson; *Burns* v. *Burns* [1984] Ch. 317, 326 *per* Fox L.J., 336 *per* May L.J.

[18] *Austin* v. *Keele* P.C., unreported, July 27, 1987 *per* Lord Oliver; Sir Christopher Slade, *The Informal Creation of Interests in Land* (1984), The Child & Co. Oxford Lecture p. 4, 6.

[19] *Grant* v. *Edwards* [1986] Ch. 638, 654 *per* Browne-Wilkinson V.-C.; *Lloyds Bank plc* v. *Rosset* [1990] 1 All E.R. 1111, 1118 *per* Lord Bridge; Gray, *Elements of Land Law* (1987), p. 271 *et seq.* Underhill and Hayton, *Law of Trusts and Trustees* 14th ed., (1987), p. 331 and Thompson, *Co-ownership* (1988), p. 39 classify certain of the trusts as express trusts enforced by means of a constructive trust.

[20] See the quote from Lord Diplock's speech in *Gissing* v. *Gissing* set out in the text at n. 12.

[21] *Paul* v. *Constance* [1977] 1 All E.R. 195; a statement of an intention to transfer the property at some time in the future is not sufficient, see *England* v. *Pepper* C.A., unreported, March 7, 1989.

[22] *Ibid.*, 199 *per* Scarman L.J.

some declaration, for example, stating the reasons why the property is to go into his sole name,[23] this is unlikely to be a sufficiently clear declaration to create an express trust but merely to form evidence from which the court can infer the parties common intention.

Implied trust   There will be an implied trust where there is an intention to create a trust but no evidence of express words of trust.[24] The trust arises from the presumed intention of the parties. A

Resulting trust   resulting trust can be said to be one particular type of implied trust in that, in certain circumstances, the court will assume that the parties had a particular intention. For example, if property is conveyed into the name of one person yet paid for by another, the property will be held on resulting trust for the party providing the money.[25]

Constructive trust   The final possible type of trust is a constructive trust. This has been defined[26] as 'a trust which is imposed by equity in order to satisfy the demands of justice and good conscience without reference to any express or presumed intention of the parties.' The courts have consistently said that which is important is the actual intention of the parties and that there is no power to ascribe an intention to the parties in the absence of evidence.[27] On this basis, reference to constructive trusts would seem inappropriate.[28]

Form of trust   The most appropriate form of trust is an implied or resulting trust. The use of an implied or resulting trust confirms that it is the intentions of the parties which are of prime importance.[29] It also confirms that the non-owner has a beneficial interest in the property from the beginning and does not have to wait for the court to declare the interest. This gives greater protection to the non-owner against third parties.[30-35]

It is proposed to follow Fox L.J.'s threefold classification in *Burns* v. *Burns*.[36] Express trusts are relatively uncommon in informal sharing arrangements and are dealt with separately.[37]

Classification   The acquisition of a beneficial interest will, therefore, be

[23] See for example *Eves* v. *Eves* [1975] 1 W.L.R. 1338 (woman under 21 years of age); *Grant* v. *Edwards* [1986] Ch. 638 (woman's matrimonial proceedings still pending); *Lloyds Bank plc* v. *Rosset* [1990] 1 All E.R. 1111 (to satisfy the trustees of the husband's family trust).
[24] *Richards* v. *Delbridge* (1874) L.R. 18 Eq. 11, 14 *per* Sir George Jessel M.R.
[25] *Dyer* v. *Dyer* (1788) 2 Cox Eq. 92.
[26] See Snell, *Principles of Equity* 28th ed., (1982), p. 192 quoted with approval in *Carl Zeiss Stiftung* v. *Smith Herbert & Co. (No. 2)* [1969] 2 Ch. 276, 301 *per* Edmund Davies L.J.
[27] See the text above at ns. 8 to 10.
[28] Sir Christopher Slade, *The Informal Creation of Interests in Land* (1984), The Child & Co. Oxford Lecture, p. 4; see also Ruoff and Roper, *The Law and Practice of Registered Conveyancing* 5th ed., (1986), p. 446. *Muschinski* v. *Dodds* (1985) 62 A.L.R. 429, 450 *per* Deane J., Cretney, *Principles of Family Law* (4th ed. 1984), p. 640.
[29] *Ibid.*, p. 7.
[30-35] See *Lloyds Bank plc* v. *Rosset* [1989] 1 Ch. 350, 385 *per* Nicholls L.J. who treated the wife as having a beneficial interest as soon as she had done some work on the premises, *i.e.* well before the court order; this was despite Nicholls L.J. describing the trust as a constructive one; see also *Fryer* v. *Brook* (1984) 81 L.S.Gaz. 2856 C.A.
[36] [1984] Ch. 317, 326, see the text at n. 15 above.
[37] See above Chap. 5, Part A, p. 71

considered under the heading of 'Resulting trust' where the claimant has directly provided part of the purchase price and her interest is treated as being proportionate to her contribution. The heading of 'Implied trust' will be used where the trust is inferred from the common intention of the parties and the beneficial interest is not directly proportionate to contributions. The division should not be treated as a rigid one as the courts themselves do not take a strict analytical approach in this area. For example, indirect contributions to the purchase price may be treated as monetary contributions giving rise to an interest under a resulting trust or as evidence of common intention giving rise to an interest under an implied trust.

2. Formalities

No writing
By section 53(1)(*b*) of the Law of Property Act 1925, a declaration of trust affecting land is unenforceable unless it is evidenced in writing. A purely voluntary oral declaration of trust by the legal owner of property, therefore, confers no interest.[38] Between those sharing residential property, however, a purely voluntary oral declaration of trust is very rare. If the parties have expressed their intentions in relation to the beneficial interest in the property, there is far more likely to be an express agreement which can be enforced, even though it is oral, under the rule in *Rochefoucald* v. *Boustead*[39] or provide evidence of a common intention which may be enforced as an implied trust if it has been acted upon.[40]

The requirement for writing does not apply to the creation or operation of resulting, implied or constructive trusts.[41] Accordingly, in the present context of the court enforcing the parties inferred intentions under a resulting or implied trust, there are no formalities to be complied with.

B. Resulting trust

Basis
Where property is conveyed into the name of a person who has not provided the whole of the purchase price, the law will impose a resulting trust on that person in favour of whoever has provided the rest of the purchase money. The law presumes that it was the parties' intention that the non-owner should have an interest in the property proportionate to his contribution to the purchase price.[42] At its simplest level, if land is conveyed to A and the purchase money is provided by A as to two-thirds and B as to one-third, there will be a

---

[38] *Gissing* v. *Gissing* [1971] A.C. 886, 905 *per* Lord Diplock; if it is acted upon, it may be enforced as an express or constructive trust, see above chap. 5, Part A, p. 71.

[39] [1897] 1 Ch. 196; see above Chap. 5, Part A, p. 71.

[40] *Gissing* v. *Gissing* [1971] A.C. 886, 905 *per* Lord Diplock; *Grant* v. *Edwards* [1986] Ch. 638, 652 *per* Mustill L.J.; see below Part C, p. 89.

[41] Law of Property Act 1925, s.53(2).

[42] *Dyer* v. *Dyer* (1788) 2 Cox Eq. Cas. 92; *Wray* v. *Steele* (1818) 2 V. & B. 388.

resulting trust for A and B in those proportions.[43] The parties thus become tenants in common, unless the contributions are equal, in which case they become joint tenants.[44] If the evidence is neutral as to the parties' actual intentions in relation to the beneficial interest in the property, the presumption of resulting trust will apply.[45]

The presumption of resulting trust is always subject to contrary intention as Lord Pearson indicated in *Gissing* v. *Gissing*[46];

> "If the respondent's claim is to be valid, I think it must be on the basis that by virtue of contributions made by her towards the purchase of the house there was and is a resulting trust in her favour. If she did make contributions of substantial amount towards the purchase of the house, there would prima facie be a resulting trust in her favour. That would be the presumption as to the intention of the parties at the time or times when she made and he accepted the contributions. The presumption is a rebuttable presumption; it can be rebutted by evidence showing some other intention."

Contrary intention   Thus if there is evidence that the parties intended to hold the beneficial interest in the property in proportions different to those suggested by their contributions there will be an implied trust based on their common intention and not a resulting trust.[47] If, however, the implied trust fails for any reason, the resulting trust based on actual contributions will survive ensuring that the non-owner still has a share in the beneficial interest, albeit of a smaller size. For example, in *Re Densham (A Bankrupt)*,[48] a wife retained a one-ninth share under a resulting trust based on her contributions although she lost her half share based on an agreement between herself and her husband when the trust based on that agreement was held to be void against the husband's trustee in bankruptcy under section 42 of the Bankruptcy Act 1914.[49]

Presumption of advancement   The presumption of advancement[50] may, in limited circumstances, displace that of resulting trust. In certain special relationships, the person providing the purchase money is presumed to intend a gift. Relevant relationships are those of father and child and husband and wife; unmarried couples are outside the presumption.[51] Thus, in the absence of evidence to the contrary, if a husband pays part of the purchase price of a house taken in his wife's name, the whole of the beneficial

---

[43] See *Cowcher* v. *Cowcher* [1972] 1 W.L.R. 425, 431 *per* Bagnall J.
[44] *Lake* v. *Gibson* (1729) 1 Eq. Ca. Abr. 290.
[45] *Gissing* v. *Gissing* [1971] A.C. 886, 907 *per* Lord Diplock; *Marsh* v. *von Sternberg* [1986] 1 F.L.R. 526, 530 *per* Bush J.
[46] [1971] A.C. 886, 902.
[47] See below Part C, p. 89.
[48] [1975] 1 W.L.R. 1519.
[49] Now section 339 of the Insolvency Act 1986; see below Chap. 9, Part A1, p. 162.
[50] See Pettit, *Equity and the Law of Trusts* 6th ed., (1989), p. 123 *et seq.*; Gray, *Elements of Land Law* (1987), p. 262 *et seq.*
[51] Unless they were engaged, Law Reform (Miscellaneous Provisions) Act 1970, s.2(1).

interest will belong to the wife.[52] The presumption is now regarded as based on old-fashioned views as to people's intentions in relation to property.[53] Whilst the presumption can now easily be rebutted by evidence of contrary intention, it still provides a 'prima facie guide line'[54] in solving questions of entitlement to property. The presumption was placed in context by Lord Hodson in *Pettitt* v. *Pettitt*[55] when he said;

Limited application

> "Reference has been made to the 'presumption of advancement' in favour of a wife in receipt of a benefit from her husband. In old days when a wife's right to property was limited, the presumption, no doubt, had great importance and today, when there are no living witnesses to a transaction and inferences have to be drawn, there may be no other guide to a decision as to property rights than by resort to the presumption of advancement. I do not think it would often happen that when evidence had been given, the presumption would today have any decisive effect."

The presumption of resulting trust will also not apply if the non-owner did not contribute his money in the character of a purchaser but intended it to be a gift or loan or merely a contribution to living expenses. If money has not been contributed in the character of a purchaser there can be no question of an implied trust either.

1. Non-purchase contributions

The fact that a non-owner has contributed money at the time of purchase of a property does not automatically mean that he is entitled to a beneficial interest under a resulting trust. The money may have been paid for other reasons. The point was made by Lord Diplock in *Gissing* v. *Gissing*[56] in relation to the purchase of a matrimonial home;

> "If the land is conveyed into the name of a spouse who has not provided the whole of the purchase price, the sum contributed by the other spouse may be explicable as having been intended by both of them either as a gift or as a loan of money to the spouse to whom the land is conveyed or as consideration for a share in the beneficial interest in the land."

Loan

If the evidence establishes that the money was paid by way of loan, the non-owner will not acquire a beneficial interest but will merely be a creditor.[57] For example, in *Potter* v. *Gyles*[58] Mr Gyles failed to establish a beneficial interest in the house

---

[52] *Re Eykyn's Trust* (1877) 6 Ch.D. 115 cited with approval by Lord Upjohn in *Pettitt* v. *Pettitt* [1970] A.C. 777, 815; see also *Tinker* v. *Tinker* [1970] P. 136.
[53] *Pettitt* v. *Pettitt* [1970] A.C. 777, 824 *per* Lord Diplock.
[54] Sir Christopher Slade, *The Informal Creation of Interests in Land* (1984), The Child & Co. Oxford Lecture, p. 8.
[55] [1970] A.C. 777, 811; see also *Simpson* v. *Simpson* (1989) 19 Fam.Law 20.
[56] [1971] A.C. 886, 907.
[57] *Aveling* v. *Knipe* (1815) 19 Ves. 441; see below Chap. 8, Part F1, p. 142.
[58] C.A., unreported, October 10, 1986.

which Mrs Potter purchased as a sitting tenant despite the fact that he provided the £6,200 purchase price. The Court of Appeal found that the parties treated the house as Mrs Potter's alone and the £6,200 as a loan. The presumption of a resulting trust was, therefore, rebutted.

Gift

The same result follows if the money paid by the non-owner was intended as a gift.[59] If the property is owned by a company, payments to the company after the purchase of property will, in effect, be treated as a gift even though the property is the matrimonial home and the wife making the payments is a director of the company.[60]

Periodic payments

Whilst periodic payments can raise the presumption of a resulting trust,[61] the payments must be referable to the acquisition of the property. Payments in the nature of rent[62] or contributions to living expenses are not sufficient. For example, in *Hannaford* v. *Selby*[63] the defendants went to live with their daughter and son-in-law when the latter bought a new house. The defendants contributed £5 a week which was calculated to be one-third of the mortgage instalments and rates. The defendants' claim to a beneficial interest was rejected by Goulding J. on the grounds that, as between the plaintiffs and the defendants, the £5 was no more than a contribution to expenses in consideration of being allowed to live with the plaintiffs in the house. It could not in any reasonable way be regarded as payment for the acquisition of a capital asset.

2.   Contributions to the purchase price

If the property is purchased outright for cash, the parties interests in the property will be in direct proportion to their cash contributions at the time of purchase.[64] As Griffiths L.J. said in *Bernard* v. *Joseph*[65];

Cash purchase

"In the unlikely event that the house was bought without a mortgage, their respective contributions to the purchase price will determine their share in the equity."

The same result will follow if one of the parties borrows the cash he contributes and remains solely responsible for the repayment of the loan.[66]

Discount on purchase

Sitting tenants are sometimes permitted to purchase the house or flat in which they are living at a discount. The present policy in relation to council housing means that purchases at a discount are becoming increasingly common. For example, in *Potter* v. *Gyles*,[67] Mrs Potter purchased her council house at a price 20 per cent. less than it would otherwise have been. If a

---

[59] *Cowcher* v. *Cowcher* [1972] 1 W.L.R. 425, 431; for the evidence of gift required see *Sekhon* v. *Alissa* [1989] 2 F.L.R. 94.
[60] *Winkworth* v. *Baron (Edward) Development Co. Ltd.* [1986] 1 W.L.R. 1512.
[61] See below Part B2, p. 87 re mortgage payments.
[62] *Savage* v. *Dunningham* [1974] Ch. 181.
[63] (1976) 239 E.G. 811; see also *Gross* v. *French* (1976) 238 E.G. 39.
[64] *Cowcher* v. *Cowcher* [1972] 1 W.L.R. 425, 431 *per* Bagnall J.
[65] [1982] Ch. 391, 403.
[66] *Cowcher* v. *Cowcher* [1972] 1 W.L.R. 425, 431 *per* Bagnall J.
[67] C.A., unreported, October 10, 1986.

person living with the tenant contributes some or all of the actual cash required for the purchase, the tenant will be regarded as making a contribution of the cash equivalent of the discount. In *Marsh* v. *von Sternberg*,[68] which concerned a flat which had been purchased at a discount by the tenant and her co-habitee, Bush J. held that the beneficial share of the parties should be decided in a proportion based on their contributions. He then went on to hold[69];

> "Though the respondent's situation only had a financial value in a given set of circumstances and did not have a market price in the world at large, it was a financial benefit nevertheless and, in my view, it is possible to infer, and I do infer, that as part of their agreement or arrangement the parties regarded the realisation of that financial benefit by way of discount as a contribution by the respondent to the purchase of the flat."

It is far more likely that any property which is the subject of dispute will have been purchased with the assistance of a mortgage. The first point to note is that the payment of the initial deposit and legal expenses will, in the absence of evidence to the contrary, raise a resulting trust in favour of the payer.[70] The extent of the parties' beneficial interests, however, will largely depend on how liablity to pay the sums due under the mortgage is assumed.

Mortgage liability If part of the purchase money is provided by one party by means of a loan, secured by mortgage on the property, and that party alone undertakes to pay, and does pay, the sums due under the mortgage, his contribution will be regarded as including the sums provided by the mortgagee.[71] It is the assumption of liability for the debt which is important, not the sums actually paid to the mortgagee.[72] As the mortgage will normally be entered into by the owner of the property this will mean that his share of the beneficial interest will be greater than that of any non-owner sharing the property, even if that person has contributed equally to the deposit.[73] However, if the parties agree between themselves that they will both be responsible for the payment of the mortgage, the proportionate shares in the beneficial interest will reflect that shared responsibility. For example, if property is conveyed to A for £24,000 with A paying £8,000 cash and the remaining £16,000 being raised on mortgage for which A and B both accept liability to pay, A will be regarded as having contributed £16,000 and B as having contributed £8,000.[74] If the mortgage money is derived from rents from the property, the money will

---

[68] [1986] 1 F.L.R. 526.
[69] *Ibid.*, 531.
[70] *Gissing* v. *Gissing* [1971] A.C. 886, 907 *per* Lord Diplock; *Davis* v. *Vale* [1971] 1 W.L.R. 1022, 1026 *per* Lord Denning M.R.
[71] *Cowcher* v. *Cowcher* [1972] 1 W.L.R. 425, 431 *per* Bagnall J.
[72] *Marsh* v. *von Sternberg* [1986] 1 F.L.R. 526, 533 *per* Bush J. following *Walker* v. *Hall* [1984] F.L.R. 126 rather than *Young* v. *Young* [1984] F.L.R. 375 where account was taken only of the actual mortgage payments made.
[73] Unless there is an implied trust based on a contrary common intention—see below Part C, p. 89.
[74] *Cowcher* v. *Cowcher* [1972] 1 W.L.R. 425, 431 *per* Bagnall J.

be regarded as having been contributed by both parties and not the party actually paying the mortgage instalments to the mortgagee.[75]

The operation of the presumption of resulting trust where different types of direct contributions are involved can be seen from the case of *Marsh* v. *von Sternberg*.[76] In that case, the respondent purchased the flat of which she was tenant for £18,350 and the discount in price was valued at £7,650. The respondent provided £5,000 cash and the remaining £13,350 was obtained on mortgage which showed the applicant as the principal debtor but the applicant and the respondent as joint

Calculation   mortgagees. Bush J. held that the parties had agreed between themselves that they were to be equally responsible for the mortgage. The respondent was, therefore, regarded as having contributed the £7,650 discount, the £5,000 cash and half the mortgage sum of £6,775 and the applicant as having contributed half the mortgage sum of £6,775. The applicant was thus held to have a 25.67 per cent. beneficial interest in the property.

Even if there is no agreement between the parties as to the payment of the mortgage, a non-owner may acquire a beneficial interest by actually paying instalments of the mortgage as they

Mortgage   fall due. This can occur in one of two ways. First, the
payments   payments, combined with other evidence,[77] can raise an implied trust based on common intention.[78] Secondly, the payments can amount to contributions of purchase money for the purpose of a resulting trust. The economic realities of purchase on mortgage and the importance of mortgage instalments are recognised by the courts.[79] Thus, regular and substantial contributions to mortgage instalments can raise a resulting trust. The courts, however, tend to treat mortgage payments as evidence of a common intention for the purposes of an implied trust rather than as contributions to the purchase price to raise the presumption of a resulting trust.[80] This gives the court greater flexibility in deciding the size of each party's share and avoids having to make a distinct between payments of interest and capital in each mortgage instalment.[81] In any event, payments of mortgage instalments which are not regarded as purchase money will not found a resulting trust. Thus in *Annen* v. *Rattee*[82] the Court of Appeal held that a person who occupied a flat in the owners' absence and made direct payments to the mortgagee did not acquire a beneficial interest as the payments had been made merely as payments for occupation and not with any intention of acquiring an interest in the flat.

---

[75] *Bernard* v. *Josephs* [1982] Ch. 391, 408 *per* Kerr L.J.
[76] [1986] 1 F.L.R. 526.
[77] *Gissing* v. *Gissing* [1971] A.C. 886, 908 *per* Lord Diplock.
[78] See below Part C, p. 89, for a detailed discussion of implied trusts.
[79] *Gissing* v. *Gissing* [1971] A.C. 886, 906 *per* Lord Diplock.
[80] *Ibid.*, 908 *per* Lord Diplock; *Bernard* v. *Josephs* [1982] Ch. 391, 404 *per* Griffiths L.J.
[81] *Young* v. *Young* [1984] F.L.R. 375, 380 *per* May L.J.; see below Part C. 1(c)(i), p. 94.
[82] (1984) 273 E.G. 503, C.A.

Indirect contributions

Indirect contributions to the purchase price, for example where there is an arrangement for one party to pay the household expenses so as to enable the other party to pay the mortgage, have been held to be capable of being contributions to the purchase price for the purpose of a resulting trust.[83] More usually, indirect payments are treated as evidence of a common intention giving rise to an implied trust.[84]

C. Implied trusts

If a person has not made sufficient contributions to the purchase price to raise the presumption of a resulting trust and still wishes to claim a beneficial interest under a trust for sale, he must establish an implied trust based on the parties' common intention. An implied trust must also be established by a person who has contributed but considers that he is entitled to a greater share of the beneficial interest than that raised by the resulting trust.

It is now accepted[85] that two elements are necessary to establish an implied trust; a common intention that both parties should have a beneficial interest and action to detriment by the claimant. The position was set out clearly by Nourse L.J. in **Basis** *Grant* v. *Edwards*[86];

"In such a case as the present, where there has been no written declaration or agreement, nor any direct provision by the plaintiff of part of the purchase price so as to give rise to a resulting trust in her favour, she must establish a common intention between her and the defendant, acted upon by her, that she should have a beneficial interest in the property."

In seeking the parties' common intention, the House of Lords[86a] has recently made a distinction between two different situations. The first is where there was an agreement, arrangement or understanding between the parties that the beneficial interest in the property was to be shared, evidence of which is based on express discussions between the parties however imprecise or imperfectly remembered those may have been. The second situation is where the only evidence of common intention is the conduct of the parties and there the court will be looking for direct contributions to the purchase price. In practice, however, many cases are unlikely to fall clearly into either category and the claimant will be relying on a combination of statements, discussions and conduct.

---

[83] *Gissing* v. *Gissing* [1971] A.C. 886, 903 *per* Lord Pearson; *c.f. Grant* v. *Edwards* [1986] Ch. 638, 653 *per* Mustill L.J. In any event the payments must be regular and substantial, *Walker* v. *Hall* [1984] F.L.R. 126.
[84] See below Part C.
[85] *Grant* v. *Edwards* [1986] Ch. 638, 647 *per* Nourse L.J., 437 *per* Browne-Wilkinson V.-C.; approved by the Privy Council in *Maharaj (Sheila)* v. *Chand (Jai)* [1986] 3 W.L.R. 440, 446; *Lloyds Bank plc* v. *Rosset* [1990] 1 All E.R. 1111, 1118–1119 *per* Lord Bridge.
[86] [1986] Ch. 638, 646–647.
[86a] *Lloyds Bank plc* v. *Rosset* [1990] 1 All E.R. 1111.

Two elements

A person claiming a beneficial interest under an implied trust will, therefore, have to show either direct evidence of a common intention or conduct from which a common intention can be inferred.[87] The claimant will further have to show that he acted to his detriment on the basis of that common intention. In many instances this will not impose an additional burden as the conduct which raised the inference of common intention will also amount to acting to detriment.[88] Where the inference of a common intention is based on an arrangement or understanding between the parties, conduct by the claimant can amount to detriment which would not have been sufficient, on its own, to provide evidence of a common intention.[88a] The types of conduct from which a common intention can be inferred and those which amount to detriment are examined below. In some of the cases considered the relevant beneficiary was also a joint holder of the legal estate; that fact does not alter the principles in the cases in relation to the acquisition of a beneficial interest.

1. Common intention

Objective test

What has to be proved is a common intention that the claimant as well as the legal owner should have a beneficial interest in the property.[89] The intention can be based on oral declarations and inferred from the conduct of the parties and the surrounding circumstances.[90] When considering the parties' conduct, the test to be applied is an objective, and not a subjective, one.[91] The court applies the test of the reasonable man as Lord Diplock pointed out in *Gissing* v. *Gissing*[92];

> "As in so many branches of English law in which legal rights and obligations depend upon the intentions of the parties to a transaction, the relevant intention of each party is the intention which was reasonably understood by the other party to be manifested by that party's words or conduct notwithstanding that he did not consciously formulate that intention in his own mind or even acted with some different intention which he did not communicate to the other party. On the other hand, he is not bound by any inference which the other party draws as to his intention unless that inference is one which can reasonably be drawn from his words or conduct. It is in this sense that in the branch of English law relating to constructive, implied or resulting trust effect is given to

---

[87] See below Part C1(c), p. 93; see also Montgomery, 'A Question of Intention?' [1987] Conv. 16; *c.f.* Eekelaar, 'A Woman's Place—A Conflict Between Law and Social Values' [1987] Conv. 93.
[88] See below Part C2, p. 100.
[88a] *Lloyds Bank plc* v. *Rosset* [1990] 1 All E.R. 1111, 1119 *per* Lord Bridge.
[89] *Gissing* v. *Gissing* [1971] A.C. 886, 906 *per* Lord Diplock; *Burns* v. *Burns* [1984] Ch. 317, 326 *per* Fox L.J.; *Grant* v. *Edwards* [1986] Ch. 638, 654 *per* Browne-Wilkinson V.-C.
[90] *Gissing* v. *Gissing* [1971] A.C. 886, 902 *per* Lord Pearson; see below Part C1(c), p. 93 for factors establishing a common intention.
[91] *Burns* v. *Burns* [1984] Ch. 317, 336 *per* May L.J.
[92] [1971] A.C. 886, 906.

the inferences as to the intentions of parties to a transaction which a reasonable man would draw from their words or conduct and not to any subjective intention or absence of intention which was not made manifest at the time of the transaction itself. It is for the court to determine what those inferences are."

The objective test for common intention means that a party will be bound by his external actions, whatever his internal thoughts. Accordingly, in *Grant v. Edwards*[93] the Court of Appeal held that a common intention for both Mr Edwards and Mrs Grant to have a beneficial interest in the house in which they were living could be inferred from the fact that Mr Edwards told Mrs Grant that her name was not going on the title because it would prejudice her pending matrimonial proceedings. It was irrelevant that Mr Edwards never had any real intention of sharing the beneficial interest with Mrs Grant.

Of the same mind

There will only be a common intention if the parties are of the same mind. Intentions of either party need not be communicated if they coincide. Lack of communication, however, will prevent the establishment of a common intention if the parties are of different minds. This can be seen from *Clayton v. Johnson*[94] where Mr Clayton failed to establish a beneficial interest in a house he had conveyed to Miss Johnson because he had never said to her that he intended to retain an interest in the house and she regarded it as solely hers. Similarly in *Windeler v. Whitehall*,[95] Millett J. refused to find a common intention that Miss Windeler should have a beneficial interest in the house she shared with Mr. Whitehall because she never communicated her belief that as a common law wife she was entitled to an interest in his property.

Time of purchase

(a) **Relevant time.** When the court is deciding whether the parties had a common intention in relation to the beneficial interest in the property, it concentrates on their intentions at the time the property was bought.[96] The point was made by Fox L.J. in *Burns v. Burns*[97];

"In determining whether such common intention exists it is, normally, the intention of the parties when the property was purchased that is important."

The court, however, does not restrict itself to the factual position at the time of purchase; it considers later events and activities of the parties in so far as they throw light on the initial common intention.[98] Thus, the subsequent pattern of

---

[93] [1986] Ch. 638; see also *Crisp v. Mullings* (1976) 239 E.G. 119.
[94] C.A., unreported, November 4, 1987; see also *Thomas v. Fuller-Brown* [1988] 1 F.L.R. 237.
[95] Ch.D., unreported, May 12, 1989.
[96] *Pettitt v. Pettitt* [1970] A.C. 777, 800 *per* Lord Morris of Borth-y-Gest; *Gissing v. Gissing* [1971] A.C. 886, 900 *per* Viscount Dilhorne, 905 *per* Lord Diplock; *Bernard v. Josephs* [1982] Ch. 391, 404 *per* Griffiths L.J.
[97] [1984] Ch. 317, 327.
[98] *Gissing v. Gissing* [1971] A.C. 886, 906 *per* Lord Diplock; *Burns v. Burns* [1984] Ch. 317, 327 *per* Fox L.J.

mortgage payments by the parties may provide evidence of their original common intention.[99]

Later change   In rare cases, even if there is no common intention on purchase, a common intention may come into existence later where there is some major change in relation to the parties' contributions to the property. Thus, a later common intention may arise if one party discharges the mortgage, for example from a redundancy payment, or effects capital improvements to the property.[1] Similarly, the parties' original common intention may be superseded by a fresh agreement on a major change to contributions but such a new common intention will be unusual.[2] The possibility was conceded by Griffiths L.J. in *Bernard* v. *Joseph*,[3] a case which concerned cohabitees;

> "It might in exceptional circumstances be inferred that the parties agreed to alter their beneficial interests after the house was bought; an example would be if the man bought the house in the first place and the woman years later used a legacy to build an extra floor to make more room for the children. In such circumstances the obvious inference would be that the parties agreed that the woman should acquire a share in the greatly increased value of the house produced by her money. But this depends upon the court being able to infer an intention to alter the share in which the beneficial interest was previously held; the mere fact that one party has spent time and money on improving the property will not normally be sufficient to draw such an inference."

(b) Form of the common intention.   The common intention expressed by the parties or inferred from their conduct can take any form. It need consist of no more than an intention that the beneficial interest in the property should be shared. It is not necessary for the parties to agree the size of share each of them is to take. For example, in *Eves* v. *Eves*[4] the Court of Appeal held that the common intention was that the claimant was to have some undefined interest in the property.[5] In such a case the court will assess the size of each party's share having regard to direct and indirect contributions to the purchase of the property.[6]

Size of share   The parties common intention can go further and show the size of share each is to take. This can occur in two ways which are sometimes referred to as 'money' consensus and 'interest' consensus.[7] Both are equally enforceable.[8] In a money consensus, there is a common intention as to the proportions in which each party is to be treated as providing

---

[99] *Bernard* v. *Josephs* [1982] Ch. 391, 404 *per* Griffiths L.J.
[1] *Burns* v. *Burns* [1984] Ch. 317, 327 *per* Fox L.J.
[2] *Gissing* v. *Gissing* [1971] A.C. 886, 906 *per* Lord Diplock.
[3] [1982] Ch. 391, 404; see also *Re Nicholson, deceased* [1974] 1 W.L.R. 476.
[4] [1975] 1 W.L.R. 1338.
[5] *Ibid.*, 1345 *per* Brightman J.
[6] *Gissing* v. *Gissing* [1971] A.C. 886, 909 *per* Lord Diplock; *Grant* v. *Edwards* [1986] Ch. 638, 657 *per* Browne-Wilkinson V.-C.; see below Part D2, p. 105.
[7] See *Cowcher* v. *Cowcher* [1972] 1 W.L.R. 425, 432 *per* Bagnall J.
[8] *Re Densham (A Bankrupt)* [1975] 1 W.L.R. 1519, 1525 *per* Goff J.

the purchase price. This form of intention is not usual and more easily operates as a resulting trust.[9] In an interest consensus, there is a common intention as to the shares to be taken by each party. For example, if property is purchased on mortgage and each party contributes to the mortgage payments, directly or indirectly when they have income, although not consistently, the court may well infer a common intention that the beneficial interest is to be held in equal shares.[10] Similarly, if the parties treat the property as a joint enterprise and have a principle of sharing eveything, the court will infer a common intention that the property is to be held in equal shares.[11]

To be quantified   A final form of common intention is that the claimant should be entitled to a share in the property which was not to be quantified on purchase but was to be determined when the mortgage was repaid or the property disposed of, on the basis of what would be fair having regard to the total direct and indirect contributions made by the claimant.[12] Such a form of common intention was found by the Court of Appeal in the case of *Passee* v. *Passee*[13] where a house was shared by several members of the same family. The court's approach to the finding of the relevant common intention can be seen from the judgment of Nicholls L.J.[14];

> "Although the judge made no specific findings on the point and there is no direct evidence of the parties' intentions regarding ownership, I think it is tolerably clear from the totality of the evidence that the right inference to draw regarding the intentions of the plaintiff, the defendant and Claudia, who were three members of the same family, is that at the outset they did not intend that the property would belong to them equally or in shares then defined in proportion to their initial contributions to the acquisition cost. Their approach was much less legalistic and less rigid. They intended, or are to be taken to have intended, that each would be entitled to a share to be determined when the property ceased to be theirs on the basis of what would be fair, having regard to the contributions which in total each had by then made. Those contributions would include, in addition to the original contributions, sums contributed to the discharge of the initial mortgage and the cost of capital improvements."

(c) **Evidence of common intention.** If the parties have not entered into a clear express agreement so as to provide direct evidence of their common intention, the court has to infer the necessary common intention that the beneficial interest be shared from the conduct of the parties and the surrounding

---

[9] See above Part B2, p. 86; see also *Re Nicholson, deceased* [1974] 1 W.L.R. 476, 480 *per* Pennycuick V.-C.
[10] *Gissing* v. *Gissing* [1971] A.C. 886, 909 *per* Lord Diplock.
[11] *Midland Bank plc* v. *Dobson and Dobson* [1986] 1 F.L.R. 171.
[12] *Gissing* v. *Gissing* [1971] A.C. 886, 909 *per* Lord Diplock; *c.f.* a resulting trust which is directly related to purchase contributions.
[13] [1988] 1 F.L.R. 263; noted at [1988] Conv. 361 (J. Warburton).
[14] *Ibid.*, 270.

circumstances.[15] It is now clear that certain types of conduct, for example, payment of mortgage instalments, can provide evidence of common intention, whereas other types of conduct, for example, looking after the family, can never provide such evidence. Particular types of conduct by the parties are considered below to see in what circumstances, if any, they can provide evidence of a common intention. A general guide, however, in relation to any payments is that they will only be relevant if they are referable to the acquisition of the property.[16] Following *Lloyds Bank plc* v. *Rosset*[16a] it would appear unlikely that a claimant who is relying on pure conduct, in the absence of any evidence as to discussions of an arrangement or understanding, will succeed unless there is a direct contribution to the purchase price.

(i) *Mortgage payments.*   The courts have recognised that we now live in a 'real-property-mortgaged-to-a-building-society-owning democracy'[17] and that the payment of mortgage instalments is as important as payment of the initial deposit. As Lord Diplock pointed out in *Gissing* v. *Gissing*[18] in relation to matrimonial property;

> "The conduct of the spouses in relation to the payment of the mortgage instalments may be no less relevant to their common intention as to the beneficial interests in a matrimonial home acquired in this way than their conduct in relation to the payment of the cash deposit."

Direct contributions

Thus regular and substantial direct contributions to the mortgage instalments provide evidence that the payer should have a beneficial interest in the property.[19] The inference of a common intention is unlikely, however, if payments of mortgage instalments is the only evidence available relating to the parties' intentions[20]; evidence of contribution to the deposit or of joint enterprise,[21] for example, will be required. A common intention will not be raised by the payment of an odd one or two mortgage instalments, for example when the owner is away.[22] Nor will payments be relevant if there was in existence a contrary intention that such payments should not give rise to any interest.[23]

Capital and interest

The court will not distinguish between capital and interest when considering contributions to mortgage payments. Accordingly, payments in the early stages of a mortgage are relevant to the parties' common intention even though they will

---

[15] *Grant* v. *Edwards* [1986] Ch. 638, 655 *per* Browne-Wilkinson V.-C.
[16] *Burns* v. *Burns* [1984] Ch. 317, 328 *per* Fox L.J.; see also Eekelaar, 'The Matrimonial Home in the Court of Appeal.' (1972) 88 L.Q.R. 333.
[16a] [1990] 1 All E.R. 1111.
[17] *Pettitt* v. *Pettitt* [1970] A.C. 777, 824 *per* Lord Diplock.
[18] [1971] A.C. 886.
[19] *Gissing* v. *Gissing* [1971] A.C. 886, 907–908 *per* Lord Diplock.
[20] *Ibid.*, 908 *per* Lord Diplock.
[21] See below Part (c)(iv), p. 97.
[22] *Gissing* v. *Gissing* [1971] A.C. 886, 900 *per* Viscount Dilhorne; see also *Young* v. *Young* [1984] F.L.R. 375, C.A.
[23] *Bird* v. *Phillips* C.A., unreported, February 25, 1986.

be largely payments of interest.[24] Payment of mortgage instalments will not be relevant, however, if they were not referable to the acquisition of the property but made merely as a contribution to living expenses or as rent for the use of the premises.[25]

Undertaking liability
As well as actual payment of mortgage instalments, the undertaking of liability to pay the mortgage is also relevant. Thus, the placing of a person's name on the title deeds in order to obtain a building society mortgage is evidence that that person was intended to have a beneficial interest.[26] Similarly, a promise to pay off the mortgage in the future, when later receipt of capital is anticipated, can give rise to a common intention. For example, in *Re Nicholson deceased*[27] there was held to be a common intention for a wife to have a beneficial interest in a house owned by her husband when she had undertaken to redeem the mortgage from money to come to her under her mother-in-law's will. The relevance of the undertaking was confirmed by Pennycuick V.-C.[28];

> "It is frequently impossible to quantify in money terms the amount of an unenforceable undertaking of this kind to pay mortgage instalments or the principal under a mortgage. There is, however, no doubt that that is a factor which the court may take into account in determining what was the common intention."

(ii) *Payment of household expenses.* When people are sharing residential accommodation, particularly if the relationship is a long term one, strict accounts are unlikely to be kept. Accident, rather than design, will dictate who actually pays instalments of the mortgage and who pays the other household expenses and this fact is recognised by the court.[29] Where several people are contributing to household expenses, the court will infer a common intention that a person is to share in the beneficial common interest if the payments were made as contributions to the purchase of the property.[30] In such a situation a party is said to make indirect contributions to the purchase price.

Indirect contributions
Relevant indirect contributions can arise in one of two ways, either by increasing a common pool of income or by relieving the party paying the mortgage of other expenditure.[31] Thus Lord Diplock in *Gissing* v. *Gissing*[32] considered that payment by a wife of some of the joint household expenses out of her income could be evidence of a common intention. On

---

[24] *Passee* v. *Passee* [1988] 1 F.L.R. 263.
[25] *Annen* v. *Rattee* (1984) 273 E.G. 503; *Passee* v. *Passee* [1988] 1 F.L.R. 263 (in relation to the other members of the family resident in the house).
[26] *Crisp* v. *Mullings* (1976) 239 E.G. 119; see also *Young* v. *Young* [1984] F.L.R. 375; *Hoare* v. *Hoare* (1983) 13 Fam.Law 142, C.A.
[27] [1974] 1 W.L.R. 476.
[28] *Ibid.*, 480.
[29] *Gissing* v. *Gissing* [1971] A.C. 886, 903 *per* Lord Pearson.
[30] *Bernard* v. *Josephs* [1982] Ch. 391, 404 *per* Griffiths L.J.
[31] *Burns* v. *Burns* [1984] Ch. 317, 329 *per* Fox L.J., 344 *per* May L.J.
[32] [1971] A.C. 886, 907–908.

this basis, a wife successfully claimed a beneficial interest in a property purchased in her husband's name when she went out to work immediately after the property was purchased and thereafter contributed towards the household expenses.[33]

Household expenses

Contribution to household expenses alone will not raise a common intention.[34] It must be shown that there is some connection between the contribution and the acquisition of the property. Thus it is said that payments must be 'referable' to the purchase of the property.[35] This can be be seen from the judgment of Dillon L.J. in *Warner* v. *Warner*[36] when the Court of Appeal refused the plaintiff's appeal form the decision that she was not entitled to a beneficial interest;

> "The plaintiff's difficulty in this case lies in linking her contributions to the acquisition of the matrimonial home at all. They were payments made while they were living together, but there is not the slightest evidence that there was any thought in the minds of either of them that by making these contributions she would be acquiring an interest in the quasi matrimonial home or would be facilitating the acquisition of that home."

Payment of household expenses will be relevant if there is evidence that the owner could not reasonably afford to pay the mortgage himself,[37] or there was a clear adjustment of contributions to household expenditure on purchase of the property,[38] or there was a substantial contribution to family expenses so as to enable the mortgage instalments to be paid.[39] The court is more likely to infer a common intention in the case of indirect contributions if there is other evidence of the parties' intentions, for example payment of part of the deposit.[40]

(iii) *Work on the property.* The carrying out of construction work on the property by a person sharing residential accommodation can raise an inference that the beneficial

Substantial work

interest is to be shared. The amount of work carried out must be substantial and must be referable to the acquisition of the property.[41] Thus, where a site was bought in the name of one person and then a house built by joint effort for joint occupation there was held to be a common intention for the

---

[33] *Hazell* v. *Hazell* [1972] 1 W.L.R. 301, 305–306 *per* Megaw L.J.
[34] *Gissing* v. *Gissing* [1971] A.C. 886, 909 *per* Lord Diplock; *Richards* v. *Dove* [1974] 1 All E.R. 888; see below Part (c)(vii), p. 100.
[35] *Burns* v. *Burns* [1984] Ch. 317, 328 *per* Fox L.J. disapproving Lord Denning M.R.'s dicta to the contrary in *Hazell* v. *Hazell* [1972] 1 W.L.R. 301, 304; see also *McFarlane* v. *McFarlane* [1972] N.I. 59, C.A.
[36] C.A., unreported, July 1, 1984, quoting from the transcript.
[37] *Gissing* v. *Gissing* [1971] A.C. 886, 910 *per* Lord Diplock; see also *Grant* v. *Edwards* [1986] Ch. 638, 649 *per* Nourse L.J.
[38] *Hazell* v. *Hazell* [1972] 1 W.L.R. 301.
[39] *Burns* v. *Burns* [1984] Ch. 317, 329 *per* Fox L.J.
[40] *Gissing* v. *Gissing* [1971] A.C. 886, 907–908 *per* Lord Diplock.
[41] *Button* v. *Button* [1968] 1 W.L.R. 457.

non-owner to have a beneficial interest.[42] Similarly, physical work in helping to put the property into repair can be evidence of a common intention.[43] Supervising builders and undertaking decoration is not, however, conduct which will raise evidence of a common intention in relation to the beneficial interest.[43a]

Substantial work on the premises will not raise the inference of a common intention if there is evidence that the work was done for other reasons. For example, in *Thomas* v. *Fuller-Brown*[44] grant improvement work carried out by the claimant on the house in which he was living did not give him a beneficial interest as there was evidence that the work was the agreed payment for his board and lodging.

Generally, the carrying out of improvements to the property will not be evidence of a common intention. The point was made by Lord Diplock in *Pettitt* v. *Pettitt*[45] in relation to matrimonial property;

Improvements

> "If the husband likes to occupy his leisure by laying a new lawn in the garden or building a fitted wardrobe in the bedroom whilst the wife does the shopping, cooks the family dinner and bathes the children, I for my part, find it quite impossible to impute to them as reasonable husband and wife any common intention that these domestic activities or any of them are to have any effect on the existing proprietary rights in the family home."

Thus, the court refused to infer a common intention from the fact that a man redecorated, reglazed the windows and knocked two rooms into one in a house in which he had been living for 10 years.[46]

A major improvement, such as the building of a extension to the premises,[47] may provide evidence from which the court can infer that the improving non-owner is to have a beneficial interest but this is very unusual.[48] In the case of matrimonial property, section 37 of the Matrimonial Proceedings and Property Act 1970 confers a beneficial interest on a spouse who makes a substantial improvement to the property. For these purposes, the installation of central heating has been held to be a substantial improvement.[49]

(iv) *Joint enterprise.* The court has regard to the surrounding circumstances when considering whether a common intention in relation to the beneficial interest can be inferred. This is particularly important where the parties are married or co-habiting as evidence that the parties treated other activities, as well as the property, as a joint enterprise will provide evidence

---

[42] *Latimer* v. *Latimer* (1970) 114 S.J. 973; *Smith* v. *Baker* [1970] 1 W.L.R. 1160; *Cooke* v. *Head* [1972] 1 W.L.R. 518.
[43] *Eves* v. *Eves* [1975] 1 W.L.R. 1338, 1345 *per* Brightman J.
[43a] *Lloyds Bank plc* v. *Rosset* [1990] 1 All E.R. 1111.
[44] [1988] 1 F.L.R. 237.
[45] [1970] A.C. 777, 826.
[46] *Grant* v. *Sanderson* C.A., unreported, April 20, 1983 (cohabitees).
[47] *Burns* v. *Burns* [1984] Ch. 317, 327 *per* Fox L.J.
[48] *Bernard* v. *Josephs* [1982] Ch. 391, 404 *per* Griffiths L.J.; see also above Part C1(a), p. 91.
[49] *Re Nicholson, deceased* [1974] 1 W.L.R. 476.

Sharing assets

about their intention in relation to the property in which they are living. In *Midland Bank plc* v. *Dobson and Dobson*[50] evidence that the parties had a principle of sharing everything in their marriage was held to be evidence on which a common intention that the beneficial interest in the house held by the husband should be shared could be based. However, in *Lloyds Bank plc* v. *Rosset*[51] the House of Lords held that a common intention that a house was to be renovated as a joint venture or a common intention that the house was to be shared by parents and children as the family home, did not amount to evidence of a common intention in relation to the beneficial interest in the property.

Banking arrangements

The court often looks to the parties' banking arrangements for evidence of joint enterprise. Where savings, either before or after the purchase, are joint, there will be evidence of a common intention in relation to the property.[52] The placing of insurance moneys, received after damage to the property, into a joint account has similarly been held to provide evidence of the parties' intentions.[53] The fact that the parties never had any form of joint account is equally relevant.[54]

(v) *Relationship between the parties.*   There is no recognition of the concept of 'family' property in English law[55] and the courts have stated that the same principles apply in

Cohabitees

determining the beneficial interest of married and unmarried couples.[56] Despite this, the relationship between the parties is a factor which is considered by the court. The point was made by Griffiths L.J. in *Bernard* v. *Josephs*[57];

> "The legal principles to be applied are the same whether the dispute is between married or unmarried couples, but the nature of the relationship between the parties is a very important factor when considering what inferences should be drawn from the way they have conducted their affairs. There are many reasons why a man and a woman may decide to live together without marrying, and one of them is that each values his independence and does not wish to make the commitment of marriage; in such a case it will be misleading to make the same assumptions and to draw the same inferences from their behaviour as in the case of a married couple."

Thus, the court may be more inclined to find a common intention that the beneficial interest be shared if a property is

---

[50] [1986] F.L.R. 171. The trust was not enforced, however, because Mrs Dobson had not acted to her detriment, see below Part C2, p. 100.
[51] [1990[1 All E.R. 1111, 1117 *per* Lord Bridge.
[52] *Re Densham (A Bankrupt)* [1975] 1 W.L.R. 1519; *Smith* v. *Baker* [1970] 1 W.L.R. 1160.
[53] *Grant* v. *Edwards* [1986] Ch. 638, 650 *per* Nourse L.J.
[54] *Cowcher* v. *Cowcher* [1972] 1 W.L.R. 425.
[55] *Pettitt* v. *Pettitt* [1970] A.C. 777; proposals for statutory reform, Law Comm. No. 86: Third Report on Family Property, have not been implemented.
[56] *Bernard* v. *Josephs* [1982] Ch. 391; noted [1982] Conv. 444 (J. Warburton).
[57] *Ibid.*, 402; see also *Richards* v. *Dove* [1974] 1 All E.R. 888.

purchased in contemplation of marriage[58] but that factor on its own is not enough.[59]

Female owner

On the same basis, evidence that cohabitees do not intend to marry and, in effect, regard the relationship as one of landlady and lodger will prevent a finding that there was any common intention that the beneficial interest be shared.[60] The courts have indicated that where it is the woman that is the legal owner they will be less inclined to find a common intention.[61]

In the case of children providing a home for elderly parents, the relationship between the parties does not appear to be a factor giving rise to a common intention.[62] It may become a factor, however, if the non-owners are dependent upon the owners for care.

Statements of intention

(vi) *Declarations and representations.* An express declaration of trust may be enforced as an express trust even if it is oral.[63] Statements by the owner falling short of an express declaration of trust may still be relevant, however, as evidence from which a common intention that the beneficial interest is to be shared can be inferred. The implied trust based on such declarations and representations will only be enforced if there is some form of contribution or other detrimental act by the non-owner.[64]

Eves v. Eves

The relevance of statements at the time of purchase can be seen from *Eves* v. *Eves*[65] which concerned a house lived in by an unmarried couple. The house was in the man's name but at the time of purchase he had said to the woman that the house was not being placed into joint names because she was under 21 years of age. The woman moved into the house and did a considerable amount of work on it. The Court of Appeal held that she was entitled to a beneficial interest in the house and the Court's approach can be seen from the following extract from the judgment of Brightman J.[66];

> "The defendant clearly led the plaintiff to believe that she was to have some undefined interest in the property, and that her name was only omitted from the conveyance because of her age. This, of course, is not enough by itself to create a beneficial interest in her favour; there would at best be a mere 'voluntary declaration of trust' which would be 'unenforceable for want of writing': *per* Lord Diplock in *Gissing* v. *Gissing* [1971] A.C. 886, 905. If, however, it was part of the bargain between the parties, expressed or to be implied, that the plaintiff should contribute her labour towards the reparation of a house in which she was

---

[58] See *Tanner* v. *Tanner* [1975] 3 All E.R. 776, 779 *per* Lord Denning M.R.
[59] *Burns* v. *Burns* [1984] Ch. 317; see below Part (c)(vii), p. 100.
[60] *Thomas* v. *Fuller-Brown* [1988] 1 F.L.R. 237.
[61] *Potter* v. *Gyles* C.A., unreported, October 10, 1986.
[62] See *Hannaford* v. *Selby* (1976) 239 E.G. 811.
[63] See above Chap. 5, Part A, p. 71; see also *Re Gorman (a bankrupt)* [1990] 1 All E.R. 717 where an unsigned declaration of trust was treated as evidence of the parties' intention.
[64] See below Part C2, p. 100.
[65] [1975] 1 W.L.R. 1338.
[66] *Ibid.,* 1345.

to have some beneficial interest, then I think that the arrangement becomes one to which the law can give effect."

Similarly, in *Grant* v. *Edwards*[67] the defendant's statement to the plaintiff that her name was not being placed on the title deeds because it would prejudice matrimonial proceedings between herself and her former husband was held to provide evidence of a common intention. The statement must relate to the ownership of the property, however, and not merely to its use, for example, as a family home.[67a]

(vii) *Housekeeping and looking after the family.* In order to raise the inference of a common intention that the beneficial interest in the property is to be shared, there must be payments or other conduct which is referable to the acquisition of the property.[68] Accordingly, payment of housekeeping expenses, such as food, will be disregarded by the court if they in no way assisted in the purchase of the property.[69] Similarly, the purchase of household goods and the payment of family expenses will not be evidence of any common intention.[70]

Not sufficient contribution Despite earlier statements to the contrary,[71] it is now clear that the work and effort of looking after the family will not provide any evidence relevant for property purposes.[72]

The need for payments to be referable to the purchase of the property can be seen from *Burns* v. *Burns*[73] and *Hannaford* v. *Selby*.[74] In the first case, an unmarried couple had shared the same house, held in the man's name, for 17 years. During that period the woman had looked after the two children and the house, paid the rates and telephone bills and provided some household equipment. None of this activity was held to raise a common intention. In the second case, an elderly couple went to live with their daughter and son-in-law when the children bought a larger house. The parents contributed towards the family living expenses and worked in the garden to provide food. It was held that neither of these activities provided evidence of a common intention that the parents should have an interest in the house.

2. Detriment

Equity will not assist a volunteer and in the context of implied trusts this means that it is not sufficient merely to establish a common intention that the beneficial interest is to be shared,

---

[67] [1986] Ch. 638, 649 *per* Nourse L.J.
[67a] *Lloyds Bank plc* v. *Rosset* [1990] 1 All E.R. 1111.
[68] *Burns* v. *Burns* [1984] Ch. 317, 328 *per* Fox L.J.; noted [1984] Conv. 381 (S. Coneys), (1984) 43 C.L.J. 227 (R. Ingleby), (1984) 47 M.L.R. 735 (J. Dewar).
[69] *Richards* v. *Dove* [1974] 1 All E.R. 888, 894 *per* Walton J.; see above Part (c)(ii), p. 95.
[70] *Gissing* v. *Gissing* [1971] A.C. 886; *Burns* v. *Burns* [1984] Ch. 317.
[71] *Hall* v. *Hall* (1982) 3 F.L.R. 379, 381 *per* Lord Denning M.R.
[72] *Burns* v. *Burns* [1984] Ch. 317.
[73] *Ibid.*, see also *Button* v. *Button* [1968] 1 W.L.R. 457.
[74] (1976) 239 E.G. 811.

the claimant must go further and show that he has acted to his detriment on the faith of that common intention.[75] This dual requirement is based on Lord Diplock's speech in *Gissing* v. *Gissing*[76] when he emphasised that the court will only intervene where it is inequitable for the owner to deny the claimant's equitable interest.

    The need to show detrimental action is not as onerous as at first sight it might appear. In many cases the conduct from which the court has inferred the parties' common intention will also provide the necessary action to detriment. For example, **Contributions** direct[77] or indirect[78] contributions to the purchase price will provide evidence from which the court can infer a common intention and also show that the claimant has acted to his detriment.[79] The requirement does impose an additional burden where the common intention is based on an express agreement between the parties or is inferred from statements or representations of the owner[80] or evidence of joint **Additional burden** enterprise.[81] The importance of action to detriment in such circumstances can be seen from *Midland Bank plc* v. *Dobson and Dobson*.[82] In that case there was direct evidence of a common intention in relation to the matrimonial home in that the parties had orally agreed that the house was to be jointly owned and, further, they had treated all matters as a joint enterprise. Mrs Dobson, who had made no direct or indirect contributions to the acquisition of the property, failed to establish a beneficial interest in the house as she had not acted to her detriment on the basis of the common intention.

    In order for any conduct to amount to action to detriment, it must satisfy two conditions[83]; first it must be a type of conduct accepted by the court as involving detriment and, secondly, the conduct must be referable to the common intention. The courts now appear to be placing less emphasis on the second condition[84] and once the first condition is satisfied, the satisfaction of the second may be presumed.

(a) *Types of conduct.* The most obvious form of action to detriment is a direct contribution to the purchase of the property, whether as a contribution to the deposit or payment of instalments of the mortgage. Indirect contributions to the **Financial** purchase also count as action to detriment. For example, in **contribution** *Grant* v. *Edwards*[85] the claimant made substantial contributions

---

[75] *Grant* v. *Edwards* [1986] Ch. 638; *Maharaj (Sheila)* v. *Chand (Jai)* [1986] A.C. 898. *Lloyds Bank plc* v. *Rosset* [1990] 1 All E.R. 1111.
[76] [1971] A.C. 886, 905, see the passage quoted at n. 14 above.
[77] See above Part C1(c)(i), p. 94.
[78] See above Part C1(c)(ii), p. 95.
[79] See *Grant* v. *Edwards* [1986] Ch. 638, 647 *per* Nourse L.J., 655 *per* Browne-Wilkinson V.-C.
[80] See above Part C1(c)(vi), p. 99.
[81] See above Part C1(c)(iv), p. 97.
[82] [1986] 1 F.L.R. 171.
[83] *Grant* v. *Edwards* [1986] Ch. 638, 651 *per* Mustill L.J.
[84] *Grant* v. *Edwards* [1986] Ch. 638, 656 *per* Browne-Wilkinson V.-C.; see below Part 2(b), p. 102.
[85] [1986] Ch. 638; noted (1986) 45 C.L.J. 394 (D. J. Hayton), [1986] Conv. 291 (J. Warburton), (1987) 50 M.L.R. 94 (B. Sufrin).

to the housekeeping which enabled the owner to pay the mortgage instalments. The claimant was held to have acted to her detriment on the faith of the common intention that she was to have a beneficial interest inferred from the owner's statements at the time of purchase.[86] The carrying out of work on the premises can also amount to acting to detriment.[87-88] Also, selling the property at an undervalue has been held to be a detrimental act.[89]

Work on the premises

Whilst conduct amounting to detriment need not be of the magnitude necessary to raise an inference of common intention, certain types of conduct are not regarded as sufficient by the courts. Routine maintenance and decoration of the premises will not amount to a detrimental act for the purposes of acquiring a beneficial interest[90]; nor will the payment of general household expenses which are unconnected with the purchase of the property.[91] Moving into the premises to live with the owner will not be regarded by the court as a detrimental act either.[92]

Maintenance

The distinction between conduct which amounts to detriment and that which does not was summarised by Nourse L.J. in *Grant* v. *Edwards*[93] as follows;

"In my judgment it must be conduct on which the woman could not reasonably have been expected to embark unless she was to have an interest in the house."

In the same case, however, Browne-Wilkinson V.-C. indicated[94] that he would accept as sufficient detriment any act done by the claimant detrimental to the lives of the parties, as opposed to the purchase of the property. Such a wide view of detriment is probably still restricted to proprietary estoppel[95] and if a claimant has not contributed in some way to the acquisition of the property that alternative remedy should be considered.

Wider view

(b) *Referable to the common intention.* Lord Diplock's speech in *Gissing* v. *Gissing*[96] has been interpreted to mean that there must be a conscious connection between the parties' common intention and the claimant's detrimental act, in other words the claimant must show that he had been acting with the intention of acquiring a beneficial interest. Some judges[97] have seen the

Connected to common intention

---

[86] See above Part C1(c)(vi), p. 99.
[87-88] *Eves* v. *Eves* [1975] 1 W.L.R. 1388, 1345 *per* Brightman J.
[89] *Clayton* v. *Johnson* C.A., unreported, November 4, 1987.
[90] *Midland Bank plc* v. *Dobson and Dobson* [1986] 1 F.L.R. 171. See also *Lloyds Bank plc* v. *Rosset* [1990] 1 All E.R. 1111.
[91] *Ibid.*; *Burns* v. *Burns* [1984] Ch. 317, 327 *per* Fox L.J.
[92] *Layton* v. *Martin* [1986] 2 F.L.R. 227; *Christian* v. *Christian* (1981) 131 New L.J. 43.
[93] [1986] Ch. 638, 648.
[94] *Ibid.*, 657.
[95] See below Chap. 7, Part B3, p. 118.
[96] [1971] A.C. 886, 905, see the passage quoted at n. 14 above.
[97] *Midland Bank plc* v. *Dobson and Dobson* [1986] 1 F.L.R. 171, 175 *per* Fox L.J.; *Grant* v. *Edwards* [1986] Ch. 638, 652 *per* Mustill L.J.

requirement in terms of a bargain between the parties and if the claimant's act does not coincide with, either what the parties expressly agreed, or what the court infers was to be the claimant's side of the bargain, no equitable interest will be acquired.

The requirement of bargain or conscious reliance imposes an undue burden on the claimant and the courts have recently taken a more liberal approach. In *Grant* v. *Edwards* Browne-Wilkinson V.-C.[98] accepted that there had to be some 'link' between the common intention and the acts relied on as detriment but he was not prepared to go as far as to say that there must be a conscious reliance on the common intention. The correct approach is probably contained in the following extract from the judgment of Nicholls L.J. in *Lloyds Bank plc* v. *Rosset*[99]

More liberal approach

"I can see no reason in principle why, if the parties' common intention is that the wife should have a beneficial interest in the property, and if thereafter to the knowledge of the husband she acts to her detriment in reliance on that common intention, the wife should not be able to assert an equitable interest against the husband just as much as she could in a case where the common intention was that, by acting in a certain way, she would acquire a beneficial interest. In each case the question is whether, having regard to what has occurred, it would be inequitable to permit the party in whom the legal is vested to deny the existence of the beneficial interest which they both intended should exist."

D. Beneficial interests

Where a person sharing residential accommodation acquires a beneficial interest in the property, whether under a resulting or an implied trust, the legal estate will be held on a statutory trust for sale even if there is a sole owner of the legal estate.[1] The benefits accruing, therefore, depend upon the general law applicable to trusts for sale.[2] One of the major reasons for claiming under a resulting or implied trust is that the beneficial interest can, in many instances, be enforced against third parties.[3] In relation to the owner, the holder of a beneficial interest will be seeking either to remain in possession or to

---

[98] [1986] Ch. 638, 656.

[99] [1989] 1 Ch. 350, 381; noted (1988) 104 L.Q.R. 507 (R. J. Smith), [1988] Conv. 453 (M. P. Thompson). See also *Lloyds Bank plc* v. *Rosset* [1990] 1 All E.R. 1111.

[1] *Bull* v. *Bull* [1955] 1 Q.B. 234, confirmed in *Williams & Glyn's Bank Ltd.* v. *Boland* [1981] A.C. 487, 507 *per* Lord Wilberforce; see Thompson, *Co-ownership* (1988), p. 15; Gray, *Elements of Land Law* (1987), p. 366.

[2] See Megarry and Wade, *The Law of Real Property* 5th ed., (1984), p. 411 *et seq.*; see also The Law Commission's proposals for a trust to retain with a power to sell, The Law Commission, *Transfer of Land Trusts of Land* (Law Comm. No. 181) (1989).

[3] See below Chap. 8, Part F6, p. 150.

share the proceeds of sale. The right of occupation, because of the nature of the trust for sale, is limited but the beneficiary is always entitled to a proportion of the proceeds of sale. The amount of money actually received depends upon the size of the beneficiary's share, the valuation of the property and any necessary equitable accounting.[4]

1. The right of occupation

Permissive occupation

The House of Lords in *City of London Building Society* v. *Flegg*[5] confirmed that a beneficiary under a trust for sale has no interest in the land itself but an interest in the proceeds of sale and the net rents and profits until sale.[6] Until sale, however, a beneficiary may be entitled to occupy the property but that will depend upon agreement between the beneficiaries and the purpose for which the trust was originally created. Thus, a person sharing residential accommodation who has acquired a beneficial interest has no automatic right to occupation; his only right is to a share of the proceeds of sale.

Purpose of the trust

In most cases of implied and resulting trusts involving the sharing of residential accommodation, the main purpose of the trust will be to provide a home for all the parties. The court will, in that situation, refuse to grant an order for possession to the legal owner against any other beneficiaries. Thus in *Bull* v. *Bull*[7] the Court of Appeal refused to grant possession to a son against his mother who was living in his house. They had both provided part of the purchase price and she was entitled to remain in possession as the house was bought as their joint home. If the property was not purchased as a joint residence but, for example, as an investment, it is highly unlikely that a beneficiary residing in the premises will be able to resist an action for possession.[8]

Refusal of sale

The court can also protect a beneficiary in possession by refusing the owner an order for sale under section 30 of the Law of Propety Act 1925.[9] It is now settled that the court will not order sale if the purpose of the trust is still in existence. Thus, if the house was purchased as a family home and is still required for that purpose because one party is living there with the children, the court will refuse an order for sale.[10] Similarly, if the house was bought specifically to provide a

---

[4] See below Part D2, p. 105.
[5] [1988] A.C. 54; noted (1987) 103 L.Q.R. 507 (R. J. Smith), [1987] Conv. 451 (W. J. Swadling), (1987) 46 C.L.J. 329 (C. Harpum).
[6] See section 35 of the Law of Property Act 1925.
[7] [1955] 1 Q.B. 234 approved in *Williams & Glyn's Bank Ltd.* v. *Boland* [1981] A.C. 487, 507 *per* Lord Wilberforce; for the position in relation to third parties see below Chap. 8, Part F6, p. 150.
[8] See *Barclay* v. *Barclay* [1970] 2 Q.B. 677.
[9] *City of London Building Society* v. *Flegg* [1988] 1 A.C. 54, 82 *per* Lord Oliver; see also Megarry and Wade, *The Law of Real Property* 5th ed., (1984), p. 411 *et seq.*; Thompson, *Co-ownership* (1988), p. 54 *et seq.*; Schuz, 'Section 30 Law of Property Act 1925 and Unmarried Cohabitees' (1982) 12 Fam.Law 108; Thompson, 'Cohabitation, Co-ownership and Section 30' [1984] Conv. 103; see above Chap. 1, Part D4, p.16.
[10] *Re Evers' Trust* [1980] 1 W.L.R. 1327; *c.f. Burke* v. *Burke* [1974] 1 W.L.R. 1063, 1067 *per* Buckley L.J.

home for an elderly parent who is still living in the premises, the court will not order sale even if the children, who are co-beneficiaries, have left.[11] Whilst a party in possession is strictly only liable to pay an occupation rent if he has ousted the other party,[12] the court, in other cases, may only refuse to order sale if an undertaking is entered into to pay such a rent.[13]

If the purpose of the trust has gone because the parties have separated[14] or can no longer live in harmony,[15] the court will order sale and thus deprive the beneficiary in occupation of possession. For example, in *Ali* v. *Hussein*[16] a house had been jointly purchased to provide a home for two families. The two wives quarrelled and one family left. Goff J. held that the purpose for which the trust was created had ended and that the property should be sold. In an endeavour to alleviate hardship, the court may hold that the purpose of the trust is deemed to continue beyond the separation of the parties until the party in possession has found alternative accommodation.[17] More often the court will give the beneficiary in possession an opportunity to purchase the other (owner)-beneficiary's interest by suspending the operation of the order for possession for a short period.[18]

2. Sharing the proceeds of sale

A person sharing residential property who has succeeded in establishing that he has a beneficial interest in that property will be entitled to part of the proceeds of sale when the property is sold or a comparable sum when the trust terminates. The actual amount of money received will depend upon the size of his share, the value of the property and the result of any necessary equitable accounting.

(a) *Size of the beneficial interest.* In the case of a resulting trust,
Resulting trust the size of the beneficial interest will depend upon the proportion of the beneficiary's contribution to the purchase price.[19] If the parties had no common intention in relation to the beneficial interest and the contributions were clearly unequal, the court will not award equal shares even if the parties are married or co-habiting on a permanent basis.[20]
Implied trust In the case of an implied trust, the form of the parties' common intention is important. The original common intention may itself define the size of the parties' beneficial interests, particularly if the intention was inferred from evidence of joint

---

[11] *Charlton* v. *Lester* (1976) 238 E.G. 115; for the position where one party is bankrupt see below Chap. 9, Part B2, p. 165.
[12] *Dennis* v. *McDonald* [1982] Fam. 63.
[13] See *Bernard* v. *Josephs* [1982] Ch. 391, 411 *per* Kerr L.J.
[14] *Jones* v. *Challenger* [1961] 1 Q.B. 176; *Bernard* v. *Josephs* [1982] Ch. 391.
[15] *Rivett* v. *Rivett* (1966) 200 E.G. 858.
[16] (1974) 231 E.G. 372.
[17] *Cousins* v. *Dzosens* (1984) 81 L.S.Gaz. 2855.
[18] *Bernard* v. *Josephs* [1982] Ch. 391.
[19] See above Part B, p. 83, and the text at n. 76.
[20] *Gissing* v. *Gissing* [1971] A.C. 886, 903 *per* Lord Pearson; *Walker* v. *Hall* [1984] F.L.R. 126, 134 *per* Dillon L.J.

Common intention

enterprise.[21] Common intention as to shares can also be inferred from surrounding circumstances, for example that money from the property was placed in a joint account.[22] If the common intention was inferred from direct[23] or indirect[24] contributions to the purchase price, the court will take a broad view of those contributions in an endeavour to find the parties' intention in relation to the size of the beneficial interests.[25] In so doing, the court does not restrict itself to the circumstances at the time the property was acquired but looks to the whole of the contributions by the parties.[26] The courts' approach to the payment of mortgage instalments can be seen from the following extract from the speech of Lord Diplock in *Gissing* v. *Gissing*[27];

> "If the contribution of the wife in the early part of the period of repayment is substantial but is not an identifiable and uniform proportion of each instalment, because her contributions are indirect or, if direct, are made irregularly, it may well be a reasonable inference that their common intention at the time of acquisition of the matrimonial home was that the beneficial interest should be held by them in equal shares and that each should contribute to the cost of its acquisition whatever amounts each could afford in the varying exigencies of family life to be expected during the period of repayment."

Broad view

If the parties common intention was of the form that the size of the share was to be left to be determined when the property was sold on the basis of what would be fair having regard to the parties' total contributions, the court will take a wide view of the contributions made by the parties. Rather than entering into a precise mathematical calculation the court will 'paint with a broad brush' giving some allowance for inflation as regards earlier contributions.[28]

Assessment of contributions

Where the parties intend that the beneficial interest should be shared but have no common intention at all in relation to the size of the share, the court will assess the size of the beneficial interest. If the contribution by one party was in the form of work on the premises, the court must assess the value of that work.[29] Similarly, if the parties have made financial contributions, the value of those financial contributions has to be assessed. The court cannot fall back on the maxim 'equality if equity' except as a last resort in the absence of evidence about the size of the share.[30] In assessing the value of financial

---

[21] See above Part C1(c)(iv), p. 97; *Midland Bank plc* v. *Dobson and Dobson* [1986] 1 F.L.R. 171, 174 *per* Fox L.J.
[22] *Grant* v. *Edwards* [1986] Ch. 638, 650 *per* Nourse L.J.
[23] See above Part C1(c)(i), p. 94.
[24] See above Part C1(c)(ii), p. 95.
[25] *Gissing* v. *Gissing* [1971] A.C. 886, 908 *per* Lord Diplock.
[26] *Bernard* v. *Josephs* [1982] Ch. 391, noted [1982] Conv. 444 (J. Warburton); see also *Re Gorman (a bankrupt)* [1990] 1 All E.R. 717, 724 *per* Vinelott J.
[27] [1971] A.C. 886, 908.
[28] *Passee* v. *Passee* [1988] 1 F.L.R. 263, 271 *per* Nicholls L.J.
[29] *Cooke* v. *Head* [1972] 1 W.L.R. 518.
[30] *Burns* v. *Burns* [1984] Ch. 317, 345 *per* May L.J. Equal shares are more likely if the property is in joint names.

contributions, the court does not carry out a strict mathematical account but takes a broad view, making allowance for periods when either party was temporarily unable to make contributions.[31]

(b) *Value of the property.*   If the property is actually sold, the beneficiary will receive the relevant proportion of the sale price after deduction of any outstanding charges and costs.

Value at sale   Alternatively, if the trust is terminated by one party buying the share of the other as in *Bernard* v. *Josephs*,[32] the property is valued at the date the interest is purchased. It was at one time considered,[33] in relation to property acquired for joint occupation, that the property should be valued when one party left. In times of inflation this clearly put the beneficiary leaving at a disadvantage as he acquired a share of the lower valuation at separation rather than a share of the higher valuation on sale. The correct approach in relation to resulting and implied trusts is to be found in the judgment of Kerr L.J. in *Turton* v. *Turton*[34];

> "Their inferred intention could only be that if and when they should separate, then each of them would still have whatever may be their appropriate beneficial share in the property, which would remain until such times as it might be sold or one might buy out the interest of the other. But there would never be any basis for attributing to them any implied intention that their respective shares should be valued specifically at the time of separation."

Thus, in all cases the latest valuation is taken.

(c) *Equitable accounting.*   Often, one party is left in possession of the premises and pays the whole of the mortgage instalments

Mortgage payments   until the property is sold or the trust terminates. In that situation the party in possession is given credit for mortgage instalments of capital which he has paid on behalf of the other party, *i.e.* if he is entitled to a two thirds share he receives credit for one third of the payments.[35] No credit is given for payments of mortgage interest as this is regarded as equivalent to an occupation rent[36] for the use of the premises.[37] If part of the premises are let, credit is given after the rent received has been deducted from the mortgage payments.[38]

If either party has incurred expenditure on improvements to the premises or costs which are not reflected in the size of

[31] *Bernard* v. *Josephs* [1982] Ch. 391, 404 *per* Griffiths L.J.
[32] [1982] Ch. 391.
[33] *Hall* v. *Hall* (1982) 3 F.L.R. 379; *Gordon* v. *Douce* [1983] 1 W.L.R. 563.
[34] [1987] 2 All E.R. 641, 650, noted [1987] Conv. 378 (J. Warburton); see also *Walker* v. *Hall* [1984] F.L.R. 126.
[35] *Crisp* v. *Mullings* (1975) 239 E.G. 119; *Walker* v. *Hall* [1984] F.L.R. 126; *Marsh* v. *von Sternberg* [1986] 1 F.L.R. 526. For the probable position in relation to endowment mortgages see Thompson, *Co-ownership* (1988), p. 52.
[36] See above the text at n. 12.
[37] *Leake* v. *Bruzzi* [1974] 1 W.L.R. 1528; *Suttill* v. *Graham* [1977] 1 W.L.R. 819; for the position where one of the co-owners is bankrupt see *Re Gorman (a bankrupt)* [1990] 1 All E.R. 717, 727 *per* Vinelott J.
[38] *Bernard* v. *Josephs* [1982] Ch. 391.

Improvements the share, credit is given for the amount expended. For example, in *Bernard* v. *Josephs*[39] the property was held in equal shares but Mr Joseph was held to be entitled to credit for £2,000 spent on improvements and £650 paid towards initial costs.

E.   Practical considerations

A claim to a beneficial interest in property is most likely to succeed where the claimant has been involved with the purchase from the beginning and has then, or subsequently, made financial contribution. It is highly unlikely that a claim will succeed where the sharing of accommodation starts well after the property was purchased.[40] The absence of financial contribution in some form or the carrying out of work on the premises is fatal as there will be no resulting trust and even if a common intention is established[41] there will be no acting to
Alternative detriment[42] to raise an implied trust. If the only conduct by
remedy the claimant is housekeeping and looking after the family,[43] proprietary estoppel should be considered.[44]

    The courts are unlikely to declare that the claimant is entitled to a beneficial interest if the sharing has been on a
Temporary temporary basis without any long term commitment.[45] In that
sharing situation, a contractual licence should be considered.[46] The courts have shown a reluctance to assist a man trying to claim a beneficial interest in a house owned by a woman.[47]

    It is important to obtain as much detail as possible about the financial arrangements between the parties and the basis on
Financial which all payments were made. The difference between
arrangements contributing to living expenses and indirect contributions to the purchase price is crucial.[48] Detailed evidence about the parties actions and discussions at the time of purchase is equally important.[49]

---

[39] [1982] Ch. 391.
[40] *Warner* v. *Warner* C.A., unreported, July 11, 1984.
[41] See above Part C1(c)(iv), p. 97 and Part C1(c)(vi), p. 99.
[42] See above Part C2(a), p. 101.
[43] See *Burns* v. *Burns* [1984] Ch. 317.
[44] See below Chap. 7.
[45] See above Part C1(c)(v), p. 98.
[46] See above Chap. 2, Part B, p. 24.
[47] *Thomas* v. *Fuller-Brown* [1988] 1 F.L.R. 237; *Potter* v. *Gyles* C.A., unreported, October 10, 1986.
[48] See above Part C1(c)(ii), p. 95 and see above Chap. 1, Part C3, p. 8.
[49] See above Part C1(a), p. 91 and see above Chap. 1, Part C2, p. 7.

7 PROPRIETARY ESTOPPEL

The doctrine of proprietary estoppel[1] provides the most useful and flexible remedy for the solution of the legal problems raised by the informal sharing of residential accommodation. The fact that it is no longer necessary to satisfy rigid criteria before a claim based on proprietary estoppel can succeed means that the doctrine is particularly useful in those situations where the parties never recorded or clearly articulated their intentions or where there was no intention to create legal relations.

Alternative remedy

The courts, themselves, turn to the remedy of proprietary estoppel when other potential solutions prove to be impossible or inappropriate.[2] It is advisable, therefore, always to consider proprietary estoppel, even if there is, prima facie, a more obvious solution. For example, a claim for a beneficial interest in the property under a resulting trust may not succeed because of lack of sufficient financial contribution but there may be sufficient detriment to establish a claim based on proprietary estoppel.[3] In such a case, proprietary estoppel must be separately pleaded, as a pleading of resulting trust is not wide enough to cover proprietary estoppel.[4]

Broad doctrine

Proprietary estoppel, in its present form, is a very broad doctrine and it is difficult to define its operation with certainty. Further uncertainty stems from the variety of interests which the courts have awarded to satisfy the equity raised by the doctrine in any one case. This causes particular problems for third parties.[5] The uncertainty, however, is inherent in the process of adopting an existing doctrine to cover a field, that of informal sharing arrangements, which has previously been largely ignored by the law.

In *Crabb* v. *Arun District Council*,[6] Scarman L.J. suggested[7] that when faced with a case of proprietary estoppel the court;

Basic criteria

"Having analysed and assessed the conduct and relationship of the parties has to answer three questions. First, is there an equity established? Secondly, what is the

---

[1] To be distinguished from promissory estoppel and estoppel by representation, see Snell, *Principles of Equity* 28th ed., (1982), pp. 554 *et seq.*
[2] *Grant* v. *Edwards* [1986] Ch. 638.
[3] See the discussion of *Burns* v. *Burns* [1984] Ch. 317 in *Coombes* v. *Smith* [1986] 1 W.L.R. 808, 816.
[4] *Walker* v. *Walker* C.A., unreported Bound Transcript No. 173, 1984.
[5] See below Chap. 8, Part F7, p. 156.
[6] [1976] Ch. 179; discussed in (1976) 92 L.Q.R. 174 (P. S. Atiyah), (1976) 92 L.Q.R. 342 (P. J. Millett).
[7] *Ibid.*, at pp. 192–193.

extent of the equity, if one is established? And, thirdly, what is the relief appropriate to satisfy the equity?"

The first question involves ascertaining the basis of the doctrine and its application to particular facts. The remaining two questions go together and involve determination of the actual interest to be granted as a result of the successful use of the doctrine.

A. Basis of the doctrine

The doctrine of proprietary estoppel is of mixed parentage and has had a troubled birth and development. Several of its constituents remain open to debate. A reasonable summary, which has been used by the courts,[8] is that contained in Snell's *Principles of Equity*[9];

Summary

"Yet the equity is based on estoppel in that one (A) is encouraged to act to his detriment by the representations or encouragement of another (O) so that it would be unconscionable for O to insist on his strict legal rights."

1.   History[10]

Ramsden v. Dyson

The starting point in the modern history of proprietary estoppel is the case of *Ramsden v Dyson*.[11] The later difficulties in the application of the doctrine stem from the fact that Lord Cranworth L.C. and Lord Kingsdown stated the principle in two different ways. Two versions of the doctrine developed, one based on common expectation, sometimes referred to as estoppel by encouragement or estoppel by acquiescence and the second based on mistake as to true legal rights.

Lord Kingsdown L.J.'s[12] view of proprietary estoppel was as follows;

"If a man, under a verbal agreement with a landlord for a certain interest in land, or, what amounts to the same thing, under an expectation created or encouraged by the landlord, that he shall have a certain interest, takes possession of such land, with the consent of the landlord, and upon the faith of such promise or expectation, with the knowledge of the landlord, and without objection by him, lays out money upon the land, a Court of equity will compel the landlord to give effect to such promise or expectation."

Common assumption

In this version of proprietary estoppel the court has particular regard to the parties common assumption and, where reliance is placed upon that common assumption gives effect to it. Examples include refusing possession so as to

[8] See for example, *Brinnand v. Ewens* (1987) 19 H.L.R. 415, 416.
[9] 28th ed., (1982), p. 558.
[10] See *Taylor Fashions Ltd v. Liverpool Victoria Trustees Co. Ltd* [1982] Q.B. 133 (note), 144 *et seq.*; Gray, *Elements of Land Law* (1987), p. 388 *et seq.*
[11] (1866) L.R. 1 H.L. 129.
[12] *Ramsden v. Dyson* (1866) L.R. 1 H.L. 129, 170.

permit a son to remain in a bungalow built on his father's land where the father had encouraged an assumption that the son was to be allowed to remain there for his life[13] and ordering the granting of an easement where one party had acted in reliance on an agreement that a right of way was to be granted.[14]

The alternative version of proprietary estoppel was given by Lord Cranworth L.C.[15];

Silent consent

"If a stranger begins to build on my land supposing it to be his own, and I, perceiving his mistake, abstain from setting him right, and leave him to persevere in his error, a Court of equity will not allow me afterwards to assert my title to the land on which he had expended money on the supposition that the land was his own. It considers that, when I saw the mistake into which he had fallen, it was my duty to be active and to state my adverse title, and that it would be dishonest in me to remain wilfully passive on such an occasion, in order afterwards to profit by the mistake which I might have prevented."

In this approach to proprietary estoppel far greater emphasis is placed on the state of mind and acts of the non-owner. It was in this type of case, where the owner had remained silent, that Fry J. in *Willmott* v. *Barber*[16] set out his five probanda for the establishment of proprietary estoppel;

Five probanda

"In the first place, the plaintiff must have made a mistake as to his legal rights. Secondly, the plaintiff must have expended some money or must have done some act (not necessarily upon the defendant's land) on the faith of the mistaken belief. Thirdly, the defendant, the possessor of the legal right, must know of the existence of his own right which is inconsistent with the right claimed by the plaintiff. If he does not know of it he is in the same position as the plaintiff, and the doctrine of acquiescence is founded upon conduct with knowledge of your legal rights. Fourthly, the defendant, the possessor of the legal right, must know of the plaintiff's mistaken belief of his rights. If he does not, there is nothing which calls upon him to assert his own rights. Lastly, the defendant, the possessor of the legal right, must have encouraged the plaintiff in his expenditure of money or in the other acts which he has done, either directly or by abstaining from asserting his legal right."

The courts began to apply the five probanda to all cases of proprietary estoppel, insisting on a clear mistake as to legal rights[17] where the approach of Lord Kingsdown would have been more appropriate. The difficulties caused by the rigid application of *Willmott* v *Barber*[18] and the wider range of

[13] *Inwards* v. *Baker* [1965] 2 Q.B. 29.
[14] *Crabb* v. *Arun District Council* [1976] Ch. 179.
[15] *Ramsden* v. *Dyson* (1866) L.R. 1 H.L. 129, 140.
[16] (1880) 15 Ch.D. 96.
[17] See for example *E. & L. Berg Homes Ltd* v. *Grey* (1980) 253 E.G. 473.
[18] (1880) 15 Ch.D. 96.

circumstances in which the doctrine of proprietary estoppel was being invoked caused the court to place the doctrine on a more flexible base.

2.   The modern doctrine

The need to place the doctrine of proprietary estoppel on a more modern footing and to avoid the mistakes of history was recognised by Oliver J. in *Taylor Fashions Ltd.* v. *Liverpool Victoria Trustees Co. Ltd.*[19] He stated[20] the present position in this form;

Taylor Fashions case

"Furthermore, the more recent cases indicate, in my judgment, that the application of the *Ramsden* v. *Dyson* principle (whether you call it proprietary estoppel, estoppel by acquiescence or estoppel by encouragement is really immaterial) requires a very much broader approach which is directed to ascertaining whether, in particular individual circumstances, it would be unconscionable for a party to be permitted to deny that which, knowingly or unknowingly, he has allowed or encouraged another to assume to his detriment rather than to inquiring whether the circumstances can be fitted within the confines of some preconceived formula serving as a universal yardstick for every form of unconscionable behaviour."

This wider formulation of the doctrine has now been confirmed and accepted by the courts.[21]

Whilst the five probanda in *Willmott* v. *Barber*[22] are still referred to,[23] it is now recognised that proprietary estoppel is wider than the type of situations envisaged in that case.[24] The probanda, thus, become factors to be considered in deciding whether a party is estopped, with different weight to be given to each factor in different factual circumstances. For example, the knowledge of the party to be estopped will be of more relevance in cases where he has stood by without protest, whereas the detriment suffered will be of more relevance in cases of encouragement.

The modern doctrine is thus a broad one based on unconscionability. When considering the doctrine, the courts[25] have referred to the necessity for four ingredients. These are not as detailed as the 'five probanda' but do provide some

---

[19] [1982] Q.B. 133; discussed in (1981) 97 L.Q.R. 513. An earlier move towards placing proprietary estoppel on a basis of inequity can be seen in *Inwards* v. *Baker* [1965] 2 Q.B. 29.

[20] [1982] Q.B. 133, 151–152 and see also the earlier statement of Browne-Wilkinson J. in *Re Sharpe (A Bankrupt)* [1980] 1 W.L.R. 219, 223.

[21] *Amalgamated Investment and Property Co. Ltd* v. *Texas Commercial International Bank Ltd* [1982] Q.B. 84, 103; *Att.-Gen. of Hong Kong* v. *Humphreys Estate (Queen's Gardens Ltd)* [1987] A.C. 114; *Re Basham (decd.)* [1986] 1 W.L.R. 1498.

[22] (1880) 15 Ch.D. 96.

[23] See for example *Swallow Securities Ltd* v. *Isenberg* (1985) 274 E.G. 1028; *Coombes* v. *Smith* [1986] 1 W.L.R. 808.

[24] *Re Basham (decd.)* [1986] 1 W.L.R. 1498.

[25] *Brinnand* v. *Ewens* (1987) 19 H.L.R. 415 *per* Nourse L.J.

Unconscionability

judicial guidance as to how the doctrine will be applied. The four ingredients are first, that the claimant must show that he has incurred expenditure or otherwise prejudiced himself or acted to his detriment and, secondly, that such action, must have taken place in the belief either, that he had a sufficient interest in the property or, that he would obtain such an interest. The third ingredient is that the belief must have been encouraged by the owner of the land or some one acting on his behalf and the final ingredient is that there is no bar to the equity.

B.   Elements of proprietary estoppel

1.   Encouragement or assurance

A claim of proprietary estoppel will fail unless the claimant can show some form of encouragement or assurance as to rights in the property by the owner. The point was made by Cumming-Bruce L.J. in *Swallow Securities Ltd.* v. *Isenberg*[26];

> "It is an essential ingredient of the equity that the conduct of the plaintiff in whom the legal right is vested must have been such as to induce in the defendant an expectation that the defendant's rights are different from and more extensive than the defendant's strict legal rights."

Whilst proprietary estoppel has now been placed on a broader footing, it still does not extend to the situation of pure expenditure on the land of another with consent.[27] The basic rule remains that the mistaken improver is without remedy in the absence of encouragement or acquiescence as to entitlement.[28] Accordingly, a tenant of part of a house who carried out repairs and improvements to the whole property could not rely on proprietary estoppel to establish a beneficial interest in the whole house when it was established that he knew that the defendant had bequeathed the house to her son and that there had been no encouragement by the defendant as to entitlement to the whole house.[29] Similarly, in *Thomas* v.

Mistaken improver

Fuller-Brown[30] a man who carried out substantial improvements to his mistress' house was held not to be entitled to an interest in the house as he knew that his mistress wanted to own her own house exclusively and that she had left the house to her children in her will.

The encouragement or acquiescence relied upon by the claimant must have come from the party to be estopped, *i.e.*

---

[26] (1985) 274 E.G. 1028.
[27] *Savva and Costa* v. *Harymode Investments Ltd* C.A., unreported, October 9, 1980; *Spence* v. *Brown* (1988) 18 Fam.Law 291.
[28] Goff & Jones, *The Law of Restitution* 3rd ed., (1986), pp. 137–138.
[29] *Stilwell* v. *Simpson* (1983) 133 New L.J. 894. If the improver has no reason to suppose that the land is not his, continuing silence by the owner can amount to acquiescence, see *Ramsden* v. *Dyson* (1866) L.R. 1 H.L. 129, 168 *per* Lord Wenslydale.
[30] [1988] 1 F.L.R. 237.

the owner of the relevant legal estate. Thus, the owner of the fee simple cannot be estopped as a result of representations by his tenant.[31] The owner can be estopped, however, by the actions of his agent. A tenant, for example, can rely on the statements of the landlord's managing agent or employee.[32] If the owner is a limited company, encouragement or assurance from a director is sufficient, certainly if the director has a controlling interest.[33]

Encouragement by owner

Form

The encouragement or assurance can be in any form. It may consist of writing, words or conduct or any combination thereof. Statements relied upon need not be as clear as would be necessary to found a contract; the equivocal nature of any promises is, however, a factor to be considered in determining whether it would be unconscionable for the owner to rely on his strict legal rights.[34] Passive conduct, unaccompanied by words, is sufficient to constitute encouragement if it is reasonable in the circumstances for the claimant to construe it in that way.[35]

Whatever the form of the encouragement or assurance, the owner must intend that his words or actions should be relied upon. Thus a mere expression of opinion by the owner, for example that the claimant is unlikely to be evicted from the land, will not be sufficient.[36] In the case of passive acquiescence over a period of time, there must be knowledge on the part of the owner that his acquiescence is being relied upon.[37]

Intent

There is no condition that the owner should be fully aware of his strict legal rights when he gives any encouragement or assurance to the claimant; knowledge of the true position by the party to be estopped is merely a factor to be considered. Similarly, it is not necessary to show that the party to be estopped knew that the claimant was mistaken as to his legal rights where there is some positive act of encouragement or assurance. All that is necessary is a common assumption of some present or future entitlement to the property on the part of the claimant. Knowledge of the claimant's state of mind and his mistake as to his legal rights remains a relevant factor, however, where the only form of acquiscence alleged is purely passive conduct.[38] Thus in *Brinnand* v. *Ewens*[39] tenants of

State of mind

---

[31] *Swallow Securities Ltd* v. *Isenberg* (1985) 274 E.G. 1028.
[32] *Ibid.*
[33] See *Savva and Costa* v. *Harymode Investments Ltd* C.A., unreported, October 9, 1980 where the court treated the defendant company as the alter ego of the second defendant, Mr. Reid; see also *Philip Lowe (Chinese Restaurant Ltd)* v. *Sau Man Lee* C.A., unreported, July 9, 1985.
[34] *Jones* v. *Watkins* C.A., unreported, November 26, 1987. The vaguer the promises, the clearer the evidence of detriment required.
[35] *Warnes* v. *Hedley* C.A., unreported, January 31, 1984 and see also *Willmott* v. *Barber* (1880) 15 Ch.D. 96.
[36] *E. & L. Berg Homes Ltd* v. *Grey* (1980) 253 E.G. 473; see also *Stuart* v. *Harris* C.A., unreported, November 23, 1989.
[37] *Savva and Costa* v. *Harymode Investments Ltd* C.A., unreported, October 9, 1980.
[38] *Taylors Fashions Ltd* v. *Liverpool Victoria Trustees Co. Ltd* [1982] Q.B. 133, 147, 152 *per* Oliver J.
[39] (1987) 19 H.L.R. 415; see also *Gross* v. *French* (1976) 238 E.G. 39.

part of a house did not succeed in a claim based in proprietary estoppel to an interest in the whole house when the only assurance was passive acceptance by the landlord of work carried out by the tenants and the landlord had no knowledge of the tenant's belief that they had a right to the whole premises.

Rights in or over land

The encouragement or assurance must relate to rights in or over land. General statements about future security are not sufficient. For example, the plaintiff failed to found a claim of proprietary estoppel for a beneficial interest in property in *Layton* v. *Martin*[40] where the assurance took the form of a promise of 'What emotional security I can give, plus financial security during my life and financial security after my death.' Similarly, in *Coombes* v. *Smith*[41] an assurance that the plaintiff would always be looked after and would always be provided with a roof over her head was insufficient to found a claim in proprietary estoppel. By comparison, in *Pascoe* v. *Turner*[42] the plaintiff was assured that the house she was living in would be hers and succeeded in a claim of proprietary estoppel.

The courts will imply a reference to particular property where there is no other explanation for the assurance. Thus, in *Greasley* v. *Cooke*[43] the assurance to the unpaid housekeeper was in the form of a statement that she had no need to worry and that she would be looked after. In the context of the fact that she had lived with the family for 42 years in the same house, it was held that there was an assurance that she would be allowed to remain in the house rent free for as long as she wished.[44] A general description of property is also acceptable. Thus a valid claim has been accepted on an assurance in relation to the owner's residuary estate.[45]

Future rights

It was once considered that the encouragement or assurance must relate to an existing right.[46] It is now clear that an assurance that the claimant will obtain an interest in the future is sufficient. This can be seen from in *Re Basham dec'd.*,[47] where the plaintiff had worked without payment for her step-father for many years and later looked after him when he retired, as a consequence of the step-father indicating several times that she would get his property when he died. It was held that the assurance as to future rights was sufficient to found a claim of proprietary estoppel to the deceased's estate.

Type of right

The assurance can relate to any form of right in or over property. For example, a tenant can receive assurance that he will have a right of pre-emption,[48] a mistress can be

---

[40] [1986] 2 F.L.R. 227.
[41] [1986] 1 W.L.R. 808, 818. Note, this may be a hard decision as the five probanda were applied strictly.
[42] [1979] 1 W.L.R. 431.
[43] [1980] 1 W.L.R. 1306.
[44] *C.f. Coombes* v. *Smith* [1986] 1 W.L.R. 808 where the plaintiff lived in two different houses provided by, and separate from, the defendant.
[45] *Re Basham (decd.)* [1986] 1 W.L.R. 1498.
[46] See *Willmott* v. *Barber* (1880) 15 Ch.D. 96.
[47] [1986] 1 W.L.R. 1498; see also *Crabb* v. *Arun District Council* [1976] Ch. 179, 193–194 *per* Scarman L.J.
[48] *Stilwell* v. *Simpson* (1983) 133 New L.J. 894.

encouraged in her belief that she will be allowed to remain in
the house until her child reaches 17 years old[49] or that she will
have the fee simple of the house[50] or a son may be assured that
his grandmother will leave him her house if he goes to look
after it for her.[51] The acts of encouragement or acquiescence
relied upon may lack clarity and be open to more than one
interpretation. It is important, therefore, to plead all possible
alternative rights as a result of the proprietary estoppel. For
example, acquiescence to repairs and improvements to the
property may not found a claim for a beneficial interest in the
property but may support a claim for an irrevocable licence[52]
or may support a claim for a tenancy but not the fee simple.[53]

2. Reliance

It is not sufficient for a claimant to a right founded on the
doctrine of proprietary estoppel simply to incur some
detriment; he must incur that detriment because of, or in
reliance on, the encouragement or acquiescence as to a right in
the property given by the owner. The assurance or
encouragement must be an operative cause of the detriment.
The importance of reliance was stressed by Slade L.J. in *Jones
v. Watkins*[54] when he said;

> "If, however, on an assessment of the evidence as a whole,
> the court takes the view that, on the balance of
> probabilities, there is no causal connection between the
> encouragement or representation relied on and an alleged
> item of detriment, that item cannot, in my judgment,
> found a claim based in proprietary estoppel."

**Other
explanations**
This requirement of reliance can cause particular problems
in the context of sharing residential property. There will often
be far more cogent reasons than an expectation of a right in the
property to explain the various acts of detriment alleged to have
been suffered by the claimant. Tenants[55] or licensees[56] who
improve the house or flat in which they are living will do so
primarily to make their own lives more comfortable and not in
the expectation of a new tenancy or greater interest. The
claimant failed for that reason in *Warnes v. Hedley*.[57] In that
case, Mr and Mrs Hedley lived in a house which had been
purchased by Mrs Warnes, Mr Hedley's mother. Mr and Mrs
Hedley spent a considerable sum of money refurbishing the
premises, in particular in providing a nursery. The Court of
Appeal rejected Mr and Mrs Hedley's claim to a beneficial

---

[49] *Coombes v. Smith* [1986] 1 W.L.R. 808.
[50] *Pascoe v. Turner* [1979] 1 W.L.R. 431.
[51] *Watts v. Story* (1984) 134 New L.J. 631.
[52] See for example, *Savva and Costa v. Harymode Investments Ltd* C.A.,
     unreported, October 9, 1980.
[53] See for example, *Jones v. Watkins* C.A., unreported, November 26, 1987.
[54] C.A., unreported, November 26, 1987.
[55] *Stilwell v. Simpson* (1983) 133 New L.J. 894; *Brinnand v. Ewens* (1987) 19
     H.L.R. 415.
[56] *E. & L. Berg Homes Ltd v. Grey* (1980) 253 E.G. 473.
[57] C.A., unreported, January 31, 1984.

interest in the house based on the doctrine of proprietary estoppel on the grounds that the refurbishment work would have been carried out even if they knew or had been told that they had merely a licence determinable on reasonable notice.

Mistresses

Mistresses will often fail to establish a right in the property in which they have been living for the same reason. Thus, in *Layton* v. *Martin*[58] Mrs Layton failed to found a claim in proprietary estoppel as the court held that she went to live with Mr Martin simply to be his wife in all but name and not in reliance on any representation that had been made to her. Similarly, in *Coombes* v. *Smith*[59] the plaintiff was unable to rely on any detriment she might have suffered on moving to the defendant's house when it was held that she moved because she preferred to live with the defendant rather than with her husband and not because of any assurance she received about future provision.

Family situations

The requirement of reliance can be troublesome where the parties are closely related. Many acts which would otherwise be regarded as detrimental can be explained as merely part of family arrangements and to prevent bad feeling. For example, in *Rogers* v. *Eller*[60] a sister and her husband failed to establish an interest in a house belonging to her brother in which they were living rent free. They had carried out work on the premises but this was held to be for their own comfort and to keep the brother content rather than in reliance on any expectation of an interest in the house. The greater the detriment, however, the more likely it is that the acts have been done in reliance on some expectation of an interest in the property. Thus, in *Re Basham (dec'd.)*[61] it was held that the plaintiff's acts went well beyond what was called for by natural love and affection.

Quasi-family situations

The same problem arises in quasi-family situations. A claim may fail on the grounds that the claimant's acts were done merely because she was treated as a member of the family. Thus in *Philip Lowe (Chinese Restaurant) Ltd* v. *Sau Man Lee*[62] the claimant who was a 'little wife,' *i.e.* a mistress who lived with the family, failed to establish an interest in the house in which she was living because the works of repair and redecoration she had carried out had been done for the sake of the family and not in reliance on any representations. However, if the work is out of all proportion to any quasi-family ties, reliance will be found.[63]

Following the case of *Greasley* v. *Cooke*,[64] the burden is on the owner of the property in question to show that particular items of detriment were not done in reliance on his

---

[58] [1986] 2 F.L.R. 227.
[59] [1986] 1 W.L.R. 808, 820.
[60] C.A., unreported, May 20, 1986.
[61] [1986] 1 W.L.R. 1498, 1505. For the facts of this case see above Part B.1, p. 115.
[62] C.A., unreported, July 9, 1985.
[63] *Greasley* v. *Cooke* [1980] 1 W.L.R. 1306.
[64] *Ibid.*; noted in [1981] Conv. 154 (R. Annand); (1981) 44 M.L.R. 461 (G. Woodman).

Burden of proof encouragement or assurance. The position was set out by
Jonathan Parker Q.C., sitting as a deputy High Court judge, in
Coombes v. *Smith*[65] as follows;

> "I take it to mean merely that where, following assurances
> made by the other party, the claimant had adopted a
> course of conduct which is prejudicial or otherwise
> detrimental to her, there is a rebuttable presumption that
> she adopted that course of conduct in reliance on the
> assurances."

3. Detriment

A claimant will not succeed in founding a claim in proprietary
estoppel unless he has suffered some detriment in reliance on
the encouragement or assurance given by the owner of the
property. This requirement is sometimes catergorised as
prejudice[66] or alteration of position.[67]

The classic example of a detrimental act is improvement to
the property in question. The work on the property must be
more than normal repairs and maintenance.[68] An occupier
must show work beyond that which is necessary to keep the
Work on the premises in a habitable state. Thus, expenditure of £4,000 in
property 1974 in refurbishing a flat and in providing new kitchens and
bathrooms was held to be a detriment[69] and the installation of
gas and replumbing of a house together with exterior repairs
has also been held to be a sufficient detriment.[70]

Detriment is not restricted to permanent improvements to
the premises nor need it involve the expenditure of money.
Indeed, it has been said that the categories of detriment are not
closed.[71] It can consist of unpaid work in the property owner's
Work for the business[72] or on his farm.[73] Time and effort are capable of
owner being a detriment for the purposes of proprietary estoppel.[74]
Thus, a woman who had looked after a family without pay for
a considerable number of years was held to have acted to her
detriment.[75] Moving house at the request of the owner of the
relevant property is also a sufficient detriment. For example,
there will be a valid claim in proprietary estoppel if the
claimant gives up his house and job in order to go and look
after an elderly relative's house.[76] In *Jones (A.E.)* v. *Jones
(F.W.)*[77] a son was held to have acted to his detriment when
he left his house and job in Kingston-upon-Thames in order to

---

[65] [1986] 1 W.L.R. 808, 821; see also *Re Basham (decd.)* [1986] 1 W.L.R.
1498, 1507.
[66] *Watts* v. *Story* (1984) 134 New L.J. 631.
[67] *Re Basham (decd.)* [1986] 1 W.L.R. 1498, 1504.
[68] *Appleby* v. *Cowley, The Times,* April 14, 1982.
[69] *Warnes* v. *Hedley* C.A., unreported, January 31, 1984.
[70] *Pascoe* v. *Turner* [1979] 1 W.L.R. 431.
[71] *Watts* v. *Story* (1984) 134 New L.J. 631 *per* Slade L.J.
[72] *Re Basham (decd.)* [1986] 1 W.L.R. 1498.
[73] *Jones* v. *Watkins* C.A., unreported, November 26, 1987.
[74] *Ibid.*
[75] *Greasley* v. *Cooke* [1980] 1 W.L.R. 1306.
[76] *Watts* v. *Story* (1984) 134 New L.J. 631.
[77] [1977] 1 W.L.R. 438.

go and live in a house near to his father in Blundeston in Suffolk. On the same basis, not moving away from the area and thus giving up the possibility of better employment[78] or not seeking employment at all in order to look after an elderly owner and his land[79] can amount to a detriment.

Not all changes in personal circumstances amount to detriment for the purposes of proprietary estoppel. In *Coombes* **Leaving home**   v. *Smith*,[80] for example, the acts of detriment relied upon by the claimant in support of her claim for an interest in the house in which she was living included leaving her husband to go and live with the defendant, allowing herself to become pregnant by him and looking after their daughter and the house which he provided for them. None of these acts was held to be sufficient. Failure to seek alternative accommodation can amount to detriment if the claimant's prospects of obtaining another home would have been substantially more favourable at an earlier date.[81]

Common forms of detriment alleged where residential property has been shared include contributions to household **Contributions to**   living expenses and the carrying out of routine repairs. Such **living expenses**   acts are generally regarded as part of the general joint living arrangements and not sufficient, on their own, to found a claim in proprietary estoppel.[82] The contrast with the carrying out of improvements to the premises was made by Goff L.J. in *Griffiths* v. *Williams*[83];

> "but part of it had been spent in paying outgoings. In so far as the expenditure was of the latter character, I doubt whether it would raise an equity in Mrs Williams' favour, because it would be regarded simply as current payments for the benefits which she was enjoying by being allowed to live in the house. But in so far as money was spent upon permanent improvements such as I have mentioned, it would be capable of creating what is known as a promissory estoppel."

In most cases of sharing residential property there is unlikely to have been any detailed discussion as to legal entitlement but merely a tacit assumption that the claimant will not be asked to leave. It is in that sort of situation that the court is looking for some clear act of detriment or prejudice before any claim based on proprietary estoppel will succeed. However, if there has been clear representation that the claimant is entitled to a particular interest in the property, then even the paying of part of general household expenses or looking after home and family may be sufficient acts of detriment.[84]

---

[78] *Re Basham (decd.)* [1986] 1 W.L.R. 1498.
[79] *Jones* v. *Watkins* C.A., unreported, November 26, 1987.
[80] [1986] 1 W.L.R. 808.
[81] *Stevens* v. *Stevens* C.A., unreported, March 3, 1989.
[82] *Griffiths* v. *Williams* (1977) 248 E.G. 947; see also *Hannaford* v. *Selby* (1976) 239 E.G. 811.
[83] (1977) 248 E.G. 947.
[84] See *Grant* v. *Edwards* [1986] Ch. 638, 657 *per* Browne-Wilkinson V.-C.

Balancing benefits and detriments

It is for the court to decide whether the alleged acts of detriment or prejudice suffered by the claimant are sufficient detriment to found a claim in proprietary estoppel. All such acts are to be judged at the time that the owner goes back on his previous encouragement or assurance.[85] Thus, there is a balancing procedure by the court. The alleged acts of detriment suffered will be considered against any benefits received. It is a process which is approached with some degree of caution by the courts as can be seen from the following statement by Slade L.J. in *Watts* v. *Story*[86];

> "I do not think it is possible, or even desirable, to define the nature and extent of the prejudice or detriment which has to be established in a case such as the present by a claimant who is relying on alleged detriment or prejudice other than expenditure of money. All I would say is that, before allowing the claim in such a case, the court in my opinion, has to be satisfied that, when all the circumstances are taken into account, the detriment or prejudice is such that it would be inequitable to allow the party who made the relevant representation to go back on it."

In that case a claimant who had given up the tenancy of his flat and prospects of employment in Leeds in order to go and live in his grandmother's house in Nottinghamshire was held not to have acted to his detriment so as to found a claim to an interest in the house. The fact that he had moved had to be balanced against the facts that he had had the benefit of a rent free house and had received other benefits under his grandmother's will.

Proof

The type and extent of the detriment suffered by the claimant in reliance on the owners encouragement or assurance is the major factor in the courts determination of whether it would be inequitable for the owner now to assert his full legal rights. It is, therefore, important for all potential items of detriment sought to be relied upon to be specifically alleged and proved.[87]

4. Equity

Courts approach

In answering the first question posed by Scarman L.J. in *Crabb* v. *Arun District Council*[88]—is an equity established?—the courts approach the particular case before them with a degree of caution.[89] The reason for that cautious approach is that the effect of the doctrine of proprietary estoppel may be to confer on the claimant a permanent, irrevocable interest in the land of

[85] *Jones* v. *Watkins* C.A., unreported, November 26, 1987 *per* Slade L.J.
[86] (1984) 134 New L.J. 631.
[87] *Jones* v. *Watkins* C.A., unreported, November 26, 1987 *per* Slade L.J.
[88] [1976] 1 Ch. 179; see p. 109.
[89] *Watts* v. *Story* (1984) 134 New L.J. 631.

another, even though he has given no consideration for such acquisition by way of contractual arrangement, and no legally effective gift of it has been made in his favour.[90]

The courts are also influenced by the fact that if the doctrine of proprietary estoppel was to be applied liberally, owners of land would be deterred from allowing any concessions at all to others for fear of losing their land. The point was made by Ormrod L.J. in *E & L Berg Homes Ltd.* v. *Grey*[91];

> "Also I think it is important that this court should not do or say anything which creates the impression that people are liable to be penalised for not enforcing their strict legal rights. It is a very unfortunate state of affairs when people feel obliged to take steps which they do not wish to take, in order to preserve their legal rights and prevent the other party acquiring rights against them. So the court in using its equitable jurisdiction must, in my judgment, approach these cases with extreme care."

Refusal of relief

The court in answering the first question may refuse to find an equity in the claimant's favour for a variety of reasons. Grounds for refusal can include lack of encouragement or acquiescence as in *Swallow Securities Ltd.* v. *Isenberg*,[92] absence of reliance as in *Layton* v. *Martin*[93] or a combination of the two as in *Coombes* v. *Smith*.[94] More usually the court will decide not to find an equity because the claimant has not suffered sufficient detriment.[95] Whatever the reason given the court, in effect, is deciding whether it would be unconscionable for the owner now to be permitted to deny that which he had previously encouraged or acquiesced in.[96]

Misconduct

Even if the claimant proves that he has acted to his detriment in reliance on the encouragement or assurance of the owner that he has some right in the property and the court would otherwise find an equity in his favour, he may still not succeed in a claim founded on proprietary estoppel if there has been some misconduct on his part. The doctrine of proprietary estoppel is an equitable one and the maxim "that he who comes to equity must come with clean hands" applies.[97] Thus, a claimant who sought to bolster his case by producing a false letter from a builder detailing items of work carried out on the premises, failed to establish a right to remain in the premises on the basis of proprietary estoppel.[98]

---

[90] *Ibid.*
[91] (1980) 253 E.G. 473.
[92] (1985) 274 E.G. 1028; see above Part B1, p. 113.
[93] [1986] 2 F.L.R. 227; see above Part B2, p. 116.
[94] [1986] 1 W.L.R. 808.
[95] *Watts* v. *Story* (1984) 134 New L.J. 631; *Jones* v. *Watkins* C.A., unreported, November 26, 1987; see above Part B3, p. 118.
[96] See *Taylors Fashions Ltd* v. *Liverpool Victoria Trustees Co. Ltd* [1982] Q.B. 133 (note), 151–152 *per* Oliver J.; see above Part A2, p. 112.
[97] *Williams* v. *Staite* [1979] Ch. 291; *Willis (J.) & Son* v. *Willis* (1986) 277 E.G. 1133.
[98] *Willis (J.) & Son* v. *Willis* (1986) 277 E.G. 1133; Thompson, 'Estoppel and Clean Hands' [1986] Conv. 406.

The type and seriousness of misconduct which will defeat a claim for proprietary estoppel is a matter for the discretion of the court. The degree of misconduct will be less than would be required to cancel an already existing equitable licence.[99] Whilst the presentation of a false document will bar the equity, exaggeration on affidavit and in the witness box of work done on the premises and time and effort devoted to the owner's business will not operate as a bar.[1] Conduct adverse to the owner such as to make it difficult for the owner to enjoy and occupy his premises may also bar the equity,[2] for example by making obscene gestures at the owner's visitors and disturbing their sleep by sounding a car horn continually at night.[3] This final criterion could present difficulties where the owner and claimant have been sharing the relevant premises and the conduct of the claimant has made life so intolerable for the owner that he has been forced to leave.[4]

C.   Remedies

In answering the second question raised by Scarman L.J. in *Crabb* v. *Arun District Council*[5]—what is the extent of the equity?—the court looks to the conduct giving rise to the equity, *i.e.* the detrimental or prejudicial acts and the encouragement or assurance relied on.[6] When considering the third question—what is the relief appropriate to satisfy the equity?—the court takes a wider view and considers all the

All circumstances considered

circumstances up to and including the date of trial.[7] Indeed, events between the owner going back on his previous encouragement or assurance and the trial can seriously affect the remedy granted. In *Crabb* v. *Arun District Council*[8] the natural remedy was for the owner to grant the claimant an easement for a consideration. However, the actions of the owner in the meanwhile of locking out the claimant from his land meant that the Court of Appeal ordered that an easement be granted without consideration.

It has been argued[9] that the doctrine of proprietary estoppel merely sanctions the informal creation of property rights which has already occurred as a result of the actions of the parties. This has been seriously disputed[10] and the better

---

[99] *Ibid.*

[1] *Jones* v. *Watkins* C.A., unreported, November 26, 1987. The relevant items of work may be discounted, however, leading to a conclusion that the plaintiff, on balance, has not suffered any detriment.

[2] *Williams* v. *Staite* [1979] Ch. 291, 300 *per* Cumming-Bruce L.J.

[3] See *Brynowen Estates Ltd* v. *Bourne* (1981) 131 New L.J. 1212.

[4] For an example of the possible family tensions, although in that case jointly generated, see *Hannaford* v. *Selby* (1976) 239 E.G. 811.

[5] [1976] 1 Ch. 179, 193.

[6] *Williams* v. *Staite* [1979] Ch. 291, 298.

[7] *Ibid.*: *Pascoe* v. *Turner* [1979] 1 W.L.R. 431, 438.

[8] [1976] 1 Ch. 179, 199.

[9] Moriarty, 'Licences and Land Law: Legal Principles and Public Policies' (1984) 100 L.Q.R. 376.

[10] Dewar, 'Licences and Land Law: An Alternative View' (1986) 49 M.L.R. 74; Thompson, 'Estoppel and Clean Hands' [1986] Conv. 406; Evans, 'Choosing the Right Estoppel' [1988] Conv. 346.

Rights from the court view appears to be that property rights do not arise until the decision of the court, the extent of those rights being at the discretion of the court. Whilst the right granted by the court will usually be as close to the representation or common expectation as possible, the court may award a right greater or lesser than that contemplated by the parties. Thus in *Pascoe* v. *Turner*,[11] the claimant, who could reasonably have expected a licence to occupy the premises for her life, was granted the fee simple. By contrast, in *Cushley* v. *Seale*,[12] a plaintiff who anticipated being awarded a right to possession of premises for the remainder of the term of the defendant's lease, was granted reimbursement of the sums she had spent on improvements to the premises.

1. Potential remedies

The greatest remedy that can be awarded to satisfy the equity raised by proprietary estoppel is to require the owner to **Legal estate** transfer his estate to the claimant. This remedy may be granted when there was a clear statement of intention by the owner to transfer the fee simple[13] or to leave the property to the claimant on his death.[14] The owner may also be required to transfer his estate if that is the only way to give sufficient security and protection to the claimant.[15] Alternatively, the court may require the owner to grant, or confirm the grant of, a lease to the claimant.[16]

Instead of a legal estate, the court may award the claimant **Equitable interests** a beneficial interest in the property. The owner thereafter holds the property on trust for himself and the claimant in the proportions declared by the court. Thus in *Jones (A.E.)* v. *Jones (F.W.)*[17] the son was held to have a quarter beneficial interest in the house as a tenant in common.

In the situation of informal sharing of residential property, a common award is a grant to the claimant of a right to **Occupation for life** occupy the relevant premises rent free for life. This was the right granted in *Greasley* v. *Cooke*.[18] Alternatively, the claimant may be granted a similar right to occupy until certain conditions are satisfied, for example until a child of the owner and claimant reaches 17 years old.[19] Whilst such irrevocable licences are a natural solution to the common expectations of the parties in many informal sharing arrangements, their precise legal nature is obscure. The claimant is protected against the owner by the courts refusal to grant possession but his position in relation to third parties, such as purchasers,

---

[11] [1979] 1 W.L.R. 431.
[12] C.A., unreported, October 28, 1986.
[13] *Dillwyn* v. *Llewelyn* (1862) 4 De G. & F. 517, 521–522.
[14] *Re Basham (decd.)* [1986] 1 W.L.R. 1498.
[15] *Pascoe* v. *Turner* [1979] 1 W.L.R. 431; see below Part C2, p. 125.
[16] *Siew Soon Wah* v. *Yong Tong Hong* [1973] A.C. 836.
[17] [1977] 1 W.L.R. 438, for the facts of this case see p. 118; see also *Grant* v. *Edwards* [1986] 1 Ch. 638, 657 *per* Browne-Wilkinson V.-C.
[18] [1980] 1 W.L.R. 1306, 1312, for the facts of this case see p. 115.
[19] See *Coombes* v. *Smith* [1986] 1 W.L.R. 808.

mortgagees or a trustee in bankruptcy is not settled or
secure.[20]

The grant of an irrevocable licence for life raises further
problems as it can be argued[21] that the claimant's life interest
makes him a tenant for life under the Settled Land Act 1925.
Settled Land Act If correct, this would have the effect of endowing the claimant
1925 with far greater powers than was intended. The problem was
considered in *Dodsworth* v. *Dodsworth*[22] where the defendants
expended money on the deceased plaintiff's bungalow in the
expectation, encouraged by her, that they would be allowed to
remain in the bungalow for as long as they wished to do so.
Russell L.J. set out the position as follows;

> "If immediate and direct effect is given to the expectations
> of the defendants, to take effect in priority to the
> respondents' entitlement and statutory duties, we cannot
> see but that it will lead, by virtue of the provisions of the
> Settled Land Act, to a greater and more extensive interest
> than was ever contemplated by the plaintiff and the
> defendants. The defendants would necessarily become
> joint tenants for life. As such they could sell the property,
> or quit and let it."

One solution adopted by the courts to this problem is to direct
Long lease the owner to grant to the claimant a long lease determinable on
the claimant's death at a nominal rent and subject to an
absolute covenant not to assign.[23]

The solution chosen by the courts need not necessarily
include a right of occupation and may simply be an order that
the owner pay the claimant monetary compensation. Such an
order is likely to be made if the claimant has already left the
premises[24] or it is impossible for the owner and the claimant to
Repayment continue sharing the premises.[25] An order for monetary
compensation may be secured by a right to remain in
occupation of the premises until payment. The solution finally
adopted in *Dodsworth* v. *Dodsworth*[26] was that the defendants
be reimbursed the money they had spent on improvements to
the bungalow and be paid a reasonable sum for their time spent
on such work and that no order for possession to be made until
such sum was paid.

An order for reimbursement may also be secured by
granting the claimant a lien or charge over the property. Such
an order was envisaged by Browne-Wilkinson L.J. in *Walker* v.
With security *Walker*,[27] a family house sharing case, when he said;

---

[20] See below Chap. 8, Part F7, p. 156.
[21] The argument would appear to be flawed by the fact that there is no deed or
    other instrument within section 1 of the Settled Land Act 1925, unless the
    order of the court is the instrument—see *Griffiths* v. *Williams* (1977) 248
    E.G. 947, 949–950 *per* Goff L.J.; see above Chap. 2, Part C.1, p. 35.
[22] (1973) 228 E.G. 1115; *c.f. Ungurian* v. *Lesnoff* [1989] 3 W.L.R. 840.
[23] *Griffiths* v. *Williams* (1977) 248 E.G. 947, 950.
[24] *Cushley* v. *Seale* C.A., unreported, October 28, 1986.
[25] *Dodsworth* v. *Dodsworth* (1973) 228 E.G. 1114, 1114 *per* Russell L.J.; see
    also *Re Sharpe (A Bankrupt)* [1980] 1 W.L.R. 219 which although argued as
    a constructive trust case proceeded on the principles of proprietary estoppel.
[26] (1973) 228 E.G. 1114.
[27] C.A., unreported, April 12, 1984.

"Applying that principle of proprietary estoppel to the facts as they emerged at the trial, the father might have been able to make a case that he was entitled to such an "equity" on the basis that he had made, not an outright gift of the money to the son, but a gift on the understanding that he would have a room in the new house and be provided with his keep, which understanding was encouraged by the words or actions of the son. If such a case had been made out, the court could have enforced the "equity" arising under the propietary estoppel in such manner as was just, for example by requiring repayment of the whole or part of the monies and by imposing a charge on the new house to secure such repayment."

2. Relevant considerations

The terms of any representation or forms of encouragement and type and extent of detriment are clearly matters which are considered by the court when deciding how to satisfy the equity raised by proprietary estoppel. The court will attach different weight to the various elements depending on the way the equity has arisen. Where there has been a clear representation by the owner that the claimant is to have some interest in the property, the court will pay greater attention to the terms of the representation than to acts of detriment and compel the owner to give effect to his representation.[28] Where there has been merely tacit acquiescence by the owner in the acts of the claimant, the court will have more regard to the acts of detriment and the state of mind of the claimant.[29]

A major concern of the court when considering how to satisfy the equity is the security of the claimant. The point was made by Goff L.J. in *Griffiths* v. *Williams*[30]

Claimant's security

'The court ought to see, having regard to all the circumstances, what is the best and fairest way to secure protection for the person who has been misled by the representations made to him and subsequently repudiated.'

Accordingly, the court is less likely to order a grant to the claimant of an interest in the land if he already has some interest, for example a protected tenancy, which protects his right of occupation.[31] On the same reasoning, in *Savva and Costa* v. *Harymode Investments Ltd.*[32] one of the factors which influenced against granting the plaintiff a beneficial interest in the house in which she was living was that the owner had not disturbed her occupation and disclaimed any intention of seeking possession.

The desire to protect the claimant can lead to the court granting the claimant a greater interest than might reasonably

---

[28] *Dillwyn* v. *Llewelyn* (1862) 4 De G. F. & J. 517.
[29] See above Part B1, p. 113, and Part B3, p. 118.
[30] (1977) 248 E.G. 947, 950.
[31] See *Stillwell* v. *Simpson* (1983) 133 New L.J. 894; *Brinnand* v. *Ewens* (1987) 19 H.L.R. 415.
[32] C.A., unreported, October 9, 1980.

Pascoe* v. *Turner be expected. In *Pascoe* v. *Turner*[33] the defendant had expended a large part of her savings in carrying out repairs and improvements to the house in which she was living. The plaintiff owner, who had previously lived with the defendant for 10 years, assured her that the house was hers. The Court of Appeal considered granting the defendant a licence but ordered the plaintiff to transfer his legal estate to her. The Court's reasoning was set out by Cumming-Bruce L.J.[34];

> "We take the view that the equity cannot here be satisfied without granting a remedy which ensures to the defendant security of tenure, quiet enjoyment, and freedom of action in respect of repairs and improvements without interference from the plaintiff. The history of the conduct of the plaintiff since April 9, 1976, in relation to these proceedings leads to an irresistible inference that he is determined to pursue his purpose of evicting her from the house by any legal means at his disposal with a ruthless disregard of the obligations binding upon conscience. The court must grant a remedy effective to protect her against the future manifestations of his ruthlessness. It was conceded that if she is granted a licence, such a licence cannot be registered as a land charge, so that she may find herself ousted by a purchaser for value without notice. If she has in the future to do further and more expensive repairs she may only be able to finance them by a loan, but as a licensee she cannot charge the house. The plaintiff as legal owner may well find excuses for entry, in order to do what he may plausibly represent as necessary works and so continue to derogate from her enjoyment of the licence in ways that make it difficult or impossible for the court to give her effective protection."

Effect of potential remedy A relevant consideration is the practical effect of potential remedies. This is particularly important where the parties are, or have been, sharing residential property. Thus in *Dodsworth* v. *Dodsworth*[35] one reason why the judge at first instance refused to grant the defendants a right to occupy the bungalow was because the plaintiff was still alive and the effect of such an order would be to require her to share her home with people with whom 'she was, or thought she was, at loggerheads.'

Owner deceased If the owner has died and the claim is defended by his personal representatives, the court may order the costs of the action to be paid out of the deceased's estate. In that situation, the costs may be such that the property has to be sold. Even if the claimant succeeds in establishing an interest in the property under the doctrine of proprietary estoppel, he or she will receive only the relevant proportion of the proceeds of sale remaining after the payment of costs and lose any right to remain in the property.[36]

---

[33] [1979] 1 W.L.R. 431; noted [1979] Conv. 379 (F. R. Crane).
[34] *Ibid.* 438–439.
[35] (1973) 228 E.G. 1114; see also *Burrows* v. *Sharp* C.A., unreported, April 13, 1989.
[36] See *Needham* v. *Bowmer* Ch.D., unreported, May 12, 1989.

D.   Practical considerations

Alternative remedy

Proprietary estoppel is a very flexible solution both in the situations in which it operates and the remedies awarded by the court to satisfy the equity which arises. The doctrine should always be considered when there is any possibility that one of the other solutions may fail because of the lack of a vital element. It is particularly useful where the doctrine of part performance might otherwise be considered because there is no need for there to be an intention to create legal relations but merely a need for a common expectation that a right would be acquired.[37] It is also very relevant when the solution of an implied trust is being considered; there may not be sufficient contribution by the claimant to establish a common intention but there may be sufficient detriment to raise an equity under the doctrine of proprietary estoppel.[38]

Pleading

Whenever the doctrine of proprietary estoppel is being considered as a potential remedy, it must be separately pleaded.[39] Also, all acts which could amount to items of detriment or prejudice must be separately alleged.[40] In cases where proprietary estoppel is being alleged as an alternative to part peformance it should be remembered that items of detriment can be wider than potential acts of part peformance as they do not have to be referable to a contract. The categories of detriment are not closed and all acts of the claimant should be considered as potential items of detriment. Similarly, all statements and acts of the owner should be viewed as potential acts of encouragement or acquiescence.

Housekeeper

Elderly relatives

The practical situations in which the doctrine is most likely to be successful are those of an unpaid housekeeper[41] or child looking after elderly relatives[42] who is now the subject of possession proceedings brought by the deceased owner's next-of-kin. The solution is also relevant to deal with the situation of older people who have gone to live with their younger relatives,[43] or vice versa,[44] and who have made capital contributions to either the purchase or extension of the house in which they are living. Proprietary estoppel should also be considered as a possible solution if a mistress has made improvements to the house in which she is living at her own expense.[45]

Mistresses

Proprietary estoppel is unlikely to be of assistance, however, to a mistress who has not remained in the house[46] or who has merely 'kept' a house as opposed to improving

---

[37] See for example *Maddison* v. *Alderson* (1883) 3 App.Cas. 467; see above Chap. 4, Part B, p. 65.

[38] See *Grant* v. *Edwards* [1986] Ch. 638 and Chap. 6, Part C1(c), p. 93.

[39] *Walker* v. *Walker* C.A., unreported, Bound Transcript No. 173, 1984.

[40] *Jones* v. *Watkins* C.A., unreported, November 26, 1987.

[41] *Greasley* v. *Cooke* [1980] 1 W.L.R. 1306; see p. 115.

[42] *Griffiths* v. *Williams* (1977) 248 E.G. 947.

[43] *Re Sharpe (A Bankrupt)* [1980] 1 W.L.R. 219.

[44] *Dodsworth* v. *Dodsworth* (1973) 228 E.G. 1114; see p. 124.

[45] *Pascoe* v. *Turner* [1979] 1 W.L.R. 431; see p. 126.

[46] *Layton* v. *Martin* [1986] 2 F.L.R. 227; see p. 117.

Family situations

it.[47] Similarly, the solution is unlikely to assist a person who has been living with a member of his family if he has not made any capital contributions either in terms of money or work. This will be so even if he has been contributing to joint living expenses and carried out routine repairs.[48] Nor will proprietary estoppel assist a claimant who has done work on property in which he is living without encouragement or consent in any way from the owner; he will simply be regarded as making his life more comfortable than deserving of an interest in the property.[49]

Review

Proprietary estoppel is far from a universal panacea and the court approaches the doctrine with a degree of caution. An important factor in determining the court's use of the doctrine appears to be whether proprietary estoppel is being used as a defence or as a means to claim an interest in property. A review of the cases discussed in this Chapter shows that where property has been shared, the claimant is far more likely to succeed if proprietary estoppel is being used as a defence to a possession action[50] than if it is being used as part of a claim to a greater interest in property.[51] Even when proprietary estoppel is being used as a defence, the court has regard to the need to protect the claimant and elderly single ladies[52] tend to be more successful than younger couples[53] or single men[54] seeking to stay in residential premises.

[47] *Coombes* v. *Smith* [1986] 1 W.L.R. 808; see p. 117.
[48] *Rogers* v. *Eller* C.A., unreported, May 20, 1986; *Griffiths* v. *Williams* (1977) 248 E.G. 947; see p. 119.
[49] *Stillwell* v. *Simpson* (1983) 133 New L.J. 894; see Part B1, p. 113.
[50] See *Greasley* v. *Cooke* [1980] 1 W.L.R. 1306; *Griffiths* v. *Williams* (1977) 248 E.G. 947; *Pascoe* v. *Turner* [1979] 1 W.L.R. 431.
[51] See for example *Jones* v. *Watkins* C.A., unreported, November 26, 1987; *Brinnand* v. *Ewens* (1987) 19 H.L.R. 415.
[52] See the cases cited in n. 50. The court has also indicated that women with small children are more deserving of protection—see *Rogers* v. *Eller* C.A., unreported, May 20, 1986.
[53] See for example *Warnes* v. *Hedley* C.A., unreported, January 31, 1984; *Rogers* v. *Eller* C.A., unreported, May 20, 1986.
[54] See for example *Watts* v. *Story* (1984) 134 New L.J. 631; *Thomas* v. *Fuller-Brown* [1988] 1 F.L.R. 237.

8 THIRD PARTIES

Many informal arrangements for the sharing of residential property cause no problems until a third party becomes involved. This can occur if the owner sells the property or if a mortgagee tries to enforce his security.[1] The non-owner's rights against the third party depend on two factors; first the legal relationship between himself and the owner and any interest he may have in the property and, secondly, the general law in relation to third party rights in land law. The form of the general law will depend upon whether title to the land is registered or unregistered. Whatever the type of property, a claimant's rights will be subject to any pre-exisiting adverse interests in the property, for example, the rights of a mortgagee.

The reader is referred to the standard texts on land law[2] and conveyancing[3] for the detailed law on the enforcement of property rights against third parties. Certain areas of the law relating to both unregistered and registered land can, however, cause particular problems for people sharing residential property and they are considered in detail below together with the special rules relating to spouses. The consequences of the death of the owner and the effect of obtaining a claimant's consent to a transaction are then examined. Finally, the protection of each possible type of interest a claimant may have is considered in the context of both systems of conveyancing.

A.   Unregistered land

Legal and equitable interests
If the title to the land is not registered the legal estates and interests, as defined in Section 1 of the Law of Property Act 1925, will bind a purchaser without notice unless registrable under the Land Charges Act 1972. All other interests are equitable[4] which depend for their validity on registration under the 1972 Act, or if not within that Act, on the doctrine of notice or overreaching. The land charges system presents

[1] For the position in relation to a trustee in bankruptcy see below Chap. 9.
[2] Gray, *Elements of Land Law* (1987); Megarry and Wade, *The Law of Real Property* 5th ed., (1984); Cheshire and Burn, *Modern Law of Real Property* 14th ed., (1988).
[3] Farrand, *Emmett on Title* 19th ed., (1986); Barnsley, *Conveyancing Law and Practice* 3rd ed., (1988); Ruoff and Roper, *The Law and Practice of Registered Conveyancing* 5th ed., (1986).
[4] Law of Property Act 1925, s.1(3).

several traps for a person entering into possession of land informally and the concept of constructive notice can cause problems in certain situations.

1. Land charges

There are three particular matters of concern in relation to registration under the Land Charges Act 1972. The first and most important is the need for the interest to be entered on the register. The second problem arises from the fact that registration must be against the name of the estate owner. Finally, the Act may not be capable of protecting the actual right or interest enjoyed by the non-owner sharing the property.

Strict registration A purchaser will take free of any interest which is capable of being protected by registration if it is not so registered.[5] In the case of some interests, including an estate contract, he must be a purchaser of the legal estate.[6] It is irrelevant that the purchaser has actual knowledge of the claimant's interest,[7] or, indeed, takes specifically subject to it.[8] The rules for the registration of land charges are applied very strictly. The fact that the property is purchased by another member of the family who knew of the arrangement will not protect the claimant against the purchaser if he has not entered his interest on the register. The courts' approach to the protection of land charges can be seen from the speech of Lord Wilberforce in *Midland Bank Trust Co. Ltd.* v. *Green*[9];

> "The case is plain: the Act is clear and definite. Intended as it was to provide a simple and understandable system for the protection of title to land, it should not be read down or glossed: to do so would destroy the usefulness of the Act. Any temptation to remould the Act to meet the facts of the present case, on the supposition that it is a hard one and that justice requires it is, for me at least, removed by the consideration that the Act itself provides a simple and effective protection for persons in Geoffrey's position—*viz.*—by registration."

Occupation not sufficient This strict approach to the Land Charges Act 1972 can cause considerable hardship where arrangements for sharing residential accommodation have been made informally. The claimant will not have been advised at the time and will not only not know how to register but, even worse, will not know that his interest needs protection by registration. He may well have assumed that if he is in occupation he is protected. This is particularly relevant where the claimant has been let into possession following an agreement for the purchase or lease of

---

[5] *Ibid.*, s.199; Land Charges Act 1972, s.4(5)(6).
[6] Land Charges Act 1972, s.4(6); *McCarthy and Stone Ltd.* v. *Hodge (Julian S.) & Co. Ltd.* [1971] 1 W.L.R. 1547.
[7] *Midland Bank Trust Co. Ltd.* v. *Green* [1981] A.C. 513.
[8] *Hollington Bros. Ltd.* v. *Rhodes* [1951] 2 T.L.R. 691.
[9] [1981] A.C. 513, 528.

the property. The registration position, therefore, should always be checked and if a sale is still under negotiation, for example, it may still be possible to protect the claimant. The other effect of a strict application of the rules of registration is that the owner can deliberately convey the property to a close friend or relative in order to defeat the rights of the claimant.[10]

Under the land charges system, registration is against the name of the estate owner and not against the land or estate.[11] The correct name against which to register is the full name of the estate owner as set out in his title deeds.[12] An interest protected by entry against a version of the true name will not be enforceable against a purchaser who searches against the correct name and obtains a clear search certificate.[13] The difficulties which this can cause can be seen from the case of *Diligent Finance Co. Ltd.* v. *Alleyne*[14] which concerned the matrimonial home held in the name of Erskine Owen Alleyne.

Registration against name Mr Alleyne deserted his wife and she registered her statutory right of occupation[15] as a Class F land charge against the name "Erskine Alleyne." Mr Alleyne then negotiated an increased mortgage from the plaintiffs. The Plaintiffs searched against the name "Erskine Owen Alleyne" and received a clear search certificate. The plaintiffs subsequently brought an action for possession and Foster J. held that the plaintiffs' legal charge had priority over Mrs Alleyne's Class F land charge.

Only those interests specified in section 2 of the Land Charges Act 1972 can be protected by registration. Thus an interest arising under a trust for sale is not registrable because it is specifically excluded from the definition of general equitable charge in Class C (iii).[16] The courts are not inclined to widen the class of interests registrable under the land charges system.[17] Thus, some of the rights arising under **Proprietary estoppel** proprietary estoppel do not come within the scope of registration and are dependent on the old rules of notice for protection.[18]

2. Doctrine of notice

Those equitable interests which are not registrable are enforceable against everyone save a bona fide purchaser of the legal estate without notice. The doctrine of notice is important, therefore, in relation to some interests arising by virtue of **Beneficial interests** proprietary estoppel and beneficial interests under a trust for sale which are not overreached because the purchase, or

---

[10] See *Midland Bank Trust Co. Ltd.* v. *Green* [1981] A.C. 513.
[11] Land Charges Act 1972, s.3(1).
[12] *Standard Property Investment plc* v. *British Plastics Federation* (1987) 53 P. & C.R. 25, 32 *per* Walton J.
[13] *Oak Co-operative Building Society* v. *Blackburn* [1968] Ch. 730.
[14] (1971) 23 P. & .C.R. 346.
[15] See below Part C, p. 138.
[16] Land Charges Act 1972, s.2(4).
[17] See *Shiloh Spinners Ltd.* v. *Harding* [1973] A.C. 691.
[18] *Ives (E.R.) Investment Ltd.* v. *High* [1967] 2 Q.B. 379, (easement arising by estoppel); such rights are not overreached, *Shiloh Spinners Ltd.* v. *Harding* [1973] A.C. 691, 721 *per* Lord Wilberforce.

mortgage, money is not paid to two trustees or a trust corporation.[19]

There is no difficulty if the third party has actual notice of the relevant interest but problems can arise where the claimant is relying on constructive notice. A purchaser will be deemed to have notice of the rights and interests of any person, besides the owner, who is in occupation.[20] He will not be bound, however, if on reasonable inquiry the occupier does not reveal the nature and extent of his interest.[21] For a long time it was considered that a wife's occupation of the property could never be constructive notice of any interest she may have as her presence was explainable by her status as wife rather than by her entitlement to an equitable interest.[22] This view has now been seriously doubted and a purchaser may have constructive notice of the equitable interests of any relative living on the premises whether the owner is himself in residence or not.[23]

Wives and relatives

The courts' more liberal approach to the question of constructive notice can be seen from the case of *Kingsnorth Finance Co. Ltd.* v. *Tizard*,[24] although it has been argued that the decision places too great a burden on the purchaser.[25] In that case, the matrimonial home was held in the name of Mr Tizard but his estranged wife had an equitable interest. She did not live at the house but returned during the day to look after the two children and slept there when he was away. Mr Tizard charged the house to the plaintiffs as security for a loan after arranging for the plaintiffs' agent to survey the property when his wife was away and he had removed all traces of her presence. Judge John Finlay Q.C., sitting as a judge of the High Court, held that the plaintiffs had constructive notice of the wife's equitable interest. Notice stemmed from the fact that further enquiries were not made after the surveyor found evidence of occupation by children and he was informed that Mr Tizard, who had described himself as single on the application form, was separated from his wife who was living nearby.

Occupation

B. Registered land

If the title to the land is registered, the claimant's position is governed by the Land Registration Act 1925. That Act sets out a three-fold division of interests; registrable interests, minor

---

[19] Law of Property Act 1925, ss.2(2) and 27(2); see Part F6, p. 150.

[20] *Hunt* v. *Luck* [1902] 1 Ch. 428; *City of London Building Society* v. *Flegg* [1988] 1 A.C. 54, 80 *per* Lord Oliver; section 14 of the Law of Property Act 1925.

[21] See *Midland Bank Ltd.* v. *Farmpride Hatcheries Ltd.* (1980) 260 E.G. 493, the case is still good law on constructive notice although it is now clear that a contractual licence will not bind a third party.

[22] *Caunce* v. *Caunce* [1969] 1 W.L.R. 286.

[23] *Hodgson* v. *Marks* [1971] Ch. 892, 935 *per* Russell L.J.; *Williams & Glyn's Bank Ltd.* v. *Boland* [1981] A.C. 487, 511 *per* Lord Scarman; *Northern Bank Ltd.* v. *Henry* [1981] I.R. 1.

[24] [1986] 1 W.L.R. 783.

[25] [1986] Conv. 283 (Thompson); [1986] All E.R. Rev. 181 (Clarke).

Basic system

interests and overriding interests. Registrable interests, in respect of which title can be granted by the Registrar, consists of freeholds and leaseholds for more than 21 years.[26] Overriding interests are those interests which bind a purchaser irrespective of notice.[27] All other interests are minor interests which require to be protected on the register if they are not to be overridden.[28] A person sharing residential property may have an overriding interest but the provisions are far from clear cut. Similarly, protection of a minor interest is not straightfoward and can cause difficulties where an arrangement has been entered into informally.

1. Overriding interests

Lease

Overriding interests are defined in section 70(1) of the Land Registration Act 1925. The two most relevant in the context of sharing residential property are leases for 21 years or less[29] and the rights of persons in actual occupation.[30] A lease will only be protected in its own right if it is a legal lease[31] and granted at a rent.[32] An agreement for a lease or a lease at no rent may still be protected as an overriding interest if the tenant is in occupation.

Persons in actual occupation

Section 70(1)(g) provides that the following rights are protected regardless of entry on the register;

> "The rights of every person in actual occupation of the land or in receipt of the rents and profits thereof, save where enquiry is made of such person and the rights are not disclosed."[33]

The value of the section, from the point of view of a claimant, can be seen from the case of *Hodgson* v. *Marks*[34] where an elderly widow voluntarily transferred the title to her house to her lodger. She intended that the house should still remain hers and continued to reside there. The lodger then sold the house. It was held that the lodger was a bare trustee and that the purchaser took subject to the widow's beneficial interest because she was in occupation. The claimant will not be protected, however, if he is not in occupation in either of the two ways specified in the section. Thus, where a father allowed his step-daughter to occupy his flat, rent free, neither of them was in occupation.[35]

---

[26] Land Registration Act 1925, s.123 as amended by the Land Registration Act 1986, s.2.
[27] Land Registration Act 1925, ss.3(xvi) and 70.
[28] *Ibid.*, s.3(xv).
[29] *Ibid.*, s.70(1)(k).
[30] *Ibid.*, s.70(1)(g).
[31] *City Permanent Building Society* v. *Miller* [1952] Ch. 840, 853.
[32] The requirement as to no fine was removed by the Land Registration Act 1986, s.4(1)(4).
[33] N.B. Enquiry is to be made of the person with the potential overriding interest and not the registered proprietor, see *Hodgson* v. *Marks* [1971] Ch. 892.
[34] [1971] Ch. 892.
[35] *Strand Securities Ltd.* v. *Caswell* [1965] Ch. 958.

Rights protected

The "rights" which are protected are those which are recognised by the general law as being rights or interests in land; personal rights are not protected.[36] Accordingly, as it has now been established that a contractual licence does not create an interest in land,[37] a contractual licensee will not be able to enforce any rights against a third party simply because he is in occupation. A claimant's occupation will also not protect him against a third party whose interest already has priority under the rules of general land law.[38] Similarly, if the claimant's interest has already been overreached under section 27(2) of the Law of Property Act 1925, he will not be protected by section 70(1)(g). The point was made by Lord Templeman in *City of London Building Society* v. *Flegg*;[39]

Interests overreached

"The right of the respondents to be and remain in actual occupation of Bleak House ceased when the respondents' interests were overreached by the legal charge save in so far as their rights were transferred to the equity of redemption. As persons interested under the trust for sale the respondents had no right to possession as against the appellants and the fact that the respondents were in actual occupation at the date of the legal charge did not create a new right or transfer an old right so as to make the right enforceable against the appellants."

The section does protect an occupier entitled to a beneficial interest where the sale or mortgage is made by a sole owner and it is useful where someone has been allowed into possession under an agreement for a lease or purchase.

The question of whether someone is in "actual occupation" for the purposes of the section is a matter of physical fact. The courts' approach can be seen from Lord Scarman's speech in *Williams & Glyn's Bank Ltd* v. *Boland*[40]

Actual occupation

"I do not, therefore, read the Act of 1925 as requiring the courts to give the words 'actual occupation' in section 70(1)(g) the special meaning for which the appellants contend, namely an occupation, which by its nature necessarily puts a would-be purchaser (or mortgagee) upon notice of a claim adverse to the registered owner. On the contrary, I expect to find—as I do find—that the statute has substituted a plain factual situation for the uncertainties of notice, actual or constructive as the determinant of an overriding interest."

---

[36] *National Provincial Bank Ltd.* v. *Ainsworth* [1965] A.C. 1175, 1261 *per* Lord Wilberforce.

[37] *Ashburn Anstalt* v. *Arnold* [1989] 1 Ch. 1; see above Chap. 2, Part B1, p. 24.

[38] See *Paddington Building Society* v. *Mendelsohn* (1985) 50 P. & C.R. 244, 248 *per* Browne-Wilkinson L.J.; see Part F6(a), p. 151.

[39] [1988] 1 A.C. 54, 73; noted (1987) 103 L.Q.R. 520 (R. J. Smith), (1987) 46 C.L.J. 329 (C. Harpum), [1987] Conv. 451 (W. J. Swadling); see also Thompson, "Dispositions by Trustees for Sale" [1988] Conv. 108.

[40] [1981] A.C. 487, 511; for the problems caused by this decision see *Property Law: The Implications of Williams & Glyn's Bank v. Boland*, Law Commission No. 115, Cmnd. 8636; *Third Report on Land Registration*, Law Commission No. 158, H.C. 269.

Thus a wife or other close relative can be in actual occupation contemporaneously with the owner even if their presence is not immediately obvious.[41]

The exact circumstances of when a person is in actual occupation are still open to question, although it is now clear that continuous and uninterrupted presence is not necessary.

Examples of actual occupation

Thus, a temporary absence caused by a stay in hospital for a few days has been held not to prevent actual occupation.[42] In *Kingsnorth Finance Co. Ltd* v. *Tizard*[43] Mrs Tizard was held to be in occupation of the property although she actually slept elsewhere. Her presence during part of each day to look after the children was sufficient. A liberal approach to the question of actual occupation was taken by the Court of Appeal in *Lloyds Bank plc* v. *Rosset*.[44] In that case a semi-derelict house was purchased in the name of Mr Rosset as the matrimonial home. Mrs Rosset was held to be in actual occupation before she started living in the premises. The presence of the builder as her agent carrying out renovation of the house and Mrs Rosset's daily visits to supervise the work was sufficient.[45]

The House of Lords, however, recently stressed that some degree of permanence and continuity is required. In *Abbey National Building Society* v. *Cann*[46] it was held that the moving of furniture and possessions into the property before the claimant herself actually took up residence was not sufficient to establish actual occupation within section 70(1)(g).

Time for actual occupation

Until recently, it was considered that the relevant time for determining whether a claimant was in actual occupation and, thus, protecting his interest, was the date of registration of the transfer or charge.[47] The House of Lords has now held that the crucial time is the date of completion of the relevant transaction and not the date of registration[48] and, thus, avoided the problem of the "registration gap." Provided that the claimant is in occupation at the relevant time, his interest remains enforceable against that purchaser even if he later leaves the premises.[49]

2. Minor interests

Minor interests are all interests other than registrable interests and overriding interests and include beneficial interests arising

---

[41] See *Kling* v. *Keston Properties Ltd.* (1985) 49 P. & C.R. 212, 222 *per* Vinelott J.

[42] *Chhokar* v. *Chhokar* [1984] F.L.R. 313.

[43] [1986] 1 W.L.R. 783, see the text at n. 24 for the facts of this case, the occupation point is strictly *obiter* as the title to the land was unregistered.

[44] [1989] 1 Ch. 350; noted (1988) 104 L.Q.R. 507 (R. J. Smith), [1988] Conv. 453 (M. P. Thompson); Sparkes, "The Discoverability of Occupiers of Registered Land", [1989] Conv. 342.

[45] The point was not considered in the House of Lords.

[46] [1990] 1 All E.R. 1085, 1101 *per* Lord Oliver.

[47] Cheshire and Burn, *Modern Law of Real Property* 14th ed., (1988), p. 757.

[48] *Abbey National Building Society* v. *Cann* [1990] 1 All E.R. 1085.

[49] *London and Cheshire Insurance Co. Ltd.* v. *Laplagrene Property Co. Ltd.* [1971] Ch. 499.

Definition

under a trust for sale which are capable of being overreached on sale.[50] A purchaser for valuable consideration will take free of minor interests unless they are entered on the register.[51] Whilst it is possible for an interest to be both a minor and an overriding interest at the same time,[52] a claimant may fail to satisfy the criteria for an overriding interest at the relevant time, for example, because he is not in actual occupation. Accordingly, unless a claimant has a purely personal right such as a bare licence, his interest should be protected by an entry on the register. The two methods available to a claimant to protect his interest are a notice and a caution.

Entry on register

In *Williams & Glyn's Bank Ltd* v. *Boland*[53] Lord Wilberforce emphasised[54] that the only form of notice which was relevant was entry on the register. The basic rule is that actual notice of the claimant's interest by a third party provides no protection.[55] In two exceptional situations, the courts have allowed minor interests to be enforced even though they were not protected by entry on the register. However, neither the possibility of the purchaser being in bad faith nor a constructive trust should be relied upon.

Lack of good faith

The first exception arose from the case of *Peffer* v. *Rigg*[56] where two brothers-in-law purchased a house for their joint mother-in-law. The house was conveyed into the name of Mr Rigg alone although it was agreed that Mr Peffer had a beneficial half share. Mr Peffer's interest was not protected by entry on the register. The property was then sold by Mr Rigg to Mrs Rigg on their divorce for £1. Graham J. held[57] that a purchaser[58] took free of an unregistered interest only if he was in good faith and Mr Rigg failed to satisfy this criterion because he had clear knowledge of Mr Peffer's equitable interest. This decision has been critised[59] and was not followed in *Burr* v. *Copp*.[60]

Constructive trust

The second ground of Graham J.'s decision was that Mrs Rigg was bound by the equitable interest because she took the property on a constructive trust.[61] This second ground was also used in *Lyus* v. *Prowsa Developments Ltd*[62] to enforce an unregistered minor interest. In that case, the purchaser took the property expressly subject to the plaintiff's estate contract. This exception to the need for registration is very limited and will only be applied in the clearest cases. The point was made

[50] Land Registration Act 1925, s.3(xv).
[51] *Ibid.*, s.20(1)(4).
[52] *Williams & Glyn's Bank Ltd.* v. *Boland* [1981] A.C. 487, 507 *per* Lord Wilberforce.
[53] [1981] A.C. 487.
[54] *Ibid.*, 504.
[55] *De Lusignan* v. *Johnson* (1973) 230 E.G. 499.
[56] [1977] 1 W.L.R. 285.
[57] *Ibid.*, 294.
[58] Land Registration Act 1925, s.3(xxi), *cf.* s.20 which contains no reference to "good faith."
[59] Hayton, "Purchases of Registered Land" [1977] C.L.J. 227; Martin, "Constructive Trusts of Registered Land" [1978] Conv. 52.
[60] [1983] C.L.Y. 2057.
[61] [1977] 1 W.L.R. 285, 294; see above Chap. 5, Part A, p. 71.
[62] [1982] 1 W.L.R. 1044.

by Fox L.J. in *Ashburn Anstalt* v. *Arnold*[63] after agreeing with the actual decision in *Lyus* v. *Prowsa Developments Ltd*[62];

> "The court will not impose a constructive trust unless it is satisfied that the conscience of the estate owner is affected. The mere fact that land is expressed to be conveyed 'subject to' a contract does not necessarily imply that the grantee is to be under an obligation, not otherwise existing, to give effect to the provision of the contract."

Notice

The more effective method of protection for most interests[64] is a notice which makes all dispositions subject to the right or interest entered on the register.[65] A notice, however, will not convert an invalid claim into a valid interest in the property.[66] The difficulty about entering a notice, from a claimant's point of view, is that the land certificate must be lodged at the Land Registry for the notice to be entered.[67] Entry of a notice, thus, requires the co-operation of the owner unless the land certificate is already deposited at the Land Registry because there is a prior registered charge.[68] A lease at a rent without taking a fine[69] and a spouse's statutory rights of occupation under the Matrimonial Homes Act 1983[70] are two exceptional rights which can be protected by notice without lodgement of the Land Certificate.

Caution

If the owner will not co-operate, the only way a claimant can protect his interest is by lodging a caution against dealings. This can be entered without production of the Land Certificate[71] but a statutory declaration specifying the interest requiring protection must be lodged.[72] That interest must be a minor interest in land and includes an interest under a trust for sale[73] and a pending land action.[74] If the property is subject to a registered charge, the caution should be registered against the proprietor of the charge as well as the proprietor of the land to affect dispositions by the chargee.[75]

Limited protection

A caution does not make a claimant's interest automatically binding on a purchaser or mortgagee but merely gives the claimant a right to object to any subsequent dealings with the property. The cautioner is given notice of an intended transaction by the Registrar and the caution will be cancelled if the cautioner does nothing. The interest will only be protected if the cautioner shows cause to the Registrar why the caution

---

[63] [1989] 1 Ch. 1, 25.
[64] Land Registration Act, s.49(1).
[65] *Ibid.*, s.52(1).
[66] *Ibid.*, s.52(2).
[67] *Ibid.*, s.64(1)(c); the entry of a joint proprietorship restriction under s.58(3) suffers from the same difficulty.
[68] *Ibid.*, s.65.
[69] *Ibid.*, s.64(1)(c).
[70] *Ibid.*, s.64(5).
[71] *Ibid.*, s.54. A caution against first registration under s.53 is registered if title to the land is not yet registered.
[72] Land Registration Rules 1925, r. 215(4).
[73] *Elias* v. *Mitchell* [1972] Ch. 652.
[74] Land Registration Act 1925, s.59(1).
[75] Ruoff and Roper, *The Law and Practice of Registered Conveyancing* 5th ed., (1986), p. 825.

should continue to have effect or why the dealing should not be registered before the period of notice expires.[76] The registered proprietor can make the cautioner prove his claim before any dealing takes place by requiring the Registrar to operate the 'warning-off' procedure.[77] This similarly requires the cautioner to prove his case to the Registrar within a period of notice. Any dispute about a caution is adjudicated upon by the Registrar or the court.[78]

A further limitation on the effectiveness of a caution is that the Registrar takes the view that the function of a caution is to afford temporary and not permanent protection. If the claim is in dispute he will remove the caution unless the cautioner institutes legal proceedings.[79] The court takes a similar robustness of approach to cautions and will look favourably on an application by way of motion to vacate a caution where there are no substantial grounds for supporting the registration.[80] A caution will be entered on the register, however, whilst any appeal against an order to vacate the caution is in process.[81]

Thus, unless the claimant has a clear interest in the property a caution will provide no more than temporary protection unless he is prepared to take legal proceedings against the owner to establish his claim. A further barrier to the use of a caution is section 56(3) of the Land Registration Act 1925 which provides that if a claimant registers a caution without reasonable cause he may be liable in damages to anyone who suffers loss as a result of the registration.

C.   Spouses

Matrimonial Homes Act 1983

A spouse who does not have a legal estate in the matrimonial home has certain statutory rights of occupation under the Matrimonial Homes Act 1983.[82] They consist of a right not to be evicted or excluded and, if not in occupation, a right, with the leave of the court, to re-enter and occupy the home.[83] These statutory rights are independent from, and in addition to, any equitable interest the spouse may have in the property.[84] A spouse can enforce the statutory rights of occupation against a third party by registration. In view of the difficulties and uncertainties attached to both establishing an equitable interest and in enforcing that interest against third parties, the statutory rights should always be registered where the claimant is married to the owner of the property.

[76] Land Registration Act 1925, s.55.
[77] Land Registration Rules 1925, r. 218.
[78] For the division of responsibility see Ruoff and Roper, *The Law and Practice of Registered Conveyancing* 5th ed., (1986), pp. 828–829.
[79] Hayton, *Registered Land* 3rd ed., (1981), p. 27; Ruoff and Roper, *The Law and Practice of Registered Conveyancing* 5th ed., (1986), pp. 814 *et seq.*
[80] *Rawlplug Co. Ltd.* v. *Kamvale Properties Ltd.* (1968) 20 P. & C.R. 32, 40, *per* Megarry J.; *Alpenstow* v. *Regalian Properties plc* [1985] 1 W.L.R. 721, 727 *per* Nourse J.
[81] *Belcourt* v. *Belcourt* [1989] 1 W.L.R. 195.
[82] Section 1(1); see Thompson, *Co-ownership* (1988), pp. 71 *et seq.*
[83] Section 1(1).
[84] Section 1(11).

In the case of unregistered land, the statutory rights are
Protection of protected by registering a Class F land charge.[85] If the title to
rights the land is registered, the rights are protected as a minor
interest by entering a notice on the relevant title[86]; deposit of
the land certificate is not required.[87] Registration is in many
instances effective to stop a proposed sale of the matrimonial
home.[88] The court will remove the registration, however, if the
purpose behind it was not to protect the spouse's occupation
but to freeze the proceeds of sale.[89] Also, on a spouse's
application under section 1(3) of the 1983 Act for a declaration
as to her rights of occupation, the court will take into account
the circumstances of the purchaser and may dismiss the
application.[90]

Additional protection against a mortgagee is given by
section 1(5) of the 1983 Act which provides that mortgage
payments made by the non-owning spouse have to be accepted
Mortgagees by the mortgagee. Also, if the statutory rights of occupation
have been registered, a mortgagee must give the non-owning
spouse notice of any action to enforce the mortgage and that
spouse has a right to be made a party to the action.[91]

D. Death

The death of the owner will often cause problems for any
person sharing residential accommodation because, whilst the
owner may have been content for the sharer to remain in
occupation, his personal representatives may want to sell the
premises with vacant possession. The personal representatives,
however, take the property subject to the liabilities of the
deceased owner and the claimant can assert the same rights to
an interest in the property against the personal representatives
Deceased owner's as he could have asserted against the owner. It is possible that
will the owner may have made provision for the claimant to remain
in occupation and the terms of any will should be ascertained.

Special provisions[92] apply if the owner's interest in the
property was a statutory tenancy under the Rent Act 1977 or
Tenancies an assured tenancy under the Housing Act 1988.[93] Even if the
sharer has been left the owner's interest by will, he will only be
able to succeed to the tenancy if he satisfies the relevant

---

[85] Land Charges Act 1925, s.2(1)(7).
[86] Matrimonial Homes Act 1983, s.2(8)(*a*); the rights may not be protected by
entry of a caution, *ibid.*, s.2(9) nor are they an overriding interest, *ibid.*,
s.2(8)(*b*).
[87] Land Registration Act 1925, s.64(5).
[88] See *Wroth* v. *Tyler* [1974] Ch. 30.
[89] *Barnett* v. *Hassett* [1981] 1 W.L.R. 1385.
[90] *Kaur* v. *Gill* [1988] 2 Fam. 110.
[91] Matrimonial Homes Act 1983, s.8; for the power of the court to adjourn
possession proceedings brought by a mortgagee see Administration of Justice
Act 1970, s.36 and Administration of Justice Act 1973, s.38.
[92] For the law applying if the tenant owner died prior to the commencement of
the Housing Act 1988 see Yates and Hawkins, *Landlord and Tenant Law* 2nd
ed., (1986) pp. 438 *et seq.*
[93] Assured tenancies under the Housing Act 1980 are converted into assured
tenancies under the 1988 Act, Housing Act 1988, s.1(3).

statutory provisions.[94] If the owner had a statutory tenancy
under the Rent Act 1977, a surviving spouse or a person living
with the tenant as his or her wife or husband and occupying
the premises can succeed to a statutory tenancy.[95] Thus, a
cohabitee can now succeed automatically without having to
show membership of the family. In the absence of a surviving
Statutory spouse or a *de facto* spouse, a member of the deceased tenant's
succession family who has been living with him for at least two years can
succeed to an assured tenancy[96] under the 1988 Act. A
claimant will probably only succeed in the latter case if he
can show a legal relationship by blood or marriage to the
tenant.[97] For example, a young man was not allowed to
succeed to the statutory tenancy of an older woman with whom
he had lived in a platonic relationship for eighteen years[98] and
a *de facto* "sister" relationship for 45 years has similarly been
held to be insufficient to allow succession.[99]

In the case of an assured tenancy under the 1988 Act,
there is only a right of succession to a surviving spouse or a *de
facto* spouse occupying the premises as his or her only or
principal home where the deceased himself was not a
successor.[1] The landlord has a mandatory ground of
possession[2] on the death of the tenant who does not leave a
resident spouse and, thus, any continuing possession by the
claimant will be at the discretion of the landlord.

E. Consents

Following the widening of the circumstances in which the
presence of a person on the property will give constructive
notice of any interest he may have[3] and the liberal approach to
the question of "actual occupation" for the purposes of section
70(1)(*g*) of the Land Registration Act 1925,[4] a third party will
often ask the owner whether anyone else is in residence. If
there are others in occupation, he will then seek their consent
to the transaction. This is not, however, a foolproof method of
Limitations of protection for a third party for two reasons. First, if the title to
consents the land is registered, only enquiry of, and denial by, the
owner of an adverse interest will protect the third party. This is
so even if that person is not obviously in occupation; the fact
that his presence was not revealed by the owner is irrelevant.[5]
Secondly, the consent may be vitiated for undue influence,
particularly if it has been obtained by a mortgagee.

---

[94] *Moodie* v. *Hosegood* [1952] A.C. 61.
[95] Housing Act 1988, s.39(2) Sched. 4, para. 2.
[96] *Ibid.*, Sched. 4, para. 3; for the position if the owner is a surviving spouse
of an original tenant see Sched. 4, para. 6.
[97] See *Ross* v. *Collins* [1964] 1 W.L.R. 425.
[98] *Carega Properties S.A.* v. *Sharratt* [1979] 1 W.L.R. 928.
[99] *Sefton Holdings* v. *Cairns* [1988] 14 E.G. 58.
[1] Housing Act 1988, s.17(1).
[2] *Ibid.*, s.7 Sched. 2, Ground 7.
[3] See above Part A2, p. 131.
[4] See above Part B1, p. 133.
[5] See above Part B1, p. 133 and *Hodgson* v. *Marks* [1971] Ch. 892.

Mortgagees

Test of manifest disadvantage

Undue influence

Kings North Trust Ltd.v. Bell

The relationship between a mortgagee and an occupier whose consent is sought does not, of itself, raise a vitiating element of undue influence. The court will only set aside the transaction if it constitutes a manifest and unfair disadvantage to the person seeking to avoid it.[6] The test of manifest disadvantage is applied at the date the mortgage transaction is entered into.[7] If the mortgagor and the claimant are related and have joint finances, what is prima facie an onerous mortgage may not be to the manifest disadvantage of the consenting claimant if that is the only way the family finances can be rescued.[8]

If a mortgagee entrusts the obtaining of the claimant's signature to the consent document to a member of the family who may be expected to have influence over the consentor, the mortgagee will be liable as principal for any undue influence exerted by their agent.[9] The consent will stand, however, if the mortgagee has not expressly or impliedly constituted a member of the family his agent, even if undue influence has in fact been exercised over the consentor by an interested member of the family.[10]

The potential problems and limitations of obtaining consent to the proposed transaction from known occupiers with an interest in the property can be seen from the case of *Kings North Trust Ltd* v. *Bell*.[11] In that case the husband was the sole legal owner of the matrimonial home which he mortgaged to the plaintiffs. His wife had a beneficial interest in the property and the plaintiffs made her a party to the mortgage deed to obtain priority for their mortgage over her interest. The plaintiffs' solicitor sent the mortgage documents to the husband's solicitors who entrusted him to obtain his wife's signature to the deed. The husband failed to tell his wife the true purpose of the loan and the Court of Appeal refused to enforce the mortgage against the wife. The plaintiffs became liable for the husband's fraudulent representations. The judgment of Dillon L.J. contains valuable guidance[12];

> "The moral is that where a creditor (or intending lender) desires the protection of a guarantee or charge on property from a third party other than the debtor and the circumstances are such that the debtor could be expected to have influence over that third party, the creditor ought for his own protection to insist that the third party has independent advice.[13] That is the obvious means of

---

[6] *National Westminster Bank plc* v. *Morgan* [1985] A.C. 686; *Midland Bank plc* v. *Shephard* [1988] 3 All E.R. 17, noted [1989] Conv. 63 (Dale); *Bank of Credit and Commerce International S.A.* v. *Aboody* [1989] 2 W.L.R. 759.

[7] *Woodstead Finance Ltd.* v. *Petrou* (1986) 136 New L.J. 188; *cf. Midland Bank plc* v. *Phillips* [1986] *The Times*, March 28.

[8] *Ibid.*

[9] *Avon Finance Co. Ltd.* v. *Bridger* [1985] 2 All E.R. 281; see also *Barclays Bank plc* v. *Kennedy* (1989) 21 H.L., 132.

[10] *Colundell Ltd.* v. *Gallon* [1986] 1 Q.B. 1184 (as the mortgagee appointed solicitor agents, the son's influence over his elderly parents was irrelevant).

[11] [1986] 1 W.L.R. 119.

[12] *Ibid.*, 125.

[13] There is no need, however, to ensure that independent advice is actually obtained, *Colundell Ltd.* v. *Gallon* [1986] 1 Q.B. 1184, 1201 *per* Oliver L.J.

avoiding the risk that the creditor will be held to have left it to the debtor to procure the execution of the relevant guarantee or security document by the third party."

A mortgagee probably has no general duty to explain the nature of the transaction unless the person whose consent is sought is actually a customer of a bank mortgagee.[14] If the mortgagee does take it upon himself to explain the legal effect of the mortgage[15] and consent, he will be liable in negligence to the consentor if he omits to make a full explanation. Thus, a consentor may still have an action in damages against a mortgagee even if the transaction itself has not been set aside for undue influence.[16]

Explanation of transaction

F. Individual rights and remedies

Not all the potential rights and remedies available to a person sharing residential property provide protection against third parties, a bare licence, for example, is a purely personal arrangement with the licensor. The claimant need not have an interest in land, however, to gain a measure a protection; a loan may be protected by a charging order. The extent to which most interests are protected against third parties is now clear although, in the case of beneficial interests under a trust for sale, occasionally with harsh results. The one area in which the relationship between the claimant and third parties is not settled is that of proprietary estoppel.

1. Loans

A person intending to share residential premises will sometimes make a loan of a capital sum to the owner to assist with the purchase of the property.[17] Alternatively, a loan may be made to pay for alterations to the premises or for an extension to be built to provide suitable accommodation for the lender. Such a loan does not normally create a beneficial interest in the property under either a constructive[18] or a resulting trust.[19] The relationship between the owner and the claimant is the personal one of debtor and creditor. The creditor can, however, by obtaining a charging order against the property convert his personal contract into what amounts to a proprietary interest and gain protection against third parties. Even if the claimant has been granted an equitable licence to remain in occupation until the loan is repaid,[20] a charging order should still be

Personal contract

Charging order

---

[14] *Cornish* v. *Midland Bank plc* [1985] 3 All E.R. 513, 522 *per* Kerr L.J.
[15] In the case of a bank mortgagee, crosses the line between a normal banking transaction and going further and giving advice on more general matters germane to the wisdom of the transaction, *National Westminster Bank plc* v. *Morgan* [1985] A.C. 686, 708–709 *per* Lord Scarman.
[16] *Cornish* v. *Midland Bank plc* [1985] 3 All E.R. 513; *Midland Bank plc* v. *Perry* [1988] 1 F.L.R. 161.
[17] See, for example, *Potter* v. *Gyles* C.A., unreported, October 10, 1986.
[18] *Re Sharpe* [1980] 1 W.L.R. 219; see above Chap. 5, Part B3, p. 76.
[19] *Aveling* v. *Knipe* (1815) 19 Ves. 441; see above Chap. 6, Part B1, p. 85.
[20] See above Chap. 2, Part C, p. 35.

considered because of the doubts surrounding the enforcement of equitable licences against third parties.[21]

As a first step, the claimant should issue proceedings against the debtor for repayment of the loan and obtain judgment. The claimant can then apply to the court[22] for a charging order under the Charging Orders Act 1979 for the purpose of enforcing the judgment.[23] The charging order can relate to any land held by the debtor including an interest under a trust for sale.[24] This means, for example, that if a mother makes a loan to her son alone for the purpose of building a "granny flat" on a house he owns jointly with his wife, the mother can secure the loan by a charging order on his beneficial interest if family disharmony breaks out and she is forced to leave. The original application, if successful, will lead to an order *nisi* to be followed by an order absolute after the judgment debtor has been given an opportunity to state his case.[25]

Charging Orders Act 1979

The creditor does not have an automatic right to a charging order, the court has a discretion. By section 1(5) of the Charging Orders Act 1979 the court is directed to have regard to all the circumstances of the case and, in particular, the personal circumstances of the debtor and whether any other creditors would be likely to be unduly prejudiced by the order. If only the debtor and the creditor are involved, the creditor is entitled to expect that a charging order will be made in his favour; the burden is on the debtor to show cause why the order should not be made absolute.[26] If there are other creditors, the court has to be satisfied that it is proper to place that creditor at an advantage over the other creditors. Where the debtor is, or is about to become insolvent, an order is unlikely to be made.[27] Even if there is only one creditor, the scales are not tipped so firmly in his favour if the property to be charged is the legal estate or an equitable interest in a matrimonial home. In that case, the court has to strike a balance between the normal expectation of the creditor and the hardship to the wife and children if an order is made.[28]

Courts' discretion

When dealing with a creditor seeking a charging order on a matrimonial home, relevant circumstances in section 1(5) include the position of the creditor. The court recognises that all judgment creditors are not faceless corporations and will consider available evidence of any hardship the creditor would

Matrimonial home

---

[21] See below Part 2(c), p. 147.

[22] County Court for debts up to £5,000, County Courts Jurisdiction Order 1981, S.I. 1981 No. 1123.

[23] Charging Orders Act 1979. s.1.

[24] *Ibid.*, s.2(1); *National Westminster Bank Ltd.* v. *Stockman* [1981] 1 W.L.R. 67.

[25] For the detailed procedure see R.S.C., Ord. 50 and C.C.R., Ord. 31; Thompson, *Co-ownership* (1988), p. 99.

[26] *Roberts Petroleum Ltd.* v. *Kenny (Bernard) Ltd.* [1982] 1 W.L.R. 301, 307 *per* Brandon L.J.; *First National Securities Ltd.* v. *Hegerty* [1985] Q.B. 850, 866 *per* Sir Denys Buckley.

[27] *Rainbow* v. *Moorgate Properties Ltd.* [1975] 1 W.L.R. 788.

[28] *Harman* v. *Glencross* [1986] Fam. 81, 104 *per* Fox L.J.; noted [1986] Conv. 129 (Warburton).

suffer if the charging was not granted or its enforcement unduly postponed.[29] This is particularly important in family arrangements where the money loaned may well have been a large proportion of the creditor's savings. Repayment of the loan could be the difference between a lonely bedsit and the purchase of a warden controlled flat for an elderly relative who no longer wishes to reside with the debtor/owner. The court will also take account of the fact that the creditor could have asked for a charge on the property when the money was lent in the first place.[30] In relation to other members of the family resident in the property, relevant circumstances include the wife's ability to register her statutory rights of occupation[31] and whether enforcement of the charge would leave sufficient funds to rehouse the wife and children.[32]

Where a charging order is sought against a matrimonial home, the court's decision will also depend on whether there are any matrimonial proceedings in existence. If no matrimonial proceedings are pending when the creditor seeks a charging order, he will probably be successful,[33] although enforcement of the order may be postponed until children of the owner cease full-time education.[34] If matrimonial proceedings have been commenced, the application will usually be transferred to the Family Division.[35] The court's approach in that instance appears from the judgment of Balcombe L.J. in *Harmon* v. *Glencross*[36];

Courts' approach

> "The court should first consider whether the value of the equity in the house is sufficient to enable the charging order to be made absolute and realised at once, as in *Llewellin* v. *Llewellin* (unreported),[37] even though that may result in the wife and children being housed at a lower standard than they might reasonably have expected had only the husband's interests been taken into account against them. Failing that, the court should make only such order as may be necessary to protect the wife's right to occupy (with the children where appropriate) the matrimonial home. The normal course should then be to postpone the sale of the house for such period only as may be requisite to protect the right of occupation—a *Mesher*[38] type of order—again bearing in mind that the court is holding the balance, not between the wife and the husband, but between the wife and the judgment creditor."

The effect of a successful application is to impose on the specified property of the debtor a charge securing payment of

[29] *Ibid.*, 93 *per* Balcombe L.J.
[30] *Ibid.*, 98 *per* Balcombe L.J.
[31] *Ibid.*, 94 *per* Balcombe L.J.; see Part C, p. 138.
[32] *Ibid.*, 94 *per* Balcombe L.J.; 104 *per* Fox L.J.
[33] *Ibid.*, 99 *per* Balcombe L.J.
[34] *Ibid.*, 104 *per* Fox L.J.; *Austin-Fell* v. *Austin-Fell* [1989] 2 F.L.R. 497.
[35] *Ibid.*, 99 *per* Balcombe L.J.
[36] [1986] Fam. 81, 99.
[37] [1985] C.A. Bound Transcript 640.
[38] *Mesher* v. *Mesher and Hall* [1980] 1 All E.R. 126.

Secured debt

the money due.[39] What was a personal contract thus becomes a secure debt which has proprietary characteristics. The order is not final, however, as it can be discharged or varied by the court on the application of the debtor or of any person interested in the property.[40] "A person interested" includes anyone with an equitable interest in the property and a wife with a statutory right of occupation.[41]

Registration

Protection against third parties is available to the creditor by registration.[42] If title to the land is unregistered, the charging order should be registered against the debtor's name in the register of writs and orders affecting land under the Land Charges Act 1972.[43] In the case of registered land, the charging order may be protected by the entry of a notice.[44] If this is not possible because the debtor will not co-operate by depositing the land certificate at the Registry or there is no registered charge in existence, the charge should be protected by registering a caution against dealings.[45] Where the claimant has remained in occupation of the premises, the charging order will be protected as an overriding interest without the need for any entry on the Register.[46] In the one instance of a charge on a beneficial interest under a trust for sale of unregistered land, the charging order cannot be protected by registration because an undivided share is not land for the purposes of the Land Charges Act 1972.[47] In that situation, the charge depends for protection against third parties on the old rules of notice. The creditor should give written notice to the trustees under section 137 of the law of Property Act 1925 to retain priority in the proceeds of sale.

Enforcement

A charging order can be enforced "in the same manner as an equitable charge created by the debtor by writing under his hand."[48] The remedy of the creditor is, therefore, to apply to the court for an order for sale of the property charged[49] or for the appointment of a receiver. If the charging order affects an equitable interest under a trust for sale, the debtor can apply as "a person interested" for the sale of the whole property, and not just the equitable interest, under section 30 of the Law of Property Act 1925.[50] The court exercises its discretion in the usual way on the section 30 application having regard to

---

[39] Charging Orders Act 1979, s.1(1).
[40] *Ibid.*, s.3(5).
[41] *Harman* v. *Glencross* [1986] Fam. 81, 90 *per* Balcombe L.J.
[42] Charging Orders Act 1979, s.3(2).
[43] Section 6(1)(*a*).
[44] Land Registration Act 1925, s. 49(1)(*g*).
[45] *Ibid.*, s.59; see above Part B2, p. 135.
[46] *Ibid.*, s.70(1)(*g*); see above Part B1, p. 133.
[47] *Perry* v. *Phoenix Assurance plc* [1988] 1 W.L.R. 940, noted [1989] Conv. 133 (Price); this decision would appear to conflict with *Harman* v. *Glencross* [1986] Fam. 81 and *Midland Bank plc* v. *Pike* [1988] 2 All E.R. 434 holding, respectively, that a person entitled to a charge on an undivided share is a "person interested" for the purposes of Charging Orders Act 1979, s.3(5) and Law of Property Act 1925, s.30.
[48] Charging Orders Act 1979, s.3(4).
[49] *Matthews* v. *Goodday* (1861) 31 L.J.Ch. 282; see Baker and Langan, *Snell's Principles of Equity* 28th ed., (1982), p. 441.
[50] *Midland Bank plc* v. *Pike* [1988] 2 All E.R. 434.

whether any original purpose of the trust for sale is still in existence.[51]

2.   Licences

In general, licences are personal rights which only rarely provide protection against the actions of third parties. Even where licences do have proprietary characteristics, as in the case of equitable licences, they are not enforceable against all third parties.

Personal right

(a)   **Bare licences**   A bare licence is never more than a purely personal right. Indeed, a bare licence terminates automatically on the transfer of the relevant property by the licensor to a purchaser.[52] Thus, a bare licence provides no protection for a person sharing residential property against third parties.

No proprietary interest

(b)   **Contractual licences**   It is now clear that a contractual licence does not create an interest in land.[53] There is, therefore, no proprietary interest which can directly affect third parties.[54] The claimant is not, however, completely without remedy in all cases where persons other than the licensor become involved. The contract giving rise to the licence is binding upon any assignee of the licensor[55] and his personal representatives after his death.[56] If the licensee loses his right to occupy the land because of the intervention of a third party,

Original licensor

for example, on a sale of the property, the original licensor will remain liable in damages if the termination of the licence was in breach of the terms of the contract.[57]

Constructive trust

Although a contractual licence is not a proprietary interest, such a licence may bind a purchaser by means of a constructive trust. A constructive trust will only be imposed in very limited circumstances where the conscience of the purchaser is clearly affected.[58] A contractual licensee will only be able to resist a possession action by a purchaser if the purchaser specifically agreed to continue to give effect to the licence. Thus, if the facts of *Binions* v. *Evans*[59] were to be repeated, Mrs. Evans would be able to enforce her licence against the purchasers by means of a constructive trust. Even if the court is not prepared to impose a constructive trust, a purchaser who takes with notice of a contractual licence may be liable in damages for the

---

[51] *Re Holliday* [1981] Ch. 405, 415 *per* Buckley L.J.; see above Chap. 6, Part D1, p. 104 and below Chap. 9, Part B2, p. 165.
[52] *Terunnanse* v. *Terunnanse* [1986] A.C. 1086, 1095–1096 *per* Lord Devlin; see above Chap. 2, Part A2, p. 22.
[53] See above Chap. 2, Part B1, p. 24.
[54] *Ashburn Anstalt* v. *Arnold* [1989] 1 Ch. 1, 22 *per* Fox L.J.
[55] *Clore* v. *Theatrical Properties Ltd.* [1936] 3 All E.R. 483, 490 *per* Lord Wright M.R.; see Dawson and Pearce, *Licences relating to the use and occupation of land* (1979), pp. 133 *et seq.*
[56] See *Horrocks* v. *Forray* [1976] 1 W.L.R. 230, 234.
[57] *King* v. *David Allen & Sons, Billposting Ltd.* [1916] 2 A.C. 54; see above Chap. 2, Part B4(a), p. 31.
[58] *Ashburn Anstalt* v. *Arnold* [1989] 1 Ch. 1, 25 *per* Fox L.J.; see above Chap. 5, Part B4, p. 77.
[59] [1972] Ch. 359; see above Chap. 5, Part A2, p. 73 the text at n. 20 for the facts of this case; see also *Ashburn Anstalt* v. *Arnold* [1989] 1 Ch. 1, 23 *per* Fox L.J.

tort of interference with existing contractual rights if he seeks
to terminate the licence.[60]

(c) Equitable licences   The extent to which an equitable
licence arising from proprietary estoppel[61] provides protection

Proprietary   against the actions of third parties is not clear. It is now
characteristics   accepted that an equitable licence has some proprietary
characteristics and that it can bind a volunteer such as a trustee
in bankruptcy.[62] There has, as yet, been no case where an
equitable licence has been held to bind a purchaser for value
and it has been suggested[63] that only a purchaser with express
notice would be bound. Whatever the extent of the proprietary
characteristics of an equitable licence, it will not bind a third
party automatically and the licensee should take steps to protect
his interest.

   If title to the land is unregistered, the licence cannot be
protected by registration as an equitable licence is not within
the list of registrable interests in section 2 of the Land Charges
Act 1972. Protection is, therefore, given by the old

Notice   rules of notice. The claimant should take all possible steps to
bring his licence to the attention of potential third parties.
Simply being in occupation may not be sufficient to enforce his
licence against a purchaser for value.

   If title to the land is registered, it would appear[64] that an
equitable licence can be protected as a minor interest by entry

Registration   on the register of a notice or caution.[65] As an equitable licence
has proprietary characteristics, it should also be capable of
being protected as an overriding interest[66] under section
70(1)(g) of the Land Registration Act 1925 if the licensee is in
occupation.[67]

   It has been held that an irrevocable licence for life makes
the licensee a tenant for life under the Settled Land Act

Irrevocable   1925.[68] This has, however, been seriously doubted as giving
licence for life   the licensee far greater powers than would be intended by the
parties.[69] If a licensee is held to be a tenant for life, his
protection would flow from his holding of the legal estate.[70]

---

[60] *Binions* v. *Evans* [1972] Ch. 359, 371 *per* Megaw L.J.; see also Dawson and
Pearce, *Licences relating to the use and occupation of land* (1979), p. 161; R. J.
Smith, "Licences and Constructive Trusts—The law is what it ought to be"
[1973] C.L.J. 123, 136; Briggs, "Contractual Licences: A Reply" [1983]
Conv. 285, 290.
[61] For the position under proprietary estoppel before the court declares how
the equity is to be satisfied, see below Part 7, p. 156.
[62] *Re Sharpe (A Bankrupt)* [1980] 1 W.L.R. 219; see above Chap. 2, Part C2,
p. 37.
[63] *Ibid.*, 226 *per* Browne-Wilkinson J.; see also *Pascoe* v. *Turner* [1979] 1
W.L.R. 431, 439 *per* Cumming-Bruce L.J.
[64] See Ruoff and Roper, *The Law and Practice of Registered Conveyancing* 5th
ed., (1986), pp. 811, 818.
[65] See above Part B2, p. 135.
[66] See above Part B1, p. 133.
[67] See Ruoff and Roper, *The Law and Practice of Registered Conveyancing* 5th
ed., (1986), pp. 117–118.
[68] *Bannister* v. *Bannister* [1948] 2 All E.R. 133; *Binions* v. *Evans* [1972] Ch.
359 *per* Megaw and Stephenson L.JJ.; see also *Ungurian* v. *Lesnoff* [1989] 3
W.L.R. 840.
[69] *Binions* v. *Evans* [1972] Ch. 359, 366 *per* Lord Denning M.R.; *Dodsworth* v.
Dodsworth (1973) 228 E.G. 1115; *Griffiths* v. *Williams* (1977) 248 E.G. 947.
[70] Settled Land Act 1925, ss.4, 13.

Mortgage priority

There is one important limitation on the rights of an equitable licensee. If the licence was granted at the time the property was purchased and the property was being purchased with the assistance of a mortgage, the licensee's interest will be subject to the rights of the mortgagee. Thus, in *Bristol and West Building Society* v. *Henning*[71] Mrs. Henning's irrevocable licence to remain in the house she shared with her lover was unenforceable against the building society because the mortgage was granted to her lover to enable him to purchase the property with her full knowledge and approval.[72]

3. Leases

Legal estate

A lease is a legal estate, however short in duration,[73] and the lessee's protection against third parties flows from the fact that he has a right *in rem*. If title to the land is unregistered, a lease binds any third party without notice. In the case of registered land, a lease for 21 years or less is an overriding interest.[74] A lease for more than 21 years is the subject of substantive registration.[75]

Agreement for a lease

If the claimant has an agreement for a lease, as opposed to a lease, his interest will be an equitable one which will require protection by registration. In the case of unregistered land, the agreement must be registered as a C(iv) land charge under the Land Charges Act 1972.[76] If title to the land is registered, the agreement should be protected by the entry of a notice or caution on the Register.[77] An agreement for a lease is not protected as an overriding interest in its own right under section 70(1)(k)[78] but the agreement will bind a third party as an overriding interest virtue of section 70(1)(g) if the claimant is in occupation.[79]

Tenancy by estoppel

It is irrelevant between, the original owner and the tenant, whether the owner had power to grant the relevant lease because both parties are prevented from denying the validity of the creation of the tenancy.[80] Whilst such a tenancy will bind a successor in title of the owner,[81] the claimant will have no defence to an action for possession brought by someone with a better title. If the owner remedies the defect in his title, the tenant will automatically acquire a valid lease; the tenant's title by estoppel is "fed" by the owner's perfected title.[82] Thus, if

---

[71] [1985] 1 W.L.R. 778.

[72] The claimant will now be barred even if she has no actual knowledge of the mortgage, *Abbey National Building Society* v. *Cann* [1990] 1 All E.R. 1085; see below Part 6(a), p. 151.

[73] See Chap. 3, Part A, p. 40.

[74] Land Registration Act 1925, s.70(1)(k); see above Part B1, p. 133.

[75] *Ibid.*, s.8(1)(a).

[76] Section 2(4); see above Part A1, p. 130.

[77] See Part B2, p. 135.

[78] *City Permanent Building Society* v. *Miller* [1952] Ch. 840.

[79] See above Part B1, p. 133.

[80] *Cooke* v. *Loxley* (1792) 5 T.R. 4; *Alchorne* v. *Gomme* (1824) 2 Bing. 54; *Cuthbertson* v. *Irving* (1860) 6 H. & N. 135.

[81] *Webb* v. *Austin* (1844) 7 Man. & G. 701.

[82] *Ibid.*

the premises are held subject to a mortgage under which the owner has agreed not to grant leases, the claimant's lease will not bind the mortgagee. It is now doubtful, however, whether a lease granted whilst the owner was in occupation prior to completion of the purchase and mortgage will in fact bind the mortgagee.[83]

4. Part performance

Equitable interest

The remedy of part performance allows a person sharing residential property to enforce a contract for the conveyance or transfer of that property made before September 27, 1989 which is not in writing.[84] The claimant, thus, has an equitable interest in the form of an estate contract. The extent to which the claimant is protected against third parties will depend largely upon whether the title to the land is registered or unregistered.

Registered land

Overriding interest

If title to the property is registered, the claimant need take no steps to protect her interest provided that she remains in occupation. Her estate contract will be enforceable against a purchaser or mortgagee as an overriding interest under section 70(1)(g) of the Land Registration Act 1925.[85] As the claimant in this type of case is very often a resident housekeeper or live-in relative looking after the elderly owner, her interest will normally be protected automatically. Because of the uncertainty as to the precise meaning of "actual occupation," the claimant should protect her interest by means of a notice or caution[86] if she is going to be away from the premises for more than a short period.

Unregistered land

The claimant is in a much more difficult position if the title to the land is unregistered. She will only be able to enforce her interest against a third party if it is protected by entry on the Land Charges Register as a C(iv) land charge.[87] The fact that she is clearly in occupation or, indeed, tells a prospective purchaser about her right will not give her any protection if the purchaser subsequently tries to evict her.[88] In this instance the land charges system works harshly, as the claimant may not realise what her rights are and, even if she does know that she has some rights in the property, will certainly not know that she has to register a land charge to protect them.

5. Express and constructive trusts

A claimant under a written express declaration of trust will be protected against a third party in the same way and to the same extent as a claimant under an implied or a resulting trust.[89]

---

[83] *Church of England Building Society* v. *Piskor* [1954] Ch. 553 was said to have been wrongly decided by Lord Oliver in *Abbey National Building Society* v. *Cann* [1990] 1 All E.R. 1085, 1100.

[84] See above Chap. 4, Part A, p. 64.

[85] See above Part B1, p. 133.

[86] See above Part B2, p. 135.

[87] Land Charges Act 1972, s.2(4).

[88] *Hollington Bros. Ltd.* v. *Rhodes* [1951] 2 T.L.R. 691; see above Part A1, p. 130.

[89] See below Part 6, p. 150.

Written declaration

The advantage of the written declaration is that it provides clear evidence of the existence and size of the claimant's beneficial interest.

The extent to which a claimant under a constructive trust, whether arising under the rule in *Rochefoucauld* v. *Boustead*[90] or otherwise,[91] is protected against third parties is not settled.

Constructive trust

A third party who specifically takes the property subject to the interest of the claimant will be a constructive trustee in his own right and will be obliged to give effect to the claimant's interest.[92] A volunteer, such as a trustee in bankruptcy, will also be bound by the claimant's interest under a constructive trust.[93] Under the general rules of constructive trusts a bona fide purchaser for value without actual or constructive notice will not be bound.[94] The difficulty arises in relation to a purchaser who takes with notice but not specifically subject to the rights of the claimant. In *Re Sharpe (A Bankrupt)*[95] Browne-Wilkinson J. suggested,[96] in the context of a licence arising under a constructive trust, that a purchaser without express notice would not be bound by the claimant's interest.

To ensure that his interest does bind those third parties it is capable of affecting, the claimant should take steps to protect his interest. If the title to the property in question is

Unregistered land

unregistered, the claimant will have to be particularly vigilant to bring his interest to the attention of potential third parties because his interest cannot be protected by registration on the

Registered land

Land Charges Register.[97] In the case of registered land, the Chief Land Registrar takes the view that an interest under a constructive trust is capable of being protected as an overriding interest under section 70(1)(g) of the Land Registration Act 1925.[98] For greater security, the interest can also be protected by the entry of a notice or caution.[99]

6. Resulting and implied trusts

The interest of a claimant arising under a resulting or an implied trust takes effect as a beneficial interest behind a trust for sale[1] and the rules protecting that interest against third

Equitable interest

parties are the same in each case. The claimant will usually be seeking two forms of protection, a right to remain in occupation and a right to a share in the proceeds of sale, but the two are not conterminous. The claimant's position in

---

[90] [1879] 1 Ch. 196; see above Chap. 5, Part A1, p. 71.
[91] See above Chap. 5, Part B, p. 74.
[92] See *Lyus* v. *Prowsa Developments Ltd.* [1982] 2 All E.R. 953, 961 *per* Dillon L.J.; *Ashburn Anstalt* v. *Arnold* [1989] 1 Ch. 1, 25 *per* Fox L.J.
[93] *Re Sharpe (A Bankrupt)* [1980] 1 W.L.R. 219.
[94] *Pilcher* v. *Rawlins* (1872) L.R. 7 Ch. App. 259.
[95] [1980] 1 W.L.R. 219.
[96] *Ibid.*, 226.
[97] An interest under constructive trust is not specified in Land Charges Act 1972, s.2; see above Part A, p. 129.
[98] Ruoff and Roper, *The Law and Practice of Registered Conveyancing* 5th ed., (1986), p. 117.
[99] *Ibid.*, pp. 447, 818.
[1] See above Chap. 6, Part D, p. 104.

relation to third parties depends upon whether the property is held by a sole or joint owners and also upon whether title to the property is registered or unregistered. Following the decision of the House of Lords in *Williams & Glyn's Bank Ltd v. Boland*,[2] a holder of a beneficial interest under a resulting or an implied trust had a high degree of protection against third parties. Recent judicial decisions have considerably curtailed that protection by applying the doctrine of overreaching with full vigour[3] and by restricting the extent of the claimant's beneficial interest.[4]

(a) **Beneficial interest** The fact that a claimant has contributed in some way to the purchase of the property in which he is living and, under the normal rules[5] has an equitable interest therein, does not automatically mean that the claimant has an interest which is capable of being enforced against all third parties. Where the property is subject to a mortgage, the beneficiary will have no rights against the mortgagee in two situations. First, several recent cases have held that where property is purchased with the assistance of a mortgage, his equitable interest is subject to the rights of the mortgagee. Secondly, if a mortgage already exists before the claimant's equitable interest arises, the mortgagee will have priority. In those situations, a claimant has no rights which can be enforced against that mortgagee but he does have an equitable interest which can be enforced against other third parties.

Priority of mortgagees

The courts' approach in the first situation can be seen from the case of *Paddington Building Society v. Mendelsohn*.[6] In that case a mother and son agreed to buy a flat for £32,500. The mother provided £15,500 of the purchase price and the remainder was borrowed from the plaintiffs by the son and secured by a mortgage on the property. The flat was transferred into the name of the son alone and he was responsible for the mortgage repayments. The mother moved into occupation before the mortgage was registered. The son subsequently defaulted on the mortgage and the plaintiffs obtained an order for possession. The mother applied for the order to be set aside on the grounds that she had an overriding interest under section 70(1)(g) of the Land Registration Act 1925. Browne-Wilkinson L.J. held that the mother's equitable interest was subject to the rights of the mortgagee and, thus, could not amount to an overriding interest.[7] His reasoning was as follows[8];

Paddington Building Society v. Mendelsohn

---

[2] [1981] A.C. 487; noted [1980] Conv. 361 (Martin); for a detailed discussion of the case see Thompson, *Co-ownership* (1988), pp. 118 *et seq.*
[3] See below Part 6(b), p. 153.
[4] See below Part 6(a).
[5] See above Chap. 6.
[6] (1985) 50 P. & C.R. 244; noted [1986] Conv. 57 (Thompson).
[7] See above Part B1, p. 133.
[8] (1985) 50 P. & C.R. 244, 247; see also *Knightly v. Sun Life Assurance Society Ltd.* [1981] *The Times*, July 23; *Bristol & West Building Society v. Henning* [1985] 1 W.L.R. 778; *Lloyds Bank plc v. Rosset* [1989] 1 Ch. 350, 387 *per* Nicholls L.J.; *Abbey National Building Society v. Cann* (1989) 57 P. & C.R. 381.

"There being no express declaration of trust or agreement as to the beneficial interests of the mother and the son at the time of acquisition of the flat, the nature of the mother's equitable interest must depend on the intention to be imputed to the son and the mother at the time of the acquisition. Since the mother knew and intended that the mortgage was to be granted to the society and that without the mortgage the flat in which she claims a beneficial interest could not have been acquired, the only possible intention to impute to the parties is an intention that the mother's rights were to be subject to the rights of the society."

This method of limiting the claimant's rights against third parties based on the intention of the parties has been criticised as an unwarranted extension of the estoppel rules[9] and would also appear to involve imputing an intention to the parties[10] rather than inferring their actual intentions, contrary to the normal rules in relation to common intention.[11]

It has now been established that a claimant's interest will always be limited where the property is being purchased with the assistance of a mortgage regardless of the claimant's knowledge as to the existence or size of the mortgage. In *Abbey National Building Society* v. *Cann*[12] the House of Lords held

Further protection for mortgagees

that the claimant cannot acquire an interest in the property until it is actually purchased and at that time the mortgagee already has an interest ranking in priority. Lord Oliver reasoned as follows;[13]

"The reality is that the purchaser of land who relies upon a building society or bank loan for the completion of his purchase never in fact acquires anything but an equity of redemption, for the land is, from the very inception, charged with the amount of the loan without which it could never have been transferred at all and it was never intended that it should be otherwise."

Thus Mrs Cann could not enforce any equitable interest she might have in a house owned by her son against the building society who had provided the son with the purchase price. By comparison, a claimant's equitable interest should not be subject to any limitations where the owner, after the property has been purchased and without the claimant's knowledge, enters into a mortgage to raise money for his own purposes.[14]

If the claimant acquires a beneficial interest in a property which the owner has had for some time, for example by paying

---

[9] See Thompson, *Co-ownership* (1988), p. 124; Gray, *Elements of Land Law* (1987), p. 859.
[10] *Paddington Building Society* v. *Mendelsohn* (1985) 50 P. & C.R. 244, 248 *per* Browne-Wilkinson L.J.; *Bristol & West Building Society* v. *Henning* [1985] 1 W.L.R. 778, 782 *per* Browne-Wilkinson L.J.
[11] See above Chap. 6, Part C1, p. 90.
[12] [1990] 1 All E.R. 1085.
[13] *Ibid.*, 1100.
[14] *Paddington Building Society* v. *Mendelsohn* (1985) 50 P. & C.R. 244, 248 *per* Browne-Wilkinson L.J.

for substantial improvements,[15-19] he will not be able to enforce any rights against a mortgagee who provided a loan for the initial purchase of the property. The claimant's equitable interest will be enforceable against any later mortgagee in the usual way.

(b) Joint owners Where the property which is being shared is owned by more than one owner, a beneficiary has very little protection against third parties because of the doctrine of

Overreaching overreaching. By section 2 of the Law of Property Act 1925 any equitable interest under a trust for sale is overreached by a conveyance[20] to a purchaser where the purchase money is paid to two trustees or a trust corporation. The effect of section 2 is confirmed by section 27 which states that a purchaser is not to be concerned with trusts affecting the property if the purchase money is so paid. Accordingly, on a sale by joint owners a beneficiary loses all rights to occupation of the property and has only a right to the relevant proportion of the proceeds of sale in the hands of the trustee/owners. In the case of a mortgage, the beneficiary has a similar right to a share of the mortgage money in the hands of the trustee/owners but any rights of occupation of the property are restricted to the owners' equity of redemption. This result follows whether the title to the land is registered or unregistered or whether the beneficiary is in occupation or not. Section 14 of the Law of Property Act 1925 does not confer any additional rights on a beneficiary in occupation[21] and the rights enforcable under section 70(1)(g) of the Land Registration Act 1925 are subject to the overreaching rules.[22]

The strict application of the doctrine of overreaching was confirmed by the House of Lords in *City of London Building Society* v. *Flegg*[23] and the facts of that case illustrate the harsh effects the doctrine can have. Mr. and Mrs. Maxwell-Brown and Mrs. Maxwell-Brown's parents, Mr. and Mrs. Flegg, decided to purchase a house for their joint occupation.

City of London Building Society v. Flegg Although Mr. and Mrs. Flegg contributed more than half the purchase price, Bleak House was conveyed into the names of Mr. and Mrs. Maxwell-Brown alone. Several years later Mr. and Mrs. Maxwell-Brown borrowed £37,500 from the appellants without the knowledge of the respondents. Mr. and Mrs. Maxwell-Brown failed to pay sums due under the mortgage and the appellants sued for possession of Bleak House. Despite the fact that Mr. and Mrs. Flegg clearly had an equitable interest in the property and were in occupation at the time of the mortgage, the House of Lords held that they had

---

[15-19] See above Chap. 6, Part C1(a), p. 91.
[20] By Law of Property Act 1925, s.205(1)(ii) "Conveyance" includes a mortgage.
[21] *City of London Building Society* v. *Flegg* [1988] 1 A.C. 54, 72 *per* Lord Templeman, 80 *per* Lord Oliver; Thompson, "Dispositions by Trustees for Sale" [1988] Conv. 108.
[22] See above Part B1, p. 133.
[23] [1988] 1 A.C. 54; see Law Commission, *Transfer of Land - Overreaching: Beneficiaries in Occupation* (No. 188 1989).

no rights against the mortgagee. The position was summarised by Lord Templeman as follows[24];

> "Their beneficial interests were overreached by the legal charge and were transferred to the equity of redemption held by the Maxwell-Browns and to the sum advanced by the appellants in consideration of the grant of the legal charge and received by the Maxwell-Browns. After the legal charge the respondents were only entitled to continue in occupation of Bleak House by virtue of their beneficial interests in the equity of redemption of Bleak House and that equity of redemption is subject to the right of the appellants as mortgagee to take possession."

(c) Sole owner It is now accepted that a sole legal owner has power to sell or mortgage the legal estate even though he is holding the property on trust for other people with beneficial interests.[25] The equitable interests of the beneficiaries are not overreached on a sale or mortgage because the money is paid to only one person.[26] The basis of the beneficiary's protection is that a third party will be bound by the beneficiary's rights if he has notice of the existence of the beneficiary's interest. The way in which the third party acquires notice depends upon whether the title to the property is registered or unregistered.

Notice

Unregistered land In the case of unregistered land, the equitable interest cannot be protected by registration because it is not a registrable interest within section 2 of the Land Charges Act 1972. The beneficiary is, therefore, dependant for protection on the old rules of notice. A third party will be bound if he has actual or constructive notice of the beneficiary's interest.[27] Following the recent decision in *Kingsnorth Finance Co. Ltd* v. *Tizard*[28] the courts would appear to be taking a wide view of constructive notice and, provided there is some indication of the beneficiary's presence on the premises, a third party will be bound. It is still advisable, however, for a beneficiary to be vigilant as to the possibility of potential third parties, for example prospective purchasers being shown round the property, and to take all steps to bring his interest to their attention.

Registered land If the title to the property is registered, there are several steps which a beneficiary can take to protect his interest. He can apply for a restriction[29] to be entered on the Register that no disposition is to be registered without his consent.[30] If it is not possible to obtain the production of the land certificate to register a restriction, a caution should be entered on the

---

[24] *Ibid.*, 71–72.
[25] See for example *Caunce* v. *Caunce* [1969] 1 W.L.R. 286; *Williams & Glyn's Bank Ltd.* v. *Boland* [1981] A.C. 487.
[26] Law of Property Act 1925, s.2(2).
[27] See above Part A2, p. 131.
[28] [1986] 1 W.L.R. 783.
[29] Land Registration Act 1925, s.58(1)(5); Land Registration Rules 1925, r. 236.
[30] See Ruoff and Roper, *The Law and Practice of Registered Conveyancing* 5th ed., (1986), p. 873 for the form of the restriction.

Register. An interest under a trust for sale amounts to a minor interest for these purposes.[31] Alternatively, the beneficiary may appoint, or require the nominated persons to appoint, an additional trustee and ensure that he is registered as a proprietor.[32]

Even if the beneficiary takes no specific steps for protection, he may still be able to enforce his equitable interest

Overriding interest   against third parties as an overriding interest. An interest under a trust for sale is an interest subsisting in reference to the land and is, therefore, capable of being an overriding interest within section 70(1)(g) of the Land Registration Act 1925.[33] In view of the court's liberal approach to the meaning of "actual occupation," a beneficiary will normally be able to enforce his interest if he is living on the premises or is absent for only a short period.[34]

A beneficiary faced with an adverse claim from a third party may be concerned about both the right to remain in occupation and his right to part of the proceeds of sale. Because of the nature of a trust for sale, a beneficiary has no absolute right to occupation but he may have occupational rights arising from agreement with the owner or the purpose

Rights of   for which the trust was created originally.[35] Those rights are
occupation   enforceable to the same extent against a third party subject to his interest as against the original owner. The point was made by Lord Oliver in *City of London Building Society* v. *Flegg*[36];

> "The reason why a purchaser of the legal estate (whether by way of outright sale or by way of mortgage) from a single proprietor takes subject to the rights of the occupying beneficiary is not because section 14 of the Act[37] confers upon the latter some interest in land which is incapable of being overreached but because, having constructive notice of the trust as a result of the beneficiary's occupation, he steps into the shoes of the vendor or mortgagor and takes the estate subject to the same equities as those to which it was subject in the latter's hands, those equities and their accompanying incidents not having been overreached by the sale under the provisions of section 2(1) and section 27 of the Act."

Thus a purchaser or mortgagee will not be entitled to possession against a beneficiary where the purpose of the trust was to provide accommodation for that beneficiary.[38] Further, the court will exercise its discretion in the usual way on an application for sale by the third party under section 30 of the Law of Property Act 1925.[39]

[31] *Elias* v. *Mitchell* [1972] Ch. 652.
[32] Land Registration Act 1925, s.47.
[33] *Williams & Glyn's Bank Ltd.* v. *Boland* [1981] A.C. 487, 507 *per* Lord Wilberforce.
[34] See above Part B1, p. 133.
[35] See above Chap. 6, Part D.1, p. 104.
[36] [1988] 1 A.C. 54, 83.
[37] Law of Property Act 1925.
[38] See for example *Williams & Glyn's Bank Ltd.* v. *Boland* [1981] A.C. 487; *Kemmis* v. *Kemmis* [1988] 1 W.L.R. 1307.
[39] See above Chap. 6, Part D.1, p. 104.

A third party who takes with notice of the beneficiary's equitable interest is in the same position as the original owner and holds the property on trust for himself and the beneficiary. The beneficiary, therefore, has the usual right to his share of the proceeds of sale in the hands of the third party. The beneficiary will also have a cause of action against the owner for breach of trust for either selling without his consent[40] or mortgaging the property for unauthorised purposes.[41] If the beneficiary is only concerned to recover his part of the proceeds of sale, a potential solution is to ask the owner to appoint an additional trustee before any dealing takes place to ensure that overreaching takes effect in the normal way.[42] The court will assist by issuing an injunction against the owner restraining sale until the second trustee has been appointed.[43]

Alternative remedies

7. Proprietary estoppel

If a person sharing residential property bases his claim in proprietary estoppel, the extent of his protection against third parties depends upon whether the court has adjudicated on his claim against the owner before the third party intervenes. Once the court has determined the claimant's remedy[44] his rights against third parties depend solely on that remedy. For example, if the court holds that the remedy to satisfy the equity raised by the proprietary estoppel is a lease[45] the claimant will have an interest which will bind any third party whereas if he is granted an irrevocable licence,[46] he will be in a far less secure position. Whatever the remedy granted it should be protected in the usual way, for example, an estate contract should be registered. If the remedy granted is a beneficial interest under a trust for sale, the claimant's rights are liable to be overreached in the event of a sale by more than one owner[47]; the fact that the interest arose initially under the doctrine of proprietary estoppel is irrelevant once the equity has been satisfied by court order.

After court hearing

The position of the claimant in relation to third parties is not entirely clear where the court has not pronounced on the remedy to which the claimant is entitled before a purchaser or mortgagee becomes involved. The lack of certainty stems from the fact that, until the position between the owner and the claimant is litigated, the claimant has no more than unspecified inchoate rights.[48] These rights are best described as the "equity" raised by the owner's previous conduct.[49] Whilst for

Before court hearing

Inchoate rights

---

[40] Law of Property Act 1925, s.26(3).
[41] *Ibid*, s.28(1).
[42] See above Part 6(b), p. 153.
[43] *Waller* v. *Waller* [1967] 1 W.L.R. 451.
[44] See above Chap. 7, Part C, p. 122.
[45] See above Part F3, p.148.
[46] See above Part F2(c), p.147; *Williams* v. *Staite* [1979] Ch. 291.
[47] See above Part F6(b), p.153.
[48] See Bailey, "Estoppel and Registration of Title" [1983] Conv. 99, 100; see also *Fryer* v. *Brook* (1984) 81 L.S.Gaz. 2856.
[49] *Crabb* v. *Arun District Council* [1976] Ch. 179, 193 *per* Scarman L.J.; see Everton, "Towards a Concept of 'Quasi-Property'? " [1982] Conv. 118 and 177.

specific purposes, for example, compensation under the Town and Country Planning legislation,[50] the equity has been held to amount to an "interest in land," such inchoate rights are not usually considered to amount to a property interest.[51] This does not mean, however, that until the claimant's rights are crystallized by the court that he is without remedy against third parties.

New proprietary estoppel

If the third party himself gives assurances to the claimant who continues to act to his detriment, the claimant may have a new and separate claim in proprietary estoppel against the third party.[52] A purchaser, for example, may tell a claimant living in part of the premises that he will not seek to evict him and on the faith of that promise the claimant may do further work on the premises. This will be an independent cause of action and in addition to any rights the claimant may have against the third party based on notice of his original equity.

Types of third party

The equity arising by proprietary estoppel has been held to bind volunteers such as the trustees of the owner's estate,[53] a trustee in bankruptcy[54] and a successor local authority.[55] A purchaser with actual notice of the equity is also bound.[56] Whilst a purchaser with constructive notice of the equity has been held to be bound by the estoppel rights,[57] the reasoning in the case is doubtful[58] and Browne-Wilkinson J. in *Re Sharpe (A Bankrupt)*[59] advanced the view that a purchaser may not be bound unless he has express notice. A purchaser with neither actual nor constructive notice should not be bound by the claimant's rights.[60] These rules are not affected if there are joint owners of the legal estate; the equity created by proprietary estoppel is not capable of being overreached.[61]

Discretionary remedy

The fact that a third party is bound by the claimant's equity does not automatically mean that the claimant can enforce all the rights he would wish against that third party. In any case based on proprietary estoppel the remedy to be granted to satisfy the equity is at the discretion of the court[62] and the court may not necessarily grant to the claimant the right or interest represented as his by the owner.[63] Where the case involves a third party, the court may well regard that fact as a relevant consideration together with the circumstances in which the third party acquired notice of the claimant's equity.

[50] *Pennine Raceway Ltd.* v. *Kirklees Metropolitan Council* [1983] Q.B. 382.
[51] See *National Provincial Bank Ltd.* v. *Ainsworth* [1965] A.C. 1175.
[52] For the elements necessary to found a claim in proprietary estoppel see above Chap. 7, Part B, p. 113.
[53] *Dillwyn* v. *Llewellyn* (1862) 4 De G.F. & J. 517; *Inwards* v. *Baker* [1965] 2 Q.B. 29, see also *Jones* v. *Jones* (1977) 1 W.L.R. 438.
[54] *Re Sharpe (A Bankrupt)* [1980] 1 W.L.R. 219.
[55] *Salvation Army Trustee Co. Ltd.* v. *West Yorkshire Metropolitan County Council* (1981) 41 P. & C.R. 179.
[56] *Ives (E.R.) Investments Ltd.* v. *High* [1967] 2 Q.B. 379.
[57] *Hopgood* v. *Brown* [1955] 1 W.L.R. 213, 225 *per* Lord Evershed M.R.
[58] Based on privity of estate and *Taylor* v. *Needham* (1810) 2 Taunt. 278.
[59] [1980] 1 W.L.R. 219, 226.
[60] By analogy with the general law relating to equities, *Phillips* v. *Phillips* (1861) 4 De G.F. & J. 208.
[61] *Shiloh Spinners Ltd.* v. *Harding* [1973] A.C. 691, 721 *per* Lord Wilberforce.
[62] See above Chap. 7, Part C, p. 122.
[63] See for example *Cushley* v. *Seale* C.A., unreported, October 28, 1986.

This may result in the court awarding the claimant lesser rights against the third party than it would have granted against the original owner.

Unregistered land   If the title to the property is unregistered, a claimant cannot protect his equity by registration as estoppel rights do not constitute a land charge within section 2 of the Land Charges Act 1972.[64] The claimant is, therefore, reliant for protection on his ability to give notice of his rights to potential third parties. In the case of registered land, the Chief Land

Registered land   third parties. In the case of registered land, the Chief Land Registrar takes the view that rights arising as a result of proprietary estoppel are minor interests[65] which can be protected by a notice or caution.[66] The equity may also amount to an overriding interest within section 70(1)(g) of the Land Registration Act 1925 if the claimant is in occupation.[67]

---

[64] *Ives (E.R.) Investments Ltd.* v. *High* [1967] 2 Q.B. 379.
[65] Ruoff and Roper, *The Law and Practice of Registered Conveyancing* 5th ed., (1986), p. 135.
[66] See above Part B2, p. 135.
[67] See Bailey, "Estoppel and Registration of Title" [1983] Conv. 99, 102 *et seq.*

9 BANKRUPTCY

When a person becomes bankrupt any property he owns beneficially vests automatically, by operation of law, in his trustee in bankruptcy.[1] The trustee is then under a statutory duty "to get in, realise and distribute" the bankrupt's estate for the benefit of his creditor's.[2] Bankruptcy of the owner of property clearly presents considerable problems for anyone sharing that property. Any claims of occupants are thenceforward considered not only against the owner but also against the trustee in bankruptcy in the context of the competing claims by creditors.

Insolvency Act 1986

The law on insolvency of individuals[3] is now to be found in Parts VIII to XII and XVI of the Insolvency Act 1986 and the Insolvency Rules 1986 as amended. The extent to which the rights of persons sharing the bankrupt's property bind the trustee depends, however, on the usual rules governing third party rights. As a general rule, a trustee in bankruptcy takes the property subject to all existing third party rights, for example, a building society's rights under a mortgage. Thus a trustee takes subject to the rights of anyone with a lease of the premises[4] or a beneficial interest under a trust for sale arising under either a resulting or an implied trust.[5] Because he is not

Position of trustee in bankruptcy

a purchaser for value, a trustee in bankruptcy is also bound by the rights of an occupier with an equitable licence[6] or rights arising under the doctrine of proprietary estoppel.[7] An occupier with a bare or contractual licence has no rights against a trustee for the simple reason that such an occupier has no proprietary interest which can be enforced against any third party.[8] If a person sharing residential property has made a loan to the owner, but not in such a way as to give rise to a proprietary interest,[9] he will be in the same position as any other unsecured creditor of the bankrupt unless he has become a secured creditor by obtaining a charging order[10] absolute before bankruptcy.[11] The loan, whether secured or

Loan

unsecured, must be proved by notice to the trustee in

---

[1] Insolvency Act 1986, s.306.
[2] *Ibid.*, s.305(2).
[3] For the general law see Muir Hunter, *Personal Insolvency.*
[4] See above Chap. 8, Part F3, p. 148.
[5] See above Chap. 8, Part F6, p. 150.
[6] See above Chap. 8, Part F2(c), p. 147.
[7] See above Chap. 8, Part F7, p. 156.
[8] See above Chap. 8, Part F2(a)(b), p. 146.
[9] See above Chap. 8, Part F1, p. 142.
[10] See above Chap. 8, Part F1, p. 142.
[11] *Roberts Petroleum Ltd* v. *Kenny (Bernard) Ltd* [1983] 2 A.C. 192.

bankruptcy,[12] except by a secured creditor who intends to rely solely on his security.

Avoidance of interests

Although a trustee in bankruptcy takes subject to existing rights affecting the property, there are two situations in which he can avoid the interest of an occupier. First, a trustee in bankruptcy may apply to the court to set aside certain transactions of the bankrupt entered into at an undervalue within a specified period prior to the bankruptcy.[13] Secondly, a transaction entered into by the bankrupt with the intention of defrauding creditors can be set aside.[14]

Rights of occupation

A person sharing residential property will naturally seek to remain in occupation but this will only be possible in a limited number of cases. A lessee will be entitled to remain in possession and any purchaser will take subject to his full rights. Whilst an equitable licensee can remain in possession against the trustee, it is unlikely that such a licensee will be able to remain in occupation once the property has been sold unless the purchaser takes with express notice of the occupier's rights.[15] Similar reasoning would probably apply to a person claiming rights under the doctrine of proprietary estoppel which had not been adjudicated upon by the court.[16] A claimant under an implied or resulting trust has a right which is binding on a trustee in bankruptcy but, because of the nature of a trust for sale,[17] it is primarily a right to take a share of the proceeds of sale once the property is sold by the trustee in bankruptcy. The beneficiary can probably remain in occupation, however, until the property is actually sold.[18]

The primary remedy of a person sharing residential property on the bankruptcy of the owner is, thus, to receive the value of their interest from the proceeds of sale. In certain limited situations the claimant may be able to remain in occupation, either in his own right or as dependant on the bankrupt's right. The Insolvency Act 1986[19] gives both a spouse and the bankrupt some rights of occupation but usually for no more than a year from the bankruptcy. Further, if the claimant has a beneficial interest in the bankrupt's property, the trustee in bankruptcy will have to apply to the court for an order for sale under section 30 of the Law of Property Act 1925.[20] In exceptional circumstances, the court may refuse to order sale leaving the bankrupt and the beneficiary in possession.[21] In practice, a beneficiary may be able to continue

---

[12] Insolvency Act 1986, s.322(1); see Muir Hunter, *Personal Insolvency* paras. 3.247–3.249.
[13] See below Part A1, p. 162.
[14] See below Part A2, p. 162.
[15] *Re Sharpe (A Bankrupt)* [1980] 1 W.L.R. 219; see above Chap. 8, Part F2(c), p. 147.
[16] See above Chap. 8, Part F7, p. 156.
[17] See above Chap. 6, Part D, p. 104.
[18] *Bull v. Bull* [1955] 1 Q.B. 234; *Williams & Glyn's Bank Ltd v. Boland* [1981] A.C. 487; see above Chap. 6, Part D1, p. 104.
[19] Sections 336 and 337; see Part B1, p. 163.
[20] *Re Solomon (A Bankrupt)* [1967] Ch. 573.
[21] See Part B2, p. 165.

in possession by purchasing the bankrupt's interest from the trustee.

A.   Avoidance of rights

The trustee's main duty is to the bankrupt's creditors and in pursuit of that duty he is given various powers to avoid third party rights adverse to the bankrupt's property. Transactions entered into at an undervalue by the bankrupt are liable to be set aside under either section 339 of the Insolvency Act 1986, if the transaction occured within the statutory period, or under section 423, if the transaction was entered into with the intention of defrauding creditors. The 1986 Act applies only to transactions entered into after December 28, 1986 and the old provisions of section 42 of the Bankruptcy Act 1914[22] and section 172 of the Law of Property Act 1925[23] still apply to transactions entered into before that date. A person sharing residential property who has previously been given a proprietary interest by the bankrupt may be vulnerable, therefore, if he did not give full value for that interest.

The definition of a transaction at an undervalue is common to both sections[24] and includes a gift or transaction for no consideration, a transaction in consideration of marriage and a transaction in which the bankrupt received consideration worth significantly less, in money or money's worth, than he provided. Thus a lease granted at less than market value would be vulnerable to being set aside as would, for example, the gift of a beneficial interest in a house to a child who went to live with elderly parents. An interest granted by the court under the doctrine of proprietary estoppel would also appear to be vulnerable if the detriment suffered by the claimant is less than the value of the interest granted. The fact that the interest has been granted by the court may not make it inviolable; a property adjustment order made by the court on divorce is specifically stated to be reviewable under the Insolvency Act 1986.[25] It is arguable, however, that an interest under the doctrine of proprietary estoppel does not arise from having "entered into a transaction," and is thus outside the scope of the section.[26]

The effect of giving partial consideration can be seen from the case of *Re Densham (A Bankrupt)*.[27] Although the case was decided under section 42 of the Bankruptcy Act 1914, it provides a guide to the courts' approach to the similar powers under the Insolvency Act 1986. In that case a wife was held to have a joint beneficial interest in the matrimonial home under an implied trust based on a common intention between

Transaction at an undervalue

Proprietary estoppel

---

[22] See Muir Hunter, *Personal Insolvency* para. 3.295.
[23] See *ibid.* para. 3.467.
[24] Insolvency Act 1986, ss.339(3) and 423(1).
[25] Matrimonial Causes Act 1973, s.39; see *Re Abbott (A Bankrupt)* [1983] Ch. 45.
[26] See Muir Hunter, *Personal Insolvency* para. 3.296.
[27] [1975] 1 W.L.R. 1519.

Partial consideration

husband and wife that all their property was jointly owned.[28] If account was taken purely of her monetary contributions, she had a beneficial interest under a resulting trust of a one-ninth share.[29] Goff J. held[30] that that part of her beneficial interest under the implied trust which exceeded her interest under the resulting trust was liable to be set aside because it was not supported by sufficient consideration. Thus, any person sharing residential property with a beneficial interest based on common intention rather than direct contribution is potentially liable to have their interest set aside at the instance of the trustee in bankruptcy.

1.   Section 339

Five years of insolvency

Two years

Transactions at an undervalue can only be set aside under section 339 of the 1986 Act if they took place within the five years immediately preceeding the presentation of the bankruptcy petition.[31] All transactions at an undervalue within two years of the petition are vulnerable but a transaction more than two years after the petition is only vulnerable if the now bankrupt owner was insolvent at the time he entered into the transaction.[32] If the other party to the transaction was an "associate" of the bankrupt, insolvency will be assumed.[33]

Associates

"Associate" includes a spouse, whether actual, former or reputed, and members of the bankrupt's family.[34] Thus, in many instances of shared accommodation, the onus will be on the claimant to prove that his or her spouse, cohabitee or relative was not insolvent when the transaction was entered into which gave rise to the proprietary interest on which he now rests his case. For these purposes, a person is insolvent if he is unable to pay his debts as they fall due or the value of his assets is less than the amount of his liabilities taking into account his contingent and prospective liabilities.[35]

Court order

On the trustee in bankruptcy's application to set aside a transaction under section 339, the court may make such order as it thinks fit to restore the position to what it would have been if the bankrupt had not entered into the transaction.[36] This includes the power to order property transferred as part of the transaction to be vested in the trustee in bankruptcy.[37]

2.   Section 423

Transactions at an undervalue may also be set aside under section 423 of the 1986 Act on application by the trustee in bankruptcy or a victim of the transaction.[38] There is no

---

[28] See above Chap. 6, Part C1(c)(iv), p. 97.
[29] See above Chap. 6, Part B, p. 83.
[30] [1975] 1 W.L.R. 1519, 1529.
[31] Insolvency Act 1986, s.341(1).
[32] *Ibid.*, s.341(2).
[33] *Ibid.*
[34] *Ibid.*, s.435.
[35] *Ibid.*, s.341(3).
[36] *Ibid.*, s.339(2).
[37] *Ibid.*, s.342(1).
[38] *Ibid.*, s.424(1).

**Intention to
defraud**

statutory period after which a transaction is no longer vulnerable. The court only has power[39] to make an order, however, if the bankrupt entered into the transaction with the purpose of putting assets beyond the reach of a person who is making, or may at some time in the future, make a claim against him or otherwise of prejudicing the interest of such a claimant.[40] Simply agreeing that a spouse or cohabitee should have a joint beneficial interest or that a relative should have a lease at a low rent will not be sufficient to trigger section 423; there must be an intention on the part of the owner to defraud his creditors at that time.

B. Retaining possession

When the owner of property becomes bankrupt, there is usually a conflict of interest between, on the one hand, the creditors who want the property sold immediately to satisfy their debts and, on the other hand, the bankrupt and those living with him who wish to continue living in the property as long as possible. The Insolvency Act 1986 has gone some way towards helping those occupying the property by giving statutory rights of occupation to the bankrupt and any spouse.

**Limited statutory
rights**

Those rights, however, merely give a breathing space to allow time to find alternative accommodation before the inevitable sale. A spouse sharing residential property who has a beneficial interest, is given some statutory protection by section 336 of the 1986 Act when an application for sale of the property is being considered. Any other beneficiary has to rely on the courts' usual discretion under section 30 of the Law of Property Act 1925.

1. Statutory rights of occupation

A bankrupt's spouse is given limited rights of occupation by section 336 of the 1986 Act and a bankrupt with children is given similar limited rights by section 337. If sale is postponed under either of these sections, the trustee in bankruptcy may protect the bankrupt's estate by taking a charge on the property under section 313 of the Insolvency Act 1986.

(a) *The spouse's right*   Before 1986 a spouse's statutory right of occupation under the Matrimonial Homes Act 1983 did not bind a trustee in bankruptcy. Now, by section 336(2)(*a*) of the Insolvency Act 1986, a spouse's rights existing at the time the bankruptcy petition was presented[41] specifically bind the trustee. If the trustee wishes to sell the property free of the spouse's right he must make an application to the court having jurisdiction in relation to the bankruptcy[42] under section 1 of

---

[39] The courts' powers are set out in sections 423(2) and 425(1) and are similar to those in section 339, see the text at n. 36 above.
[40] Insolvency Act 1986, s.423(3).
[41] Insolvency Act 1986, s.336(1).
[42] *Ibid.*, s.336(2)(*b*).

the Matrimonial Homes Act 1983 for the right to be
terminated. When considering the application, the court may
make such an order as it thinks fit and reasonable having
regard to five specified factors.[43] If the application is made
more than a year after the first vesting of the bankrupt's estate
in the trustee, the court must assume, unless the circumstances
of the case are exceptional,[44] that the interests of the creditors

One year outweigh all other considerations.[45] Thus, in the vast majority
of cases, the maximum period of occupation for a spouse will
be one year from the bankruptcy and the period may well be
less if the court considers that the interests of the spouse are
not paramount.

The first factor to be considered by the court on the
trustee's application to terminate the spouse's right of

Relevant factors occupation is the interests of the bankrupt's creditors. This
will include such matters as whether the bankruptcy
commenced with a creditor's petition and the hardship suffered
by the creditors flowing from the non-payment of the debt,[46]
the latter being particularly relevant if any creditor is an
individual.[47] The second factor is the conduct of the spouse in
so far as it contributed to the bankruptcy. Thus, a spouse
whose reckless spending has at least partially caused the
bankruptcy is unlikely to be allowed to remain in occupation.[48]
The third factor is the needs and financial resources of the
spouse which involves consideration of the spouse's ability to
find alternative accommodation. The fourth factor is the needs
of any children, one particular matter being any potential
disruption to their schooling.[49] The final factor is "all the
circumstances of the case other than the needs of the
bankrupt." Relevant considerations could include such matters
as the amount of equity in the property and any pending
application for a voluntary arrangement. Although the needs of
the bankrupt cannot be considered under this heading, this
would not seem to preclude consideration of the needs of any
other dependants living with the bankrupt, for example, elderly
parents, whether or not they have any proprietary interest in
the property.

(b) *The bankrupt's right* The bankrupt is given limited rights
to occupy a dwellinghouse by section 337 of the 1986 Act but
only if he has children under eighteen years of age living with

With children him at the time of the bankruptcy. The section contains no
stipulation that the children must be the bankrupt's children,
merely that they must have their home with the bankrupt.
Thus, whilst a female cohabitee has no rights of occupation
under section 336 of the 1986 Act as a spouse, she may be able

---

[43] *Ibid.*, s.336(4).
[44] For the meaning of "exceptional circumstances" see below the text at n. 59.
[45] Insolvency Act 1986, s.336(5).
[46] See *Re Holliday (A Bankrupt)* [1981] 1 Ch. 405, 425 *per* Sir David Cairns.
[47] See *Harman* v. *Glencross* [1986] Fam. 81, 93 *per* Balcombe L.J. in the
context of charging orders.
[48] See *Re Densham (A Bankrupt)* [1975] 1 W.L.R. 1519, 1531 *per* Goff L.J.
[49] See *Re Bailey (A Bankrupt)* [1977] 1 W.L.R. 278, 282 *per* Megarry V.C.; *Re
Lowrie (A Bankrupt)* [1981] 3 All E.R. 353, 356 *per* Walton J.

to remain, relying upon the bankrupt's right under section 337, if her children are sharing the house.

The bankrupt is given a statutory right of occupation in the same form as a spouse under section 1 of the Matrimonial Homes Act 1983.[50] The right is a charge on the property in the hands of the trustee in bankruptcy.[51] If the trustee wishes **Application to** to sell the property with vacant possession, he will have to **court** apply to the court having jurisdiction in relation to the bankruptcy[52] for an order terminating the bankrupt's right of occupation. On such an application the court has power to make such an order as it considers just and reasonable having regard to the interests of the creditors, the bankrupt's financial resources, the needs of the children and all the circumstances of the case other than the needs of the bankrupt.[53] As with an application to terminate the statutory right of occupation of a spouse, if an application is made more than a year after the bankruptcy, the court will assume, except in exceptional circumstances, that the interests of the creditors are paramount.[54]

2. Resisting sale

If the bankrupt is the sole legal and beneficial owner of the property in question, the trustee in bankruptcy will have the **Sole owner** whole legal and equitable estate[55] and full power of sale. To obtain vacant possession, however, he may need to apply to the court in which the bankruptcy is proceeding for a possession order. That application and the resulting sale can only be delayed to the extent to which the court refuses to terminate the statutory rights of occupation of the bankrupt or his spouse.[56]

Joint names If the property is in joint names, the trustee in bankruptcy will not have the legal estate but only the bankrupt's beneficial interest and will have to apply to the court for an order for sale under section 30 of the Law of Property Act 1925.[57] Where the property is jointly owned by **Section 30 L.P.A.** the bankrupt and his or her spouse, the court has the same **1925** power and must have regard to the same factors as it would if considering an application to terminate the spouse's statutory right of occupation.[58] Although the court is given power to make such order as it considers "just and reasonable," the court will normally merely postpone the order for sale. In view of the direction in section 336(5) that after a year the interests of the creditors are to outweigh all other considerations, any postponement is unlikely to be for longer than a year.

---

[50] See above Part 1(a), p. 163, and Chap. 8, Part C, p. 138.
[51] Insolvency Act 1986, s.337(2)(b).
[52] Ibid., s.337(4).
[53] Ibid., s.337(5); for the effect of the various considerations see above Part 1(a), p. 163.
[54] Ibid., s.337(6), for the meaning of "exceptional circumstances" see below the text at n. 59.
[55] Ibid., s.306.
[56] See above Part 1, p. 163.
[57] Re Soloman (A Bankrupt) [1967] Ch. 573.
[58] Insolvency Act 1986, s.336(4)(5); see above Part 1(a), p. 163.

Exceptional circumstances

"Exceptional circumstances"[59] which may lead the court to refuse sale or to allow a longer postponement could include such matters as the fact that the property has been specifically adapted for a disabled member of the bankrupt's family,[60] that the bankrupt or a resident relative is seriously ill and awaiting treatment[61] or that the petition in bankruptcy was presented by a husband as a tactical move to avoid a transfer of property order on divorce in favour of his wife.[62]

In the case of joint ownership with someone other than a spouse, for example a cohabitee or a parent, there are no specific statutory provisions and the court exercises its usual discretion under section 30 of the 1925 Act. If the bankrupt is the sole legal owner but is holding on trust for sale for other beneficial owners under either a resulting or an implied trust, the trustee will similarly have to apply to the court for an order for sale under section 30 if the co-beneficiaries will not consent to the sale. Such an application is also unaffected by any specific statutory provisions.

The outcome of an application under section 30 of the 1925 Act is not a foregone conclusion and can involve substantial cost. The trustee in bankruptcy, therefore, is often willing to sell the bankrupt's interest in the property to the co-

Sale of bankrupt's interest

beneficiaries. Such a sale has the result, not only of securing the continued residence of the co-beneficiaries, but also of settling any disputes there may be as to the size of the co-beneficiaries' shares in the proceeds of sale.

The courts' approach to an application for sale of property under section 30 of the 1925 Act by a trustee in bankruptcy

Section 30 application

can be seen from *Re Turner (A Bankrupt)*,[63] a case which involved a matrimonial home. Goff J. set out the principles in the following three statements[64]:

"In my judgment, the guiding principle in the exercise of the court's discretion is not whether the trustee or the wife is being reasonable but, in all the circumstances of the case, whose voice in equity ought to prevail."

"In my judgment, there exist in equity two competing claims. On the one hand the wife, as part owner of the house, asks why she as co-owner should be turned out merely because her husband, the other co-owner is bankrupt. On the other hand, the trustee in bankruptcy says that he is not only entitled to realise the husband's interest but bound by statute to do so."

"In my judgment, weighing the two conflicting claims, that by the trustee based on his statutory duty, gives him the stronger claim and requires me to treat his voice as the one which ought to prevail in equity."

[59] *Ibid.*, s.336(5); see *In re Citro (a Bankrupt)*, The Times, June 7, 1990.
[60] See *Re Bailey (A Bankrupt)* [1977] 1 W.L.R. 278, 284 *per* Walton J.
[61] See *Re Densham (A Bankrupt)* [1975] 1 W.L.R. 1519, 1531 *per* Goff J. and see the text below at n. 75.
[62] *Re Holliday (A Bankrupt)* [1981] Ch. 405.
[63] [1974] 1 W.L.R. 1556.
[64] *Ibid.*, 1558.

Thus the normal order of the court will be for the property to be sold.[65] The fact that people living with the bankrupt will be rendered homeless is regarded as a natural consequence of the bankruptcy and not a reason to refuse sale.[66] Indeed, the court will make a possession order against a

Relevant factors co-owner who refuses to co-operate with the sale.[67] Similarly, disruption to a child's education, save perhaps in the last year of "A" levels, is not a sufficient reason to delay sale.[68] An order for sale was refused in *Re Holliday (A Bankrupt)*[69] but the facts of that case were very unusual. The bankrupt presented the petition with the intention of frustrating his wife's application for a property transfer order on divorce and in that situation the hardship to the wife and children was held to outweigh the interests of the creditors. It has been suggested[70] that the court would refuse to order sale if the property had been specially adapted for the needs of a disabled child living with the bankrupt and similar arguments would apply to property adapted for elderly relatives. In *Patel* v. *Ali*[71] Goulding J. indicated[72] that he would not order sale of a matrimonial home were the wife was so badly disabled that she could only run her home and look after her children with the assistance of friends and relatives who lived nearby.

The courts approach to an application for sale when one of the beneficiaries is suffering from a serious illness is not

Illness of entirely clear. In the case of *Re Toobman (A Bankrupt)*[73]
beneficiary postponement of an order for sale of the matrimonial home was refused even though Mrs. Toobman was suffering from a very serious heart condition. Warner J. set out his reasoning as follows[74];

> "The difficulty in this case is that—apart of course from giving Mr. and Mrs. Toobman a little more time to make arrangements to move out of the house—there is no definite period, short of Mrs. Toobman's life, for which I can usefully postpone the sale, to take account of her state of health; and her life, despite what her doctor says, may last several decades yet. It would hardly be just to the creditors to keep them out of their money for such a length of time, with only statutory interest at 4 per cent. per annum to compensate them."

By contrast in *Re Mott (A Bankrupt)*[75] Hoffman J. refused to order sale of a house jointly by a mother and her son after the son became bankrupt. The grounds for the refusal were that

---

[65] See Hand, "Bankruptcy and the Family Home" [1983] Conv. 219.
[66] *Re Lowrie (A Bankrupt)* [1981] 3 All E.R. 353, 356 *per* Walton J.; see also *In re Citro (A Bankrupt)*, *The Times*, June 7, 1990.
[67] *Re McCarthy (A Bankrupt)* [1975] 2 All E.R. 857.
[68] *Ibid.*, *Re Bailey (A Bankrupt)* [1977] 1 W.L.R. 278, 282 *per* Megarry V.C.
[69] [1981] Ch. 405.
[70] *Re Bailey (A Bankrupt)* [1977] 1 W.L.R. 278, 284 *per* Walton J.
[71] [1984] Ch. 283; see also *Re Gorman (A Bankrupt)* [1990] 1 All E.R. 717 where Vinelott J. was prepared to delay sale until the beneficiary's claim for negligence against her previous solicitors was determined.
[72] *Ibid.*, 289.
[73] *The Times*, March 1, 1982.
[74] Quoting from the transcript.
[75] [1987] C.L.Y. 212.

the mother was 70 years old and in poor health which would deteriorate if she was forced to move. It was also considered relevant that the creditors were largely the State in the form of the Inland Revenue and the D.H.S.S. It would appear that the court will not normally postpone sale in the case of ill-health on the part of a beneficiary unless a reasonable time limit can be put on the period of postponement. That time limit may arise from the age of the beneficiary or the seriousness of the condition. Such an approach is reinforced by the comment of Goff J. in *Re Densham (A Bankrupt)*[76] that the court would look favourably on a request to postpone sale for a period to allow a course of medical treatment to be completed.

Equity of exoneration

When the property is sold any beneficiaries will clearly lose possession but they will receive their relevant proportion[77] of the proceeds of sale after payment of any sums secured on the legal estate. If the property was charged to secure the debts of the bankrupt alone, however, the other beneficial co-owners may be able to claim the benefit of the equity of exoneration and require the secured debts to be discharged, as far as possible, from the equitable interest of the bankrupt. For example, if a house is owned jointly by a son and his parents and they charge the legal estate to the bank as security for the son's business debts, the equity of exoneration allows the parents to insist that the sums due to the bank are paid primarily from the son's share of the proceeds of sale if he is subsequently declared bankrupt.[78] The equity can only be used if it can be inferred that it was the joint intention of the co-owners that the burden of the secured indebtedness should fall primarily on the share of the actual debtor.[79] Thus, in *Re Pittortu (A Bankrupt)*[80] Scott J. held[81] that a wife could not claim the equity of exoneration in respect of sums borrowed and used for joint family expenses but that she could avoid liability for sums borrowed and used by her husband for purely business purposes and for supporting another woman.

C. Practical considerations

Whilst in strict law a person sharing residential property has only limited rights against the trustee in bankruptcy, in practice, as the person in possession, he may well be able to negotiate an amicable settlement with the trustee. Full details of the claim to an interest in the property should, therefore, be given to the trustee as soon as possible. The claimant should also, in the meanwhile, investigate ways in which he might raise finance to purchase the bankrupt's interest from the trustee.

Settlements

If the mortgage on the bankrupt's property exceeds the value of the equity or the property is held on a lease with

[76] [1975] 1 W.L.R. 1519, 1531.
[77] See above Chap. 6, Part D2, p. 105.
[78] See *Re A Debtor (No. 24 of 1971)* [1976] 1 W.L.R. 952.
[79] *Paget* v. *Paget* [1898] 1 Ch. 470.
[80] [1985] 1 W.L.R. 58.
[81] *Ibid.*, 62.

Disclaimer

potential liabilities, for example, for repair, the trustee may seek to disclaim the property as onerous property under section 315 of the Insolvency Act 1986. The disclaimer will not be effective, however, until the prescribed notice[82] has been given to every person in occupation of the premises[83] and any underlessee if the presmises are leasehold.[84] A person sharing the premises should then consider whether he wishes to apply to the court for the property to be transferred to him.[85] If so, the application has to be made within 14 days of receipt of the notice of the disclaimer.[86] A sub-tenant should also apply for a vesting order to protect his position.[87] If no steps are taken, the bankrupt's interest determines and he has no answer to an action for possession.[88] In practice, a lessor may be willing to grant a new tenancy to a person sharing the premises to save the trouble of taking an action for possession and finding a new tenant. There is no danger of disclaimer if the bankrupt is a statutory tenant under the Rent Act 1977 or the Housing Act 1985 as the statutory tenancy is a personal right which does not vest in the trustee.[89]

Voluntary arrangement

If the owner is in financial difficulties but has not yet been declared bankrupt, he should be encouraged to consider a voluntary arrangement with his creditors under Part VIII of the 1986 Act. The owner will then remain[90] in a position to raise additional finance on the security of his property for the benefit of his creditors. Provided the owner keeps to the terms of the voluntary arrangement, he will not become bankrupt and both he and those sharing the property with him can remain in occupation.[91]

---

[82] Insolvency Rules 1986, r. 6: 178.
[83] Insolvency Act 1986, s.318.
[84] *Ibid.*, s.317.
[85] *Ibid.*, s.320.
[86] *Ibid.*, s.318(*a*).
[87] *Re A.E. Realisations Ltd* [1987] 3 All E.R. 83.
[88] A statutory tenancy does not arise on the determination of a contractual tenancy, *Smalley* v. *Quarrier* [1975] 1 W.L.R. 938.
[89] *Sutton* v. *Dorf* [1932] 2 K.B. 304; *London City Corporation* v. *Bown, The Times,* October 11, 1989; *cf.* Housing Act 1989, s.5(3)(*a*).
[90] Building societies appear willing to lend to debtors the subject of a voluntary arrangement but not to those who have been declared bankrupt.
[91] Insolvency Act 1986, s.252(2).

INDEX